IN MEMORY

OF

DONALD J. BENTLEY

Nothing Hardly Ever Happens in Colbyville, Vermont

Peter Miller

Nothing Hardly Ever Happens in Colbyville, Vermont

and other stories and essays

Peter Miller

SILVER PRINT PRESS
COLBYVILLE, VERMONT 05676

Nothing Hardly Ever Happens in Colbyville, Vermont
©2008 Peter Miller. All right reserved. No parts of the contents of this book may be reproduced by any means without the permission of the publisher.
All photographs © Peter Miller except on pages 3 and 81. Page 3 photograph © Waterbury Historical Society. Page 81 photograph © Buchrach.

The poem on page vi is ©2000 by Randolph C. Phelps and is reprinted with his permission. First published in the *Green Mountain Trading Post*.

The chapter "Same-Sex Union and Dog Ownership" on page 113 is ©2000 by Ted Ross and was first published in *The Vermont Eagle*, April 2000, and in the book *Stick Season Grouse*, by Ted Ross, published in 2004 by Silver Print Press.

Published by Silver Print Press
20 Crossroad, Colbyville, Vermont 05676
Email: info@silverprintpress.com
Website: www.silverprintpress.com

Original book design by Peter Holm, Sterling Hill Productions
www.sterlinghill.com

Printed in the United States of America

First Edition: October 2008

Other books by Peter Miller: *The 30,000 Mile Ski Race*; *Peter Miller's Ski Almanac*; *The Photographer's Almanac* (co-author); *People of the Great Plains*; *The First Time I Saw Paris*; *Vermont People*; *Vermont Farm Women*; *Vermont Gathering Places*

PUBLISHER'S CATALOGING IN PUBLICATION

Author: Miller, Peter
Published: Colbyville, VT: Silver Print Press, 2008
Essays, reportage, satire and stories written or edited in Colbyville,
  Vermont by Peter Miller
1. Vermont—Description—1968–2008
 Subject:
    1. Country Life—Vermont
    2. Vermont: Social life and customs
    3. Sports—literature
    4. Vermont—biography
    5. Vermont—history

Material: 144 pages :ill.31 photographs
6x9 inches

Library of Congress Catalog Card Number 2008908076

ISBN: 978-0-9749890-5-1 (Hardcover)
ISBN: 978-0-9749890-6-8 (Softcover)

Library Cataloging Number
V 808.81 Essays

This book is dedicated to my daughters, Hilary and Dodie, who, when they were very young, would visit me in my Colbyville garret.

The Hing Boys' Jeep Club Oath

I come from Vermont, I do what I want

I won't mow my lawn, and you won't complain
I'll go fishin' at night, and walk in the rain

You can call me a woodchuck, I won't be offended
If my pants have a rip, they will some day be mended

My friends all drive Jeeps and four-wheel drive rigs
They all have long hair and chew on grass twigs

We spend our spare time just drivin' the ground
From here until there, then turn back around

I might chew tobacco or drink a few beers
I really am harmless, don't have any fears

So give me a wave when you pass by
I'll probably wave back, I'm that kinda guy

— Randolph C. Phelps

Contents

Acknowledgments

I would like to thank the many people whom I interviewed for these stories and who shared with me their research and knowledge. In particular I would like to thank Dave Henderson of the Vermont State Police who helped with the Ellis research. Dennis Devereaux of Belmont also added to the story.

The Vermont State Library is a wonderful and efficient asset to this state. Paul Donovan, Hans Asselin, and the charming people at the front desk assisted me in finding newspaper clips from the *Rutland Herald* about the Ellis suicide, articles that the *Herald* itself could not find. I also found (in the *Times Argus*) the Ben & Jerry CEO letter I wrote and which has disappeared from my files. The library has on microfilm almost every newspaper in Vermont.

Linda Kaiser of the Waterbury Historical Society was kind enough to open their large vault in the public library so I could copy the old photograph of my house and read the very interesting file they have on Colbyville.

Ted Ross, author of *Stick Season Grouse*, graciously gave me permission to use his story on dogs and same-sex marriage. He has been the perpetuator, sometimes unwittingly, in a number of incidents that eventually became literary fodder.

Jim Currier and his family run the fabulous Currier's Market in Glover. Jim is one of Vermont's greatest butchers, but his fame rests in his collection of stuffed wild animals and birds displayed in his store, including a complete moose in the post office. He lent me his stuffed woodchuck, which worked admirably in the field and which illustrates the chapter on human and animal woodchucks.

Introduction
Moving to Colbyville

1968—What a year! I was recently divorced, lost my house, kids, and job. Besides that, I was broke. Just about as low as you can get.

There was one free place I could find shelter—an unfinished attic in an old rambling farmhouse in Colbyville, Vermont, ten miles down Route 100 from Stowe. My brother and I owned the house, and the downstairs had been jerry-rigged into office space from where we ran a ski magazine, first called *Vermont Skiing* and then *Eastern Skiing*. The magazine went bust and the house was soon to be sold to pay bills.

The room I moved into with Parker, my Brittany spaniel, looked like an old attic, which it was, as raw in finish as my spirit. There was no floor, just joists, and overhead bare rafters and not a puff of insulation. I put in a plywood floor and a picture window facing the setting sun. That was it. Down a miserly hall were two small rooms whose walls were covered with torn patches of wallpaper printed with roses. They exposed crumbling plaster and lathe; cut nails were hammered into the two-by-fours. A bathroom was at the end. Abandoned during an earlier age sat a large porcelain tub with clawed ball feet, a wall sink, and believe it or not, a toilet that worked. There were more shreds of wallpaper over plaster and lathe. I covered the walls with ski posters and later with cedar shingles, all the rage in the sixties.

I mentioned there was no insulation? That winter I came down with pneumonia. Two friends put in a chimney and kerosene stove and insulated the ceiling and nailed on shiplap, rough side out, over the rafters. They jim-jammed into an alcove a kitchen with just the essentials—a tiny refrigerator, a compact stove, and a sink sitting on unfinished plywood for countertops.

I didn't know it then, but that old farmhouse and Colbyville would be my home for the next forty years. The only items in that house untouched and unmoved from those days are the toilet, the old tub, and the inside-out shiplap ceiling in the living room-attic.

A century and a half ago my new home was an elegant farmhouse with an attached shed and two adjacent barns. It was built, according to town records, in 1850. An old photograph of the house shows its classic lines. Some Victorian gingerbread has disappeared, and so have the shutters that framed the windows. The exterior was finished in clapboards, probably milled nearby. The photo must have been taken when the house was recently built and lived in by, I think, a Jim Greene, although the old records are fuzzy. Daniel Greene farmed there and sold the property in 1870, which included a ton of hay for twelve dollars and a sugarhouse with all the tools and firewood.

When I moved in, the house was covered with gray asphalt shingles, as were other houses in the neighborhood. Some slick salesman must have touted asphalt's insulation value, which is nil. I spiffed up the house and spray-painted the shingles barn red, which didn't help insulate anything but my spirits. Only later did I find out that the original clapboards were hidden under the asphalt.

In 1968 Colbyville was, well, funky. It was a run-down, all-used-up place between here and there. My neighbor Esther Truax kept up her house, which was built where the first home in Colbyville stood, a log cabin, constructed in 1788. Aywlard's Nursing Home, across the road and up the hill about a hundred yards, was beat-up gray. There lived out-sourced members of the Waterbury State Hospital. In fact, this little a village, an outpost of Waterbury, looked like one of those Civil War photographs shot on a grey day of some town on the edge of a murderous battle.

Colbyville exists for two reasons. It is beside the only road that heads north to Stowe, and there were two falls on the Thatcher Brook, which is across the road from my house. (The upper falls no longer exists, for the brook is wizened compared to its salad days one hundred years ago). On the lower falls was built, in the early 1800s, a carding mill, for there were more sheep than cows and people in Waterbury. At about the same time Oliver Rood built a potato-whiskey distillery on the upper falls. Old records insinuate he liked sampling his product, maybe a bit too much. However, during that era, overfondness of Vermonters for their home-distilled created a backlash and anti-drink crusaders chopped down many apple orchards. Rood went clean and sold his business, and the new owners, obviously politically correct, turned the potatoes into starch.

In 1856, George and Edwin Colby, two brothers in their twenties, bought

My house in Colbyville, circa 1855. This photo was taken from across Route 100, which now sees 14,500 cars a day. (Courtesy of Waterbury Historical Society)

the mill and began stripping the willows growing next to the brook, using them in the manufacture of children's carriages, boys' velocipedes, and sleds. The carriages were fancy indeed, ornamented and painted, the design and finish overseen by a German willow worker, Anton Landt. George Colby was a good businessman and an inventor. He designed a bark-stripping machine for the willows and, after the carriage business was booming, he invented Colby's Clothes Wringer that squeezed the water out of recently washed clothes between two rollers. The wringer was sold throughout America and Europe. It was such a success that they had an office at 508 Broadway in New York City where they showed off carriage samples and clothes washers equipped with Colby's Wringer. Their office was only a block away from where I lived in the 1980s—in the heart of Soho. Nowadays, one can rent a stretch Hummer from a limousine service located in their building.

In their heyday the Colby brothers employed between sixty and one hundred workers and constructed fifteen buildings covering forty thousand square feet. Naturally, this company town became known as Colbyville. George built the Colbyville Mansion, which is still there and in good shape. It resembles a squashed wedding cake. George went into the home development business and printed his own pamphlets—the last one was *How to Make Money*. It came out just before the brothers went bankrupt in 1870 over a legal suit involving wringer patents. A company from Michigan claimed the Colby Wringer infringed their patent. This may not be—the lawyer, who represented the Colby's, after the suit was settled, moved to Michigan and became a well-paid employee of the company that initiated the suit.

Things quieted down in Colbyville. The mills downsized and made butter and cheese boxes and clapboards. The farms appeared to prosper. In 1870 the Greene family sold their 65-acre farm to George Josyln (eventually it became known as the Towne Place), who lived in this house from 1899 to 1927. Altogether, some twenty people bought and sold and lived in my house. There is only one resident ghost who lives upstairs with me and seems quite frightened of its own presence.

Nothing much happened for the next forty years. Colbyville became weary with age, wear, and tear. There were a few spurts of weird history. On July 27, 1899, a lawyer, Columbus Clough, was killed by an electric car down the road from Colbyville toward Mill Village . . . perhaps misdirected karma payment for the lawyer who led the Colby brothers into bankruptcy. In 1897 the Stowe Electric Railroad was completed and joined the Waterbury Railroad station with Stowe, which at the time was a popular summer resort. In 1899 the state bought land for the state hospital (known as the insane asylum by locals). Eight churches existed in town from Waterbury to the Center; two of them were in Colbyville. In 1910 an albino deer was shot on Blush Hill, above my house, and was stuffed by Mr. Davis in his home in Colbyville.

A sawmill operated on Thatcher Brook until 1930. The Depression must have set in like an early blizzard and Colbyville, except for two farms, became a pass-through place on the way to Stowe.

My home, which was surrounded by sloping hay fields and variously known through the last one hundred years as the Greene Farm, Towne Place, and Smitty's Garage, was whittled down to a quarter of an acre when I bought it from a partner for thirty-three thousand dollars in 1973. I didn't think it was worth that when I set up my apartment with a bed next to the stove, and a desk, where I did my writing, under the picture window.

In the late 1960s traffic on the state highway was about five hundred cars a day and downtown Waterbury was a sleepy town indeed. It was during the summer of 1968 that I bicycled every street in the village of Waterbury, to familiarize myself with the town. It was a hot, muggy day. I bicycled down Main Street that was almost void save for a couple of cars and a few halfway people walking toward the old Waterbury Inn. In its heyday guests used to come from out of state to stay at this inn, and there was a huge ballroom. Now it too was a halfway stop, or a halfway inn. I bicycled to the state hospital and circled it. In the rear, I could hear screams coming from the second floor where there were bars over the windows.

On one street I passed a house with a divided front porch. An elderly man sat on the right, looking out, saying nothing. An elderly woman sat on the left porch, staring out, and her mouth was also zipped shut. Both appeared as glum as cold oatmeal.

On the other side of town, near the school I passed two boys sitting on a stoop, staring out at the house across the street. They looked at me as I bicycled past, saying nothing, not even acknowledging their own existence, the street, or me. A vacuum of time. The post office was downtown in an old grey building that smelled of oiled floors and dust. Prominent on the wall was a rack with FBI Most Wanted posters. About a half dozen years later Patty Hearst had star billing on the rack. I did stop in the bank across the street and asked for a loan, and the banker wanted so much collateral I moved my banking to Stowe. That bank was famous for quick foreclosures.

I had no camera with me when I did my first bicycle tour but I thought, hey, what great photo ops for Diane Arbus! She was to become a famous photographer whose psychological portraits reveal an invisible bell jar overstuffed with angst. I sent a card off to her but there was no reply. A few years later she slit her wrists.

To pay the bills I split my house into five apartments. Eventually, I couldn't stand the heat of being a landlord, (I could write a separate book about those trying experiences, but I prefer to forget them). I contracted writer and photographer's block and moved back to New York (I was born there) and lived up the block from the old Colby business. I'm probably the only Colby resident in the last one hundred years to have lived near both sites. I stayed there until the mid-1980s when the yuppies invaded New

My neighbors Deb and Neil Vallencourt. They've moved away, and so has the barn.

York and I was continually kicked out of my sublease apartments; they were co-opted. I returned to Vermont. Nowadays I visit the Colbyville Mansion regularly. Holly, who works for Dr. Wollensak, cleans my teeth in a room that, 150 years ago, must have been Mr. Colby's dining room.

Nowadays I am the only resident in my renovated farmhouse. In December 2007 I put in a photograph gallery in what had been a six-room office. In the middle of it is my writing office. On the walls are photographs of my beloved Trade Towers, shot in the 1980s, and a photograph of a bearded man pulling, in a snow storm, a cart laden with cardboard, photographed in 1961 when I was also living in New York, on Minetta Lane in the Village and working for *Life*. In the other rooms are my Vermont Icon photographs. All of these photographs are in black and white. Vermont is known for its green mowings and its eye-candy fall, but anyone who knows the soul of this state realizes it is best represented in honest, plain, stark black and white. I have a computer room for scanning my photographs, an upstairs apartment where the ghost lives, and a large deck.

In the time I have lived here Colbyville has turned the other cheek, and it is a cosmetic one. The halfway house closed, and the fire department burned it down (it's cheaper than tearing it down even though it was painted with lead-based paint), and a candy factory was built in its place. Now it is a repair center for some sort of meters. Below it is the house where Deb and Neil Vallencourt lived, and rented Esther's barn and transformed the penned yard in front of it, from my viewpoint, into a free sex zone for animals. The Vallencourts moved away and divorced. Now their home has been rebuilt into office space. A venture capital firm was one of the first occupants.

The Colby mansion, as I said, is an office building, and my dentist works there. Across the street is the old Steadman Mansion, built by another mill owner in the nineteenth century. That building is now the Thatcher Brook Inn.

Esther Truax—God rest her soul—my neighbor who supplied me with vegetables from her garden, was a good friend. She took in Bill, a refugee from New York who, when he became frail, walked behind the house and shot himself with a pistol. She sold her barn to the Kilkennys, who in the 1960s moved to Vermont from the Bronx and bought Bissette's Market, which is across the street. They moved the barn to a nearby town and built a retirement home. The Kilkennys in turn sold their market to Joe Caforia, who ran a wonderful deli and sold wine by the case at 10 percent markup. His wife divorced him and he ended up being a Pop without a Mom storeowner and it was too much for him. He burned out and, not finding a buyer, went bankrupt and moved away. Now young Shawn Cummings is trying to make a go of the store.

Last year Colbyville lost its spiritual center when the Grace Alliance Church closed. The congregation grew too large, there was little parking space on Route 100 and so they moved to a less commercial town, taking the bell with them, which they rang every Sunday morning. Their church is now a sales room for cabinets and home for the owner. Oh yes, in 1978, Fred Grout, who lives in a trailer on the other side of Thatcher Brook, purchased a ticket for the first Vermont State Lottery. He bought it at Kilkenny's market, a few hundred feet from his trailer, and he won forty thousand dollars. "After taxes," he told me, "there was about nineteen thousand left."

The biggest change, of course, was in 1985 when Ben & Jerry's built their ice cream plant a few hundred yards from my house. They didn't know they had moved to Colbyville, and I am not sure they know it now. When Esther died, they bought her house and four acres—it was a buffer between my home and their plant. Now I can spit off my deck onto their property. Unilever, a Dutch-Anglo conglomerate, bought Ben & Jerry's in 2000 for $326 million. The same month they acquired Slim-Fast for $2.3 billion. Unilever did $60 billion in revenues in 2007 and had the seventy-ninth highest gross income in the world, bigger than Egypt's GDP. Unilever is in a premium ice cream war with Nestlé; their latest move has been to buy Inmarko, the largest ice cream maker in Russia. Ben Cohen, one of the Long Islanders that started Ben & Jerry's, did not do too shabby when Unilever bought his company. He received $39 million for his stock.

Unilever scares me. For a while they were planning a theme park to make themselves the biggest tourist attraction in Vermont. Perhaps the idea was killed or perhaps it is in the freezer. The bosses who make decisions that affect my life and those who work at Ben & Jerry's live in New Jersey and London. They might not have ever visited Vermont, or Colbyville, which some people have renamed Ben and Jerryville.

Other changes have come. Route 100 is being stripped and in the last two years a Shaw's big-box grocery store, a bank, and a proposed Quizno's, the first fast-food franchise on the 217 miles of "Scenic" Route 100 (unless you consider the Dunkin' Donuts hidden behind some shops in Waterbury Center) are oozing up Route 100 toward my house. The traffic count has climbed, since I moved here, from a few hundred cars a day to fourteen thousand five hundred. A couple of times a year, during July 4 weekend and foliage season, the traffic is backed up for a couple of miles. Above my house, on a hill, have been built about the ugliest condominiums I have seen, particularly since they look down on my deck like a sociopathic mind (this is not NIMBY but NIMFY—my front yard is my deck). Waterbury has been a developer's paradise and a sense of aesthetics and taste reside elsewhere than Colbyville and Route 100. Now fifty-nine condos are planned for a patch of land near my house. The developer is, of course, from Stowe. What with encroaching ugliness, high property taxes, and out-of-sight costs for heating your home and driving your car, I don't think I'll be be able to afford to live here much longer.

My neighbor Esther, with vegetables from her garden for me. She died in 1996.

My house has been spruced up; no one would come to my gallery the way it looked a couple of years ago. I had to cut down the old big maple in the front yard that was in danger of falling on my house or Route 100. I also tore down a disreputable porch and repainted the house yellow, and planted flowers. It's finally beginning to look like a home.

The stories in this book were all written, edited, and shaped at my desk in my Colbyville house. Some I did the research in places far removed from Colbyville—in other areas of Vermont, or America, or Europe. They are, for the most part, articles that appeared in the *Stowe Reporter* (my best sarcastic work), *Ski Magazine*, where I was a writer and photographer for twenty years, a couple of other sports magazines, and books. Some of the articles are rejects, and others I wrote because, as a writer, that is what you do. This book is an excuse to publish them, to have you read these stories, and cull some sort of insight from them, for better or worse.

Ben & Jerryville, Not Colbyville!

In the fall of 1994, Ben & Jerry's held a contest—YO! I'm your CEO!—for the position of chief executive officer, which was being vacated by Ben Cohen. Twenty-two thousand people applied, including me. Here is my application essay, which was published in several Vermont newspapers.

Dear Ben & Jerry's,

I can think of no one, in your search for a new boss (YO! I'm your CEO!) who would serve you better as boss than I. I am very familiar with your operation; after all, I live only three hundred yards from your factory. I could walk to work along your sewer line and thus not pollute the world with my car. I am divorced and my children are grown so there are no distractions and no extra medical costs. I am accustomed to working fifteen- to eighteen-hour days.

Above all, I love ice cream and, as an ice cream gourmet, have written on the subject. Well, yes, it is true that I prefer Häagen-Dazs over Ben & Jerry's, but that would be to your advantage. I am also a whiz at marketing and public relations.

I read where you have committed double-digit millions to advertising your new "solid" ice cream. Much of your former success was in borrowing the idea of Steve's Ice Cream of Cambridge, Massachusetts, who first created candy add-ins and baby-boomer flavors (his texture, though was always smoother than yours, since he only used the high butterfat content milk from Jersey cows). Now you hope to match Häagen-Dazs' plain vanilla and chocolate. Your ice cream remains a slow second to their vanilla and your chocolate is not even close to the famous Sedutto chocolate of New York. I would correct this fault.

You have spent considerable effort in marketing your ice cream by aligning yourself with the green movement, so precious to the baby boomers that have been your core customers. As such, you designed an ice cream that has ridden on the coattails of the rain forest, the whales, the family farm, and Woody Jackson's caricature of sightless Holstein cows. In the 1990s your yuppie customers are aging (and poorer), and values are returning to concern over community and the local environment rather than what's happening in Balkiel or Brazil. This is where I can save your commercial soul.

If I may be euphemistic, most of your neighbors here in Colbyville don't think much of your company. First of all, we feel you don't know that you live in Colbyville, a hamlet just south of your factory that has been usurped by the Town and Village of Waterbury and heavily taxed to the point of no return.

You put in two sewer lagoons on a hill overlooking and upwind from our homes and had the Village of Waterbury, which considers Colbyville a dumping ground, approve the system. (We have never heard of a Ben & Jerry's executive who ever lived downwind of a sewer lagoon.) Two Colbyville residents spent six thousand dollars in legal fees, to try to block the lagoon to no avail.

In addition, your expansion into a tourist destination is increasing congestion and becoming an aesthetic eyesore to the residents of this hamlet. We were shocked when we heard you planned to put giant spoons and a replica of Ben & Jerry's pint lid as a sign on Route 100.

We talked cynically about pollution problems you had with the state water resources people and we laughed about your attempt to coerce a neighbor with eighteen pints of ice cream. However, we still don't laugh about how you worked Waterbury for the sewer lagoon and five years of no taxes.

In other words, we know Ben & Jerry's as a rather arrogant, callous and wealthy neighbor, who, in its haughty goodness, leaves on our doorstep, at Christmastime, two pints of Ben & Jerry's seconds.

Did you know there is a move afoot to create a new Vermont T-shirt that says, I HATE BEN & JERRY'S!

I can stop this local anger, have your neighbors love you and at the same time turn your neighborhood into a national marketing plan that will cost a lot less than the millions you are now spending. It will be twice as effective.

Colbyville is under terrible stress these days since Waterbury officials have let loose developers who plan to turn our neighborhood into a profitable and ugly mass of housing and stores; greed is surpassing the old-fashioned Vermont tradition of quality of life. I hear that scores of residences will be built in tiny Colbyville and destroy our last green areas.

Across the road is a beautiful, undulating hayfield of about 225 acres surrounded by woods that is now hayed and also used for cross-country skiing, tobogganing, horse riding, biking, walking the dog, jogging. This field is to become the center of another development and then we residents will have no green around us, no space to walk, no beauty to look at—just roads overburdened with traffic. In essence, Colbyville is being raped and our quality of life is being snuffed out for dollars to line pockets of people who do not live here.

Ben & Jerry's could change all this; with your profits you can stop the encroaching development. You could buy the land east of your factory and turn it into a park and baseball field. It is a natural location for concerts, field days, and an international ice cream tasting festival. (The last would be a wonderful promotion: Ben & Jerry's invites its competition from Cincinnati, Miami, San Francisco, New York, Boston, Paris, Rome, and Santiago to an ice cream taste-out. The profits would support towns around the world to protect their open space and what would it matter if Berthillon's from Paris wins the gold medal?)

Now here is my marketing nutshell—Colbyville should become an autonomous village separate from Waterbury, which with one hand takes our money and with the other condemns our hamlet to become a development of road, cars, and houses.

We feel with your help we could split off from Waterbury. We would then control and protect and increase our quality of life and condemn any more development. Our taxes would go down (yours too).

We could turn Colbyville into a mecca of calm and beauty and away from the madness of "economic development" that is turning Waterbury into a generic suburb that screams Wal-Mart. Yes, the residents of Colbyville would love you, and I am quite sure they would, after all this comes true (cynicism dies hard), change the name of Colbyville to Ben & Jerryville.

The publicity Ben & Jerry's would receive from keeping Colbyville a community of quality amidst suburban squalor and Route 100 stripping would be world-wide. Planner and developers could come to Ben & Jerry's think tanks to study small community development.

Ice cream lovers could enjoy the beauty of the Ben & Jerry's park and forest system, which would not be painted pink and purple but kept in a natural state, the way good ice cream should be. Ben & Jerry's International Ice Cream Festival would be so popular even Elvis would attend.

No one would mind if your ice creams cost more than Häagen-Dazs—we would make General Mills eat Holstein pies! Your bottom line eyes would absolutely bug out at the end of every quarter. And think . . . a village named Ben & Jerryville! After you!

This is what I would do as CEO. That's a lot better than having a bunch of I HATE BEN & JERRY's! T-shirts being sold around the country and mail-ordered through *Rolling Stone* and *Harper's* wouldn't it?

Please, I would like an office with a view.

———————

THIRTEEN YEARS LATER. This essay was prescient. The land across the street did not become a housing development, thank God, but The Country Club of Vermont. Anybody can join by paying initiation fees of seventy-five hundred dollars and an annual fee of forty-five hundred dollars a year to play golf and enjoy the nineteenth hole. The club allows us locals to walk on the property, and the members are a friendly bunch. No houses or condos are built along the fairways.

Sprawl has marched up Route 100, just as predicted, and a Shaw's supermarket now is the big-box store, but it could well be a Wal-Mart in the future. Waterbury remains round-heeled when it comes to development. Housing projects have proliferated on Blush Hill and a new one would add sixty-eight condominium units and further congest Route 100. One new traffic light has been put in at the access for Shaw's, another one is going in at exit 10, and two more are needed, one in Colbyville and another a half-mile north—four traffic lights in less than two miles. The cost in gas, and time lost, for fourteen thousand five hundred cars a day stopping for these traffic lights is staggering.

———————

In April 2000, Unilever, a global corporate food and health company, acquired Ben & Jerry's. This is my letter to the boss, whose headquarters is in the Unilever House in Blackfriar's, London.

April 16, 2000

Dear Mr. Unilever,

I just read in the paper that you bought Slim-Fast and Ben & Jerry's on the same day and slapped down $2.3 billion to lose weight and only $326 million to gain it back.

Seeing you now own a chunk of Vermont, I thought I should introduce myself as your new neighbor, as my home is smack dab on Ben & Jerry's property line—actually, within spitting distance. Fact is . . . I'm your closest neighbor.

Perhaps you didn't know that you bought an ice-cream plant in Colbyville, Vermont. It is a hamlet a few miles from Waterbury. Some people call it Ben & Jerryville. Route 100, which used to be a quiet country highway, splits it. Now *eight thousand* cars pass by my house every day. A lot of them stop off for a cone at your plant, although that is more of a tourist park than anything else.

I was pretty worried when Ben & Jerry's located here fourteen years ago. First thing they did after the factory was up and running was build waste lagoons upwind and uphill from my house. If you ever smelled whey you know what I was worried about. Two of my neighbors sued over those waste lagoons but lost. So far, I only smell whey about twice a year, which is more than enough.

Then there were other infractions with the State of Vermont regulators over waste removal and the $1.1 million won by stockholders in a class action suit when Ben & Jerry's inflated the price of its shares. That didn't bother me so much as the thought of five hundred tourists walking a hundred yards over the hill from your plant to gawk at me sunning on my deck. Well, I figured out how to scare them off.

Ben & Jerry's have been good neighbors. I turned some of their field into lawn and then their maintenance staff mowed it. I planted four apple trees on their land. A good Vermonter should plant a tree a year. Not that we could make up for what the conglomerates cut down, but just to show we

have the right spirit. I intend to plant more apple trees unless you, as the new owner, object.

I'm an author and photographer. I should send you a copy of *Vermont People*. It is a classic book of photographs and text of rural Vermonters, who, like Ben and Jerry, are an endangered species. Ben & Jerry's never sold my book in their shop. Perhaps they thought the book was too real, or perhaps it was because the native Vermonters in my book prefer apple pie to Cherry Garcia.

I hear you have promised millions for Ben & Jerry's Foundation and that you plan to provide seed capital for businesses run by minorities and low-income people. How about starting in Vermont? Writers, photographers, hand-crafters, even foundations in this state, are scraping the bottom of the barrel. Unilever made $43.3 million last year (1999). Rural Vermonters are more concerned about the beauty of their state and their independence than money, so that puts us out of whack with the rest of the country. We rural Vermonters are a minority.

How about funding my next book, *Vermont Farm Women*? If you don't care to support farm women, at least bring back Ben & Jerry's Christmas custom of leaving off a couple of pints of ice cream to those of us who live in the neighborhood. Perhaps they stopped it because it could be addictive and open up lawsuits. Now you wouldn't have any trouble if you included a six-pack of Slim Fast along with a couple of pints of Ben & Jerry's.

Incidentally, my house controls the corner of your property where there is an intersection. There ain't no way you will ever get a theme park as long as I live here.

Come visit some time!

Sincerely,
Peter Miller

Unilever paid Ben Cohen thirty-nine million dollars for his shares in Ben & Jerry's. Cohen was allowed to pick his own CEO, but was bypassed by Unilever for a company man. This is my Dear John letter to Ben:

November 20, 2000
Dear Ben,
I know how it must hurt when the new owners of Ben & Jerry's passed on your choice for a new boss and selected their own CEO, but, gosh, what do you expect? Unilever is a behemoth and we all know they are sharks when it comes to the bottom line. You knew that too when Ben & Jerry's was bought out so if they bypass your man for the top position, you might call that your just dessert.

And I know it must hurt that they might freeze out Ben & Jerry's social programs but they didn't get to be a multibillion company by being nice. What they paid for Ben & Jerry's, in their mind, is not more than a cube of ice in the freezer compartment of their refrigerator.

I wish you the best in your fight with them but may I cast your eyes in another direction? They paid you $39 million for your stock in Ben & Jerry's. How many pints of Cherry Garcia is that?

You know that CEOs in most stock-exchange-listed companies, and their board of directors, are bloated with salaries, fees, stock options, retirement funds, bonuses, golden parachutes, and bountiful perks; so much so that one wonders why there is any money left to spread around to the rest of America.

So why not make an example of this greed with your own winnings and give away most of it? You could still end up with $400,000 a year interest. At least! Put that together with the $200,000 annual fee you receive from Unilever for hanging around and you have quite a bit more than the $15,000, give or take a few bucks, that the average Vermonter from the little town of Victory makes in a year.

Think of it. You might be able to alter the image of American CEOs and make those greedy corporate boards feel just a bit guilty. Maybe they would follow your example. It is what we Vermonters expect of you, Ben: to be in the forefront to help the disenfranchised, the neglected, the poor, and the middle class—us.

Did you know I applied for the job of CEO of Ben & Jerry's a couple of years back? Well, you turned me down, so I know how it feels when your favorite candidate is shown the door.

Anything I can do to help, Ben, just call me up.

Your old neighbor,
Peter Miller

A Death in the Family

New York City, June, 1980

My uncle Cally died this spring, just as the shoots were greening the south sides of the hills and the woodcock were acting out their aerial mating dance. He died at home, in the Vermont farmhouse he had restored. He was seventy-three; lung cancer did him in.

Over six feet, square-faced handsome, father of four, happily married, silver haired in his later years, he had an easy way with him, warmed by a quick smile. For me he had been the perfect father and friend, picking up where a divorce had cut me off from the man who showed me how to hunt.

Cally's death rushed back memories, fresh as a mountain spring, of the days he first took me fishing and hunting thirty-five years ago. I was thirteen and living with my family in Connecticut when Cally picked me up for a day of fishing on a small mountain stream. He lent me a bamboo rod with vermilion windings and some flies in a folded brown leather case with the name L.L. Bean stamped on it. It was a day of unusual clarity, in the early spring when the sky was hued as deep as my spirits and the recently sprouted leaves were a transparent green. Boulders taller than I was anchored the stream, and rapids sparkled around the boulders and flowed into pools glazed blue by the sky. The water was a pure as the air. The beauty of this stream—the fragrance—I can still smell it—made me light-hearted.

I opened the fly case and on a layer of sheep wool were flies the color of rainbows—delicate but so beautiful to my young eyes—reds, iridescent green, deep blues, brilliant yellows—Scarlet Ibis, Royal Coachman, Parmachene Belle, Mickey Finn—favorite flies of that era for catching the brook trout that were colored as brilliantly as the flies.

Cally helped me tie one on my leader and then he went downstream as I dappled the fly in the rapids and let the current swirl it into the pool. The beauty and freshness of that stream and the magical beauty I saw in those flies and the solitude I felt became, for me, the essence of fishing. I don't even remember if we caught any fish. It wasn't important.

In the fall Cally and I went duck hunting on the small ponds hidden in the woods behind my family's home. I used a Stevens .410 over and under and Cally carried a pump 12 gauge. It was a drizzly, damp day that smelled of wet canvas and freshly fallen leaves. Water drops traced down branches to the point of no return, bloated, and then plopped loose. It was hypnotic, watching one after the other replicate itself and go airborne. It was windless and so silent; not even the squirrels chattered as we walked over the damp leaves.

We put up a solitary mallard from the end of the pond. Water sprayed from its orange feet, dropping onto the pond's surface and creating circles. Adrenalin took over. Cally shot, then I shot, and the duck kept climbing as Cally yelped.

"Hey! You just about shot me!"

"No, really. I was two feet over from you."

"Never shoot from behind, Peter. Never!" He gave me this stern look that crushed me. I knew there was no danger, but I had broken the etiquette of the field and a safety rule, and besides, I scared the hell out of Cally. I never forgot it, or the stern look on Cally's face and the inflection of his voice and the hurt, guilty feeling I had. Cally reprimanded by understatement. School, university, and the Army moved us apart, and then Cally found me my first job in journalism, at *Life* in Manhattan. In that understated way he smoothed into this country boy a little bit of a cosmopolitan sheen. He celebrated my job by taking me to lunch at 21.

I didn't stay in New York; the pull of the country was too strong and I moved back to Vermont. Cally retired shortly after and bought a farm in Vermont, surrounded by four hundred acres, on a dead-end road. He always lived in a house at the end of a dead-end road.

Assignments kept me on extended trips, but whenever I returned, we would get together and sometimes we would fish the Lamoille River. Often, though, I would go by myself, only to find Cally, a big straw hat on his head, standing in the middle of the stream, working his Orvis bamboo rod. I knew that he wished to be by himself on this stream. I would wave. He would smile and wave back, and I would fish another pool. We understood each other that way.

I meant to take Cally woodcock hunting with my Brittany spaniel, Parker, but, as these things go, we never got together, for I am as much a loner hunting woodcock as Cally was fishing for trout. Finally we made a date to hunt in one of my favorite covers, but my Brittany died suddenly in the field, and I didn't have the spirit to hunt.

I had moved back to New York when I heard from my sister that Cally was dying. I called up Corinne, his wife. Cally was sleeping, she said. He was in no pain. I told her that we had good times together and that he had been a good father to me. She said she would tell him. Our call became tearful. Corinne asked me to be a pallbearer.

I hung up and stared out the window at the Empire State Building rising above rooftops. I hadn't known it was so close, or how much Cally meant to me. I wrote him a note, and went out to get drunk. He died two days later, a few hours before the mailman delivered my letter.

At the funeral the priest asked us to reflect on some blessing we had received from Cally during his lifetime. It was all in that letter I sent him. I mentioned how important that first fishing trip was, and the lunch at 21, and how he had helped shape my life.

Cally was buried in St. Therese's cemetery in Hyde Park, under a mature maple tree, with no near neighbors. Just as he liked it . . . solitude and beauty.

After the funeral I drove down to where Cally had skunked me on the Lamoille by catching four sixteen-inch browns. I strung up my seven-foot Orvis and waded in where we had fished. The river was different. The mayflies had disappeared and in its place was the caddis, a hardier fly, not as delicate, ethereal, or as much fun to imitate. The rocks were slippery with slime. I caught nothing.

On the way home I took the back road to Stowe, where the iron bridge cover was located, so named because a rusted metal chair blocked a logging road next to it. This cover was a small jewel of four acres of alders and home for six to eight woodcock and occasionally a flight would drop in. It was in the shape of a peninsula between two open hilly stretches. I was going to station Cally on the hill so he could have open shooting.

I drove to the cover, thinking of Cally's smile and kicking myself for not taking him to this cover, and I thought of my dog's death, and the early death of a friend, twelve years ago, who introduced me to woodcock hunting, when I looked toward my cover and slammed on the brakes.

I stared, my mouth ajar, as the dust from the road slowly settled around the car. The cover was gone. Erased! Vanished! No longer! The alders were cut down. I couldn't believe it; it was as if this cover never was, that I never hunted it with Parker, that there was no past and no memory.

Then I spotted the bulldozer hidden in the next field. A house development was going to replace the cover. Who, I screamed to myself, would ever build a house on an alder cover that grew around a swamp fed by two springs? Who would ever destroy a cover so small?

It was another death, and I thought of the Lamoille River that had grown polluted and other bird covers that had become housing sites, or posted by out-of-staters who never walk their fields or woods.

Cally had built his Vermont home in an area protected by fields and forests. His nearest neighbors, when he moved up, were farmers. As the years went by, the farmers sold out and people from Connecticut restored the neighboring farmhouses. A cocktail circuit sprung up and so did paddle tennis and intimate, semi-formal dinners—all the appurtenances of suburbia that Cally had escaped. My uncle had lived in northern Vermont during the best of times. As I drove away from Cally, the Lamoille River, and the woodcock cover that was no more, I sensed an era in my life was extinguished, and it was a time to search for new covers.

The Twilight Season

This was first published in 1978 in *Outdoor Life*,
later in *Stick Season Grouse*, a book by Ted Ross.

My friend Ted is a traditionalist; he likes to hang the past into the present. For instance, bird season always commences with breakfast at his house, a breakfast of salted codfish cakes—the type that come in those thin, wooden boxes from Nova Scotia. God only knows why codfish cakes should mark the first day of the woodcock season.

"Well, Miller," Ted will say, year after year, with a brilliant smile lighting up his red face, as I walk in, suited for the occasion with frazzled canvas pants, my hunting vest, and a white plastic whistle hung around my neck with a piece of clothesline, "Here we go again. I hope that no-good dog of yours will do something decent today."

My Brittany, Parker, has hustled over to Tweed's dish and is gulping down his meal. Ted's dog, a Springer, is a fussy eater and needs to have meat mixed with his kibble. Parker will down anything, but particularly Tweed's meal. Tweed growls.

"Miller, get your dog away from there!" Ted says. Parker ambles under the table and curls up for a short nap. "I hope your geriatric creature makes it through the morning."

"Tweed is so gimpy," I retort, "he can't bust out all the birds, like he used to."

"Oh, shut up!" Ted barks. "Tweed is ten times the dog Parker ever will be. Eat your codfish cakes!"

"God, they stink to high heaven!"

But they taste better than they smell. Even the eggs are good; one thing Ted doesn't always cook well.

It is the opening of bird season, and in Vermont, there is no finer season. The color, the fragrance released by the woods when the sun melts the frost, the softness of morning fog burying the valleys, and the clarity of the air make it an absolute joy to go hunting birds with an old friend and two old reliable dogs.

Tweed is going on fourteen. Skinny and frail, but looking younger than his age, he sees Ted take the over-and-under out of the gun rack. Suddenly the Springer loses a dozen years. So does Parker. A little more than a year younger than Tweed, she was once mostly orange with good ticking over her muzzle, but now she is grizzly and overweight. She breathes heavily and her joints are stiff, but she too scents the excitement of opening day. Both have lived this long for the simple pleasure of hunting through the fall.

Parker and Tweed have never liked each other, not since they first hunted together ten years ago. Parker, a female and quite a femme fatale in her heyday, never could stomach Tweed, who is a bit effeminate, a characteristic that has won him the nickname Mildred. Tweed would sniff up Parker, Parker would growl, and Tweed would stiff-leg it out of range. Still, they learned to accommodate each other in the house, in the car, and in the field. Who would ever think you could hunt a pointer and flusher together? Well, you can't when they're young. You trade one off on the other. But at this age it works out fine.

Both dogs live at home and have the run of our houses, sharing our lives. They have been by our sides during financial disaster, divorce, a number of affairs, some very drunken evenings, and some very good times.

"Look at it this way, Miller," Ted said to me ten years ago after my marriage disintegrated and he loaded me and the remnants of my life into his station wagon, the Easter Pig, and moved me from my house to an apartment, "you have your fishing rod, your shotgun, and your dog. What else do you need?"

A few years later, when Ted went through the same treatment, I fed him back the same advice. If our two dogs could write, they would publish a saga about American marriage, and the emasculating technology of the American divorce, then follow it up with some rousing stories about bachelorhood. Good old Park and Tweed remained the only stability during this transitional period.

It is as traditional for us to hunt the potato field as it is to eat codfish cakes for breakfast. The cover is about twenty acres bounded on the south by a lake and marsh. The river that sustains the lake cleaves the cover from a wooded hillside. To the north is the potato field, which in some years becomes a cornfield. To the west is a small lagoon, surrounded by trees and a steep hill. The soil is moist and rich with angleworms, judging from the number of woodcock that summer there, and the flight birds that settle in sporadically during the season. The cover also holds partridge, that feed on the alders, poplar, and wild grapes that grow thickly in two sections. Occasionally we see a deer sneak through the woods in front of us. Beaver have cut small waterways and made trails. They have done much to keep the cover from growing over and turning fallow. So have the spring floods that will scour a portion of the cover, leaving behind a new layer of topsoil.

There is an old road that goes partially into the cover, then becomes a tractor trail. It is about a half mile long, and because it seems to lead nowhere but to a plowed potato field, few hunters know about it. Only once did I see a trespasser in there, an old man whom I saw from a distance, with hip boots, going across the stream with a black-and-white setter. He hid from me as I hid from him, afraid to give up our secret. I have the sneaking suspicion that Ted and I have shared this cover with him for years. We usually hit the potato field no more than three or four times a season, and maintain a steady harvest so the native woodcock will return, and the partridge will produce another year.

I found the cover more than a dozen years ago, before I had a dog. The potato field was the first cover I took Parker to hunt in. I had expected little from Parker, for although I had trained her on all the commands, the young pup had refused to point at the grouse wing I had. Yet on the first day I hunted her, the first day of the season, she pointed. I was so surprised I missed my shot twice. Then she pointed throughout the potato field, down the gully near the beaver canal, on the ridge between the thin alder cover and the marsh, in the poplars, where there is always a bird. I shot my limit that first day with Parker, hugged her, kissed her, and readily forgave her for not retrieving the birds. She would find them, worry them, but not retrieve. That first day Parker and I became a very close team, and confidants in a secret life too. My home at the time was a battlefield, heavily infiltrated by the enemy. Skirmishes were continual, and Parker and I, the brunt of these attacks, found relief, and about our only joy, in the woods.

Later, when Ted and I became friends, and we learned to trust one another enough to divulge to each other our favorite woodcock covers, and to hunt with each other safely and with confidence, we worked the cover, sometimes with Tweed, a headstrong pup, sometimes with Parker. Tweed delighted in busting out birds ahead of us. Parker was not too bad, at times, but did her share of bumping them and hunting out of range. Ted would call his dog in and scream at him awhile, I'd gnash my teeth, then Parker would bump birds, or vanish beyond whistle range, and Ted would say, "It certainly isn't Parker's day, is it?" and I would gnash my teeth again. When I would miss an easy shot, blowing out lead from both barrels of my Parker shotgun before I could even aim, Ted would stand there, screaming, "Miller, how could you?" as we both watched the bird curve around an alder and fly down the river to the other bank.

Yet we had our good moments in the potato field and other covers through the years. We hit a number of partridge in 1969, and the cover was so thick we thought we missed, but Tweed had retrieved three of them. We hunted over some classic points. We would analyze the bird's escape route and then, with Parker steady, head down, one of us crept in, the other holding outside, hoping to have a shot. One of us usually brought down a bird. We never went home empty-handed, and roasted woodcock, served with trail on toast and a currant glaze, became one of the delights of October.

Now the dogs were old. Their combined life span, in our age, was 174 years. Ted and I had moved on a bit too. We had survived our marriages to become hardened bachelors, and learned to look at anything but hunting and fishing with a slightly cynical eye. Our infirmities were beginning to show. My hip, with an old football injury, bothered me on cold days, and my knees pained me when we hunted hillside covers. Ted moved slower, and his hearing in one ear was quite dull. It took longer for each of us to recover from celebrating the delights of hunting the night before.

But, the dogs were much worse off than us. Tweed was almost totally deaf and could hunt only by sight and scent. His ticker was so decrepit that two digitalis pills kept him moving. Pain killers eased his arthritis. Parker, in this twilight season, had also gone stone-deaf. She couldn't hear my whistle. Her arthritis was so bad that at times I would have to carry her into the car and up the stairs. Her eyes were glazing over with cataracts and her lungs sounded bad. She still hunted with élan, but she wheezed like a steam locomotive.

Ted and I discussed this before the season. "Well, Christ, Miller, both these dogs live for hunting. They'd die quicker if we didn't hunt them, and what better way for them to go than in the field? I'd just as soon go that way myself," Ted said. "How would you like to be kept home and petted while your dog went hunting?"

"Depends on who does the petting," I retorted, but we both knew we would hunt our dogs until they couldn't walk, and our dogs would appreciate us for it. Neither of us would consider acquiring a younger dog. That would cause heartbreak, and I know it would kill Parker. She didn't like young dogs at all, and to see another dog invade her home would be like divorcing one woman and marrying another, and living with both in the same house.

Ted and I worked our dogs before the season. Ted would jog a couple of miles with his dog. I would sniff around new covers, looking for birds and giving Parker and myself a workout. The first days my dog was breathing so heavily we had to stop and rest, and I feared old Park would need to be carried home. Day by day she improved, and I mixed meat and boiled egg into her kibble, and stuck in a vitamin pill for dessert. On a trip to New York, she even had an electrocardiogram, and she appeared to the city doctor to be in superb shape.

It was our tenth opening day spent at the potato field with Tweed and Parker. We parked our car in the woods so nobody would see it, belled our dogs, and unsheathed our guns. As the dogs grew nervous and raring to go, the same old giddy feeling crept over me that I had when I was six and my father was taking me and his setter Lady out for the opening day. I was all lightness and smiles inside.

When the dogs were young we would hunt one or the other. Later, they could hunt together, Tweed quartering to the right, my dog to the left. Occasionally, Parker would go on point, Ted would order Tweed to hold, and we would flush and shoot the bird with Tweed doing the fetching. Both dogs, to tell the truth, weren't much good at all until they had passed their fifth birthdays. Parker came into her prime when she was six and didn't slow down until she was ten. She was always a slow hunter, and so am I, and that is why we would account for thirty woodcock every season

for game dinners through Christmas. When Parker turned nine, arthritis was setting in her hindquarter, and her hearing wasn't the best when I blew the whistle. Tweed, on the other hand, would have been dead from a heart attack at ten if it wasn't for the double dose of digitalis pills. His hearing had started to go when he was eleven.

Now both of our dogs couldn't hear a bloody thing. However, we still carried whistles around our necks to honor tradition, and sometimes to blow in frustration.

"Hunt 'em up!" I would say to the dogs, and Ted and I invaded the cover, the dogs running in front. Naturally, they didn't hear the command. They just did what came naturally.

We had learned, hunting with our old dogs, that the roles were reversed. As pups, the dogs hunted wildly, and slowly we trained them to hunt for us. Now we hunted for our dogs. They would go their way, and we would follow. Whistles wouldn't help to bring them in. Parker would jump up to look for me, and I'd wave my hand. When she was close enough so the cataracts weren't bothering her vision, I could direct her with hand signals. If she wandered off too far, she would cut a circle, find my scent, and then home in on me. Tweed would do the same. At first, Ted and I did a bit of cussing, but we learned to relax about it. Our old dogs hunted more efficiently, for they knew instinctively they didn't have the strength. They became more thorough in chasing up birds, and because they worked closer, we had more shots. We learned to pace ourselves to our dogs' pace, and every so often we would rest, enjoy the beauty of the woods, savor the woods' aroma as our dogs lay around us, panting and slowly regaining their strength. Then we'd be off again. We would hunt several hours, relax, then hunt again. On longer days we would round-robin the dogs, leaving one in the car as we hunted with the other and moved from cover to cover.

We were resting in the potato field cover, near the stream after I had downed two woodcock over points, and Ted had brought one down in a flush. It had taken us longer than usual to find the birds—the cover was thick and Tweed was losing his nose. Parker even found one. It was a warm day after the sun burned off the fog. Ted was reminiscing about hunting with geriatric dogs.

"You know," he told me, mopping his brow and holding his red crusher hat to fan his face. "I was trained by an old dog. He belonged to a friend of my father, and was called Nod. He was about thirteen, about two years older than me. When we got off the schoolbus, Nod would be there waiting. We would run home, get our guns, and Nod would lead us into the woodcock cover. He would point perfectly and wait for us to miss, for neither of us could hit anything unless we were very lucky. If we knocked a bird down, the dog would retrieve it and keep hunting for us. When we missed, the dog would turn around and go home. Nod was a patrician, and strictly in charge. He lived to be sixteen."

Our dogs were in charge as we moved upstream to the wild-grape tangle. Parker started to make scent, moving forward, her tail pumping. I knew it was a partridge. Tweed was working downwind, out of sight. "Parker's on a grouse," I yelled, and ran forward as the grouse flushed. Instead of flying over the stream, the bird flew along the bank. "Overhead!" I yelled after I shot twice and missed, and damned myself for shooting too fast. Parker gave me one of those looks. We moved to the riverbank and worked downstream to where we thought the bird was. Tweed started his scent dance, Ted warned me, and the bird flew out of the thin alders and across the stream. We both shot. A puff of feathers immobilized itself behind the bird, and then drifted downstream as the bird fell thirty yards away into the stream near the far bank. "Fetch!" commanded Ted to Tweed. Tweed went two steps into the water, came out, and gave his master a look as if to say, "Not on your life, buddy!" Parker wouldn't even think of going into the stream, and both headed back to the alders, expecting us to follow.

"Well, Miller, I guess we're the retrievers," Ted remarked. We headed into the stream, going in over our boots. The partridge was caught in a swirl next to a rock, and I went down to retrieve it. The dogs looked on from the other shore, then Parker swam across.

Tweed followed, but the current carried him down and the dog began to tread water. "He's in trouble," yelled Ted, and handed me his gun as he scrambled down the bank. He slipped and landed in the stream up to his neck and gave me a look that was about the same as Tweed's. "Help!" Ted takes to water like a pussycat. He grabbed Tweed and the two of them, soaked like dishrags, made it to shore. I was on my knees, choking with laughter as Parker sat beside me.

Water was dripping off Ted's nose, and I could hear it gurgle and slosh in his hunting vest. "What's so Goddamned funny?" We walked upstream to find a crossing, carried the dogs across, and left for home.

We dried the dogs off, changed our clothes, and finished the potato field cover in the afternoon. Parker made a staunch point, head down, not moving a muscle. Quiet filled the vacuum this dog and I and woodcock made, as I heard myself breathing. I flexed my muscles and moved in, balancing on both feet, slightly swinging, scanning with my eyes unfocused, left and right, waiting for the bird to flush. Suddenly it was up, moving fast. For some reason, this season's woodcock did not tower, they shot up in a hurry. The gun moved up in that unconscious motion I had learned through the years, and the bird was down.

Parker had not budged. She was still on point, head down. I walked up, retrieved the bird, brought it back, and dropped it in front of her. She broke then, mouthed the bird once, and gave me a look of pride and satisfaction that said we had both done our jobs. She had not heard my shot, nor had she seen the bird flush, nor had she seen me retrieve the bird. I knew then, and it made me shiver a bit, that we were perhaps partaking of our last season.

Tweed scouted another woodcock for Ted, and then Tweed and Parker vanished. We could not hear their bells, and we began scouting, each going in a different direction. I thought Parker might be on point and kept ducking down, looking around. Ten minutes later I found her lying down, her front paws crossed as she does at home sometimes, giving me that "where-have-you-been" look. "Park, whatcha doing there? Come on," but Parker remained quiet, taking it easy. Suddenly I understood. The woodcock flushed and moved to the right, scrambling around a poplar. I was on it, thank God, and the bird was down. Parker found it, mouthed it, and gave me a look as if to say "about time," then moved on.

In the lazy warmth of the afternoon we lifted Tweed and Park into the back of the station wagon and drove home. It was a good opening for the first day of the season with two geriatric, stone-deaf dogs and their over-the-hill hunters. We flushed eight woodcock. Parker pointed five and I shot four: Ted brought down two over Tweed, and we shared one partridge. A typical opening day in the potato field. That night we celebrated with a woodcock meal with two lady friends. Our dog friends were zonked out, not moving.

The fall of '77 was a good one. The leaves rattled off the trees early in October as the winds skeletized the covers and opened up the shooting. Although the flights did not appear, we found singles and doubles of woodcock, and the most partridge in a decade. Many times I hunted only with Parker in covers known by names that mean something special to the two of us—the Iron Bridge Cover, the Cows That Scared Parker Cover, the Love Cover, the Where I Got the Double Cover. These were patches of alders and poplars scattered throughout Vermont, worthless pieces of wetland and small brooks and hillside overgrown mowings that were of value only to a dog such as Parker and a hunter like me.

It was a dark wet day in late October, but I had time to hunt and the scent would be good so I drove to the Swimming Hole Cover, named because there is a curve in the brook that is deep and rock-edged. A willow leans over the hole and a rope hangs from a branch. During the summer the local kids use it. Occasionally, in the fall, Parker or I scare a trout that darts upstream, a dark arrow in a narrow stream. Alders line the stream and are kept open by grazing cows. Higher up are the apple trees, more alders, and thick second-growth hardwoods. I hit a flight in there once, with Park, and came out with a limit. We were again looking for it.

The stream meanders in a serpentine fashion so you must cross it several times. We found no birds in the first two patches along the stream, not even chalk, so I decided to move to the higher cover. Parker was working my right, and I expected her to move up the hill after I crossed. She didn't show, and I walked back to the stream thinking she was on point.

I spotted her downstream, stretched out, lifeless, the water streaming over her. My God, I muttered, dropped my gun, ran into the water, and dragged her out to the bank, which was grassy and clean where the heifers had browsed. I opened her mouth, pulled the tongue and began beating her chest. But she hadn't drowned, she had just died. She was gone. I lay there on the ground, my hands on her, the water soaking her, and rested my head on her flank. "Oh God, Parker," I whispered. "Park, oh Park."

I carried her about a half mile to the car and took her home. In the old bathtub I washed the dirt and gravel from her. She looked so old, so different. I put her in a plastic sack, took the shovel out of the garage, and drove up to the potato field.

In the corner we always hunted first, and where there was always a bird, and only about one hundred yards from where she had pointed her first woodcock twelve years ago, I buried her with her collar, the bell I used that was hung on a leather ski strap I had cut down, and the white plastic whistle I used, tied to the old piece of soft clothesline. I marked the grave by carving the date on a nearby tree, then squatted down by the raw earth. There was a slight wind blowing and it was damp, a hunter's type of damp, good scent weather. A songbird fluttered overhead, stopped on a branch, and looked at us. Branches from the alders moved softly in the wind. Most of the leaves were down, and the colors were gray and mauve, the early colors of November. That evening Ted came over and we mournfully drank our way through the night.

The Woodcock Hunter's Lament

"It's been a long time, Ray, and gosh, it's good to see you!"

"And you, Brad! You look like you did back then. Still got the Parker 16?"

"Blew the barrels. Now she's a 20."

"Parker your Brittany?"

"Died in '77. Been traveling too much to get another. Cutter must be gone now."

"Killed by a Goddamned car. I have Cutter the Second now."

"Sherry?"

"Well, we've been divorced five years. Brad, I'm sorry over that . . . what happened."

"Water over the dam, forget it. Tell me about the covers. Remember the Two Dead Drunks cover? That morning in the mist when the two of them, drunk out of their minds, sang as they stumbled by in their pajamas and the dogs went wild?"

"Judith and George. How can anyone forget? Drunk til the day they died. They seemed to enjoy it though. Their house was sold and the new owners cleared the cover and put up a horse barn and riding ring there."

"Now that's a damn shame! Been into the Screaming Lady cover?"

"Well, she had a nervous breakdown and they moved away. A guy from Connecticut built a big colonial house right smack in the center of the cover. He's never there. A couple of woodcocks still nest where we scared Lena but you're hunting right on the edge of his lawn."

"The School Yard cover? God, Ray, I'll never forget the time Cutter went nuts when we hit that flight and chased all those birds to Mississippi. I was so mad, screaming at you and Cutter. We didn't get a bird."

"Well, Cutter was young then, wasn't he? Must 'a been seventy-five woodcock in that flight. Never seen one again like it. No, the School cover is gone. They dozed it flat and made a soccer field out of it."

"The Waterfall Cover?"

"Been turned into a trailer park. Funny, though, they cut down the alders and put in fill, and then the trailers. The falls is there like it was. Should have bought that land, back then."

"The Ghost Cover? That's where Parker retrieved her first and last woodcock. When Park picked up that bird she just rolled her eyes and spit it out."

"Funny how some dogs hate to pick up a woodcock. That old ghost house, now, it was torn down and they put up a saltbox summer home for a New York couple—both of them lawyers. They cleaned out the aspens, left the birch, and planted grass."

"It doesn't sound too good, Ray. How about the Hidden Cover we had to walk so far into? Best partridge and woodcock cover we had back then."

"Well, it's now a condominium project. They get $350,000 for just one of the units. They also put a golf course below the hill where the deer yarded up."

"The Three Bird cover, right in the middle of the mowing, with the spring and just a couple of alders? No one would build there."

"Big housing development went up on the hill behind, where we would find the grouse in a good apple year. When they started out they cut down

the patch of alders and put up their development sign. They call it Partridge Hill. Don't know if anyone up there even knows what a woodcock is."

"You hunt anymore, Ray?"

"Sometimes, but for woodcock I drive up to the Northeast Kingdom, 'bout forty or fifty miles."

"You still doing carpentry and ski instructing?"

"Naw, I now sell real estate for Jackson. Make a real good living. Things have changed, Brad."

"You wouldn't happen to know where Sherry's living, would you Ray?"

The Battenkill

Ray Harris, 1931–1969

John Roesler, 1939–1968

The only difference I noticed, as I parked my car, was that the choke-cherry bushes had grown much higher. The wooded area, just behind the railroad tracks, remains a backdrop for the stream, hidden from view. A sweet breeze cooled my face as I threaded my rod, put on my waders, and, carefully latching the gate behind me, walked down the edge of the pasture. Two Morgans had their necks arched as they fed on the grass. They ignored me, as they always had. The valley remained a deep green in midsummer; Equinox Mountain was softened blue by summer haze. I climbed the wire fence that we always climbed and crossed the railroad tracks. Hidden on the other side was the stream, narrow here, about thirty feet wide bordered by ferns that grew waist high in the summer. Above, the tree branches arched overhead so this tiny river here had the appearance of a nave in a long, tree-structured cathedral. The trees filtered the sun, sprinkling bright splotches of light that shimmered on the water. The water was so clean that the brown gravely bottom appeared pristine. Even in midsummer the water remained cold, cooled by shade and springs. So many times, in another era, I had fished this section with Ray Harris, my best friend. The Battenkill had been our favorite trout stream and this was our favorite fishing stretch. We called it the Jungle.

I walked into the middle of the stream and felt the cold water cool my legs and the current tug me as I scrunched my feet into the gravel and looked up and down the stream for rises. There were none. All was quiet. Too quiet, I thought, for usually the birds were singing, the warblers, thrushes, the knock-knock-knock of the woodpecker counterpointing the drumming of a partridge sixty yards across the river and deeper into the jungle. But it was a late, lazy summer afternoon.

About forty yards downstream where the trees opened up and the sun hit the water, where we could see the freight trains pass and the engineer would wave at us, a ritual we enjoyed, a fish rose, creating a dimpled circle. There were brookies in this section, precious jewels with their orange and vermillion spots, and we usually passed them by for the browns. I recalled the one day about eight years ago in the spring, when the leaves were a pale chartreuse and the fiddleheads were just uncurling their tight ball, a March brown mayfly hatch appeared. The stream was covered with them, and the fish began to rise and dappled the stream from bank to bank as if fat raindrops from a thunder squall were pocking the surface. I was in a fit; I had to change flies, and my hands were shaking so I could hardly thread the leader through the eye of the hook, while down below Ray was playing a heavy fish and then finally I was on to a good one, then another. One half hour later the rises stopped. The river appeared as if there were no fish under its surface, and the mayflies floating so perky on the skin on the water's surface was a dream. We sat on the banks, gasping, laughing, admiring the fat browns we kept. My hands were still shaking, and I smoked a cigarette, for it had been the first time in my life I was caught in the middle of a hatch where the rises were constant and furious, a frenzy of feeding.

But it was summer now, when hatches come in the evening and the rises were few. I decided to move through this cathedral to a bend where tree trunks lay in the water and big trout hid under complicated undercurrents. It was hard to fish, but it was here I learned from Ray how to backhand a cast, or side-hand it and parachute the size 18 fly just under a low branch and a few inches from the undercut bank, where the big browns lay. We fished to the rise, each of us fishing a different section. On our knees in shallow water, we crawled into casting range and using our seven-foot, bamboo Battenkill rods, flicked out the fly and leader, hoping not to scare the feeding trout.

Some fish made a smacking sound as they took a fly and we knew they were fourteen inches or bigger. Other times they dimpled the water and then we didn't know what size they were. We fished into the ghostly, gray period between evening and darkness. We held penlights in our mouths to thread our flies onto the leaders and we cast toward what we could not see, but hear.

In the late afternoon the cathedral part of the jungle is somber; light barely penetrates the trees, and I sat at the base of an alder just above the

bank and waited for a rise. A red squirrel quarreled at me from an overhead branch. It was like that the last time.

Then I saw a rise under the low-hanging branch next to the opposite shore, where the bank was undercut. I held my breath and counted.
Within thirty seconds there was another rise. It was the same spot a fish
rose the last time we were on the stream. I watched as the circle the rising
fish created widened, flattened, and disappeared. I moved into the stream
crouched over, stripped line out, and false cast upstream. I had to thread
the fly under that low-hanging branch. The fish rose again, I waited and
I cast and settled the olive quill fly neatly next to the bank with enough
curl in the leader to stop drag. I pulled in slack and the quill disappeared
and I struck quickly and reeled in slack. He played hard, as do all these
fish, and I knew he would be twelve-inch brown before I landed him.
He was a beautiful fish, with bright orange spots, a deep brown and gold
color, his nose almost black. I took my knife out, gutted him, and admired
the orange-colored flesh that all wild trout in this stream have before I
wrapped him in ferns and put him in my creel. I sat and smoked as the
sun went over the mountain and the water flattened to a dark gray. It
was a mysterious place, this cathedral section; it was always quieter then
other sections, the water was slick in its movement, it neither bubbled nor
gurgled. I waited, looking for rises as the light died. Nothing. The stream
remained dead. No hatch, no evening rise, and I moved downstream from
the cathedral, to the bend where the water was fast and I could see the first
glimmer of the moon. Then I remembered, the moon was almost full, and
although it was fun to fish under a full moon, we rarely caught anything.
I listened for the smack of a rise—sound fishing we called it—and waited
as darkness shrouded me, and remembered other times when Ray and I
waited silently so as not to disturb this sense of suspended time.

Sometimes we caught nothing; other times we kept half a dozen trout.
The ones we didn't eat right off we froze in milk cartons filled with water.
On the way home we stopped for a beer. We felt relaxed and good, and let
the night air ride through the open windows of the car.

We followed the seasons. Henricksons, quill Gordens, red quills, March
browns, light Cahills. We started with size 12, moved to size 14s, and
then, in summer, we switched to size 18. We would put on a larger light
Cahill or white Wulff for night fishing, for we could see them as a ghost

of a glimmer on the water, and they wouldn't sink. We cut our ten- or twelve-foot leaders down to eight feet and hoped that maybe a five- or seven-pounder might strike. It never happened, but we talked about it, in the late winter, after skiing.

We stretched our season into August, when the water was low and the fish wary. It was a good time; we knew the Battenkill so well, and the holes and how spring runoff destroyed some fish holes while building others, its hidden undercut banks where the big browns sulked, feeding rarely and carefully, and those tree-logged holes with the really big fish that we never fooled. So we knew that at three thirty every afternoon in late May or early June the Cahill hatch would pop up and float downstream as the mayflies dried their wings and the big browns would go berserk and so would we.

But now there were no rises. Small eddies reflected strands of fluttering moonlight. It was silent as always.

I could feel the dew on my jacket and a clamminess around my body from being encased in waders as I sat there mesmerized by the moving stream and I thought of days and years and lives that had slid past as quickly as the moon-silvered current.

I lit my flashlight and stood up, flexing my bones, shaking off the stiff-ness, and crossed the train tracks, climbed the fence, and climbed the pasture. Along the way I picked a handful of ferns and Indian paintbrushes and black-eyed Susans. I didn't need the flashlight now, the moon flooded the valley and pasture in soft luminesence.

I drove the back way home, stopped at the tiny graveyard in Landgrove. I had to make my peace, and I went to the corner where Ray Harris was buried four years ago, killed in a car accident on the night of the moon-walk, my best friend, and I left the flowers and ferns at the base of the white marble tombstone as the moon so high bathed us in its pallor. I squatted there and looked at the tombstone and thought of nothing and everything. A stream behind this tiny graveyard gurgled quietly.

Why is this stream, the Battenkill, so tied up with deaths that are part of me, that reside in my memory, so poignant, that I cannot forget?

Our insular Green Mountain life protected us from Vietnam, although it was beginning to darken our horizon. We were in our early thirties, we lived in a beautiful state, and yes, we were insulated and selfish in our country life.

My wife and I had purchased some land in Weston and were building a house. It was in a beautiful setting, next to a woods and overlooking a pasture. A fold below the house I made into a pond. I was painting the living room wall, and a neighbor, John Roesler, was helping me. Young, tall, and slim, with blond hair, he was recently discharged from active duty as a Marine officer. He and his wife (quick smile and flashing eyes, dark hair, lively, so pretty) lived a few miles away, with John's parents. John was sorting out his civilian life, and while we were painting, we talked about Vietnam.

"I think I should go back in the service," he said.

I was surprised and looked down at him from my ladder.

"Why?" I asked. "You've done your time, you have a young wife, a baby, a new life in front of you. "

"It's my duty," he said. He never took his eyes off the wall he was painting.

John, and I have found since most Marines I have known, have a strong sense of loyalty and obligation to the Corps. We argued late that night, while painting, about Vietnam, politics, our military obligations, where our responsibilities lie.

I could tell his sense of loyalty to the Marines and duty as a married man was causing tension between him and his wife. I switched the conversation to fishing and told about the big brown trout that live in the Battenkill and how we catch them. Or try to.

"Would you like to go?"

"Yes." He said immediately. "Can I bring my wife?"

"Of course!"

A few days later I drove them twenty miles to Manchester to where we parked next to the pink house. I led them down to the Battenkill and followed the path through the ferns and bamboo, to a stretch of curving river that was more like a wide brook. We crossed the stream at a narrow part, splashing across. None of us wore waders. Susan laughed quietly. I looked back; he was holding her around the waist as they crossed. It was a warm, velvet night. Just below our section was a deep, log-entangled bend before the river flowed into the Jungle. There were big fish there, I knew, but we never caught them during the day.

John and Susy did not have rods; they were observers and behaved just like kids, laughing softly, sitting on the bank and holding hands. It was comfortable midsummer night. No fish were rising at dusk and I said "Let's wait." We sat along the banks and I told a few fish stories. Just above us was a small rapids where the water tinkled. When it had turned shadowy dark I heard the first slurp, then another.

"A large fish is rising," I murmured. "Hear it?"

I put on a white Miller and began casting by feel, letting out line slowly until I thought I was at the right range—no more than twenty-five feet. The open pasture behind prevented snagged back casts. I cast about six times with no luck, letting out a little more line with each cast. There was another slurp, more of a smack than the first rise, and then I heard a third, this one a gurgle.

"There's three big fish rising," I said softly.

They had moved up from the deep pool in the bend, and from the sound they were feeding in the shallow water just below the rapids. I cast again and again, talking to John and his wife, who had never before sat by a stream on a very dark night and listened to rising fish.

I often checked my fly and kept the same length of line out, casting high behind me as I edged slowly up the bank toward the small waterfall. When I heard a rise, I struck, and, with no pull, did it again and again. I had a lot of competition from the hatch that the browns were sucking on.

Finally I connected, a heavy deep pull, an angry shaking of my rod. I lucked out. I held the rod high over my head, reeled in the slack, and played the fish from the reel putting on just enough pressure, I prayed, to keep the fish from fleeing downstream to the tangle of logs and his lair. John turned on the flashlight. For some miraculous reason the trout did not snap off. I worked it to shore and moved my hands under its gills and flopped it out. In the light of the flashlight it was a huge, torpedo-shaped brown about twenty inches long with a deep orange and yellow belly and brilliant orange and red spots from tail to cheek. It gleamed and glistened golden in the light of the flashlight.

I killed that fish. Usually I snap their necks by putting a hand in its mouth and pulling up, but this one had sharp teeth. I took my fishing knife and drove it through his head. The next evening I poached it in white wine and served it with almonds and lemon, green beans and small potatoes. Its flesh was firm, as orange as its belly, and the meat delicate as only wild trout from cold waters taste.

I called Ray up and told him about the fish.

"Good." He said and nothing more.

"Three of them were rising."

"At what time?"

"About ten, ten thirty."

"Hmmm" was all he said. I knew he would give it a try some night. We both knew that the river in this section could only hold one angler, and it was my gift to him.

Shortly thereafter I moved to northern Vermont. In a way it was a case of moving to save a marriage. It didn't work, and I ended up in my Colbyville garret. I learned to fish new streams, and did more hunting than fishing with Ray. He was thinking of moving to Montana, where the streams were cold and rapid and the trout numerous and robust. I didn't think his wife would much appreciate the idea.

Then he was killed.

John Roesler went back to active service in the Marines. He and his wife moved away. I never saw them again, nor his parents.

A few years after Ray's death, I was talking to someone about Weston when I asked about John and his wife.

"John? He was killed in Vietnam."

The image of him and his dark-haired wife reappeared: they crossed the stream, supporting each other, and the gleaming golden trout and his internal argument, between duty and honor and family.

The next time I was in Washington, DC, I went to the Vietnam Memorial and found his name on panel 35E, line 26. He had made captain. I brushed his carved name with my fingertips. He served in the Marines for six years. His Vietnam tour began on February 1, 1967. On January 24, 1968, in Quang Nam, he became, as they called it, a ground casualty from a hostile explosive device.

I have tried to contact his wife while writing this story in the summer of

2008, but with no luck. It has been forty years since he was killed, thirty-nine years since Ray died.

I think of John and Susy on the Battenkill, during the summer of 1963, holding hands, and the big brown trout gleaming golden in the flashlight, so full of life, so vibrant in color, so beautiful, lying on the bank.

I thought of about how much we hated the Vietnam War, and how I felt, when I was in the service, of our sense of duty to our squad and our confusion over the Korean War and I felt hollowed out, and sad, and angry.

I should never, ever, have killed that trout.

I Poach: Confessions of a Duck Hunting Addict Gone Astray

I wrote this article in the 1970s for *Vermont Life*. However, their editorial advisory committee screamed so it was killed. I assume they didn't approve of such politically incorrect activities.

Sam Webb, who owned the duck-hunting preserve in Swanton we poached on, was a descendent of William Seward Webb, who married into the Vanderbilt family and founded Shelburne Farms. Sam Webb has passed on and his land now belongs to the federal government. Sic transit . . .

I poach. Yessir, I do. And I can't help it, just like some can't help carousing with the ladies, playing golf while the family's singing hymns in church, or baiting in-laws. It's a disease, and it sure is fun.

Now I'm not like any old poacher. I have my morals. First of all, I don't break any game laws. I believe in conservation, ecology, and law and order—the last item in its rightful place, of course. I don't call partridge shooting on someone else's land poaching. That's common trespassing, and common trespassing is done by every hunter in Vermont, the reason being that Vermont hunters were brought up to believe that all of the wild woods and fields of Vermont belong to all Vermonters. (Most of the land that is posted seems to be owned by flatlanders who moved to Vermont and bought land so they could keep people off it.)

And I don't poach on government land. I don't fool with the feds. I also don't poach deer or bear or skunks. I don't even hunt rabbits by the light of the moon, although that might be fun.

No, I'm a snooty poacher. I poach only wild ducks, preferably black ducks, because they are one of the world's great delicacies when served with sauce à la Grand Marnier. And I poach only on one piece of property in Vermont, a piece of land that has the tantalizing, the dangerous, the adventurous condition of being patrolled by two gamekeepers.

Played hooky when you were a kid? Ran away from home once or twice? Went on a panty raid when in college? Gave a hot seat to the old maid in church? Went skinny-dipping with your friend the tomboy before everybody else started doing it? Mister (or lady, if you got the proclivity), that ain't nothing until you go poach ducks on land patrolled by two gamekeepers who are just aching to catch you by the suspenders of your waders. Wonderful shivers streak lickety-split up and down my back every time I step past the sign that in black-stenciled letters pontificates:

HUNTING SHOOTING TRAPPING
[in very heavy stencils]
and all
TRESPASSING
[in not as heavy stencil]
on these premises
STRICTLY PROHIBITED
[legible from a shotgun distance away]
Owner S. B. Webb

Uhhh . . . Mr. Webb, I hope you don't take this personally. I have nothing at all against you, and I wish you long life and the best of duck hunting wherever you go. It is, however, fateful circumstances that have thrown us together. You happen to own the best duck-hunting land I know of, and you have it posted, and you employ two gamekeepers. With these thousand or so No Trespassing signs strung around your property like a string of pearls on a kept woman's neck, I know for a fact that you don't want me in there.

You may recall, Mr. Webb, that I did try to go straight. I wrote you a letter four years ago, on September 16, 1970, to be exact. I said in that letter, if I may quote:

> . . . Now I like hunting up there. (Mr. Webb, I'm not letting on
> about where I'm talking about because we don't want every Tom,

Dick, and Joe duck hunter up there poaching on your property, right next to me.) There are plenty of black ducks and not too many hunters. But I do get frustrated. Those bloody ducks—they keep trespassing right onto your property, then they stay there. They have no respect at all.

Being a pretty respectful fellow, at least most of the time, I cuss at those ducks and at all those No Trespassing signs. I would just like to point out, Mr. Webb, that there is an awful lot of land up there that is posted. I know it is your land and I also know that the ducks belong to both of us, and that there are plenty to go around.

Well, what I'm working up to is—would it be okay with you if I did some duck hunting on your property?

Yours for unlimited ducks and good hunting,

Peter Miller

Mr. Webb, you sent that letter right back to me and scrawled on it in an even but backward slanted script that shows you to be a mite shy:

Dear Mr. Miller—I regret that I cannot grant you permission to hunt on my property. I hunt it regularly and believe that if I didn't hunt it carefully, a lot of fellows on the lake wouldn't get as many ducks as I do. Come one, come all would be ruinous for all. Good luck.

Samuel B. Webb

Mr. Webb, you missed the point. I wanted to hunt in there myself—to heck with all of the other fellows. And I must admit, come opening day of the Vermont duck season, you were hunting it carefully, going bangde-bangdebangdebang, shooting shells as if you worked for the Remington Arms Company. As a matter of fact, the ducks didn't seem to pay too much attention to your shooting that day, but we all have days like that.

Meanwhile, I was sitting out in the bay, on the outside of the No Trespassing signs that sport your stenciled name, and not getting any ducks at all—not even popping off my twelve.

That set me to work, and I did a little checking to see if I could improve my average of hunting hours per duck. I found that you had followed the stringent Vermont laws for posting—lettered the signs correctly, spaced them at proper distances, registered them with the town clerk, and paid the two-dollar fee. I possibly could get you on technicality, though, in that the date is not on the sign.

Now I also discovered that you had the land surveyed and put your No Trespassing signs on the low-water mark. That could be argued in court, as could the fact that I found a navigable channel into your property that should come under public domain.

But what the heck. I figured if you could hire two gamekeepers to put up a thousand signs to keep me out, then you could sure top me when it comes to legal fees.

So my only recourse was to poach. Mr. Webb, I was forced into it.

Let me tell you about the first time I poached. It was on a Sunday morning. A south wind came up just after dawn, blowing briskly. It wasn't cold, nor hot, but cool, an October-type of cool that feels good when you watch the sun rise and glisten off the reeds. You can hear the ducks quacking softly as they wake up, and hear the rush of their wings, and you're scanning the sky keenly, hoping to spot the ducks flying my way instead of your way.

That day, Mr. Webb, the ducks were going your way. One after another, big luscious lumbering blacks; smooth-flying mallards; darting, diving, rushing, fast-moving teal; pairs of plump ringnecks—they all settled down behind your No Trespassing signs. When the sun was up high enough so it didn't dazzle my eyes, I could see the ducks just kept riding the winds over your land. We had no shooting, and that's when it started.

I had two friends with me. As both are members of Rotary and lack the courage of public confession and have since retired from poaching, I will call them Bob and Bruce. We mutually agreed that the ducks were in there, not out here, and if we hoped to fill our limit, our only choice was to go in there.

So we advanced across the knee-deep water, through the reeds, over the fence, and past the neatly stenciled No Trespassing sign, onto a narrow point. Behind it is a small lagoon.

Mr. Webb, you won't ever know what real duck hunting is until you cross that point of no return into a land that is virtually a police state and patrolled by two gamekeepers, who are, for all I know, equipped with whips, pistols, and vicious Dobermans. What a thrill! What a risk sport! Not only do you look up in the air for ducks, and try to shoot with finesse, but you also look around trees for gamekeepers.

What shooting we had! The ducks just whistled overhead and we were banging away in absolute bliss. However, we were such lousy shots that we managed to down only three—a black, a mallard, and a ringneck. I was urging my colleagues to straighten up and shoot true blue.

Then Bob suddenly gave out with a frightful yelp, "Boys, the duck hunting's over!" Like something out of *Deliverance*, he grabbed his coat (it was warm with the high sun) and hightailed it through the woods toward where we came from—on the outside of the No Trespassing signs. I looked up and there was an old geezer not twenty-five yards away, coming right at us. A gamekeeper. Oh, he had a sour look on his face. We were in for it.

Adrenalin started to flow like liquor on opening night of duck camp. Bruce grabbed a duck, I grabbed the black (of course), and the three of us, up to our armpits in waders, ducks, coats, and shotguns, hippity-hopped through the woods toward freedom and safety, the gamekeeper right behind us.

Bob, who has a fear of all sorts of authority, particularly since he is Canadian and hoped to become a landed citizen of the United States, didn't want to blemish his record. He took off in the knee-deep water as if he intended to join a flight of ducks heading south. Have you ever seen a redhead or other diving duck take off? They wind up like old bi-wing planes in a bumpy pasture. Their wings flap, their legs pump, their feet churn water and splash, and they gain speed as they paddle, run on the surface of the water, and take off—quack, quack, quack.

That was just what Bob looked like. With a shotgun in one hand, coat and duck in the other, he was running and flapping over the water like a duck scared out of its wits, taking off toward oblivion.

However, Bob forgot one detail—the strand of barbed wire that marked the No Trespassing boundary, hidden under a few inches of water. He hit that barbed wire with his foot just as we assumed he would be airborne. Splat—gun, coat, duck, and Bob went full-length into the water so hard it looked like the splash a black makes falling from sixty yards. But no matter, he was up faster than a poacher's wink and, the last we saw of him, he was running over the water into the rushes, looking like he was ready to dive under and breathe air through a reed.

Bruce and I were laughing so hard we barely made it to the bullrushes, where we squatted out of sight and tried to stifle ourselves. All humped over, using the reeds as a cover, we finally reached our camouflaged boat and whistled Bob out of his hiding place. The whites of his eyes were bulging, his mouth was tense, and he looked around shiftily. Wet soggy reeds hung half in, half out of his waders and in his hair.

"Where is he?" he whispered.

We finally spotted the gamekeeper up in a tree, eyeballing us with binoculars. He carried no whip, no gun, and had no dog. Just a nice, ordinary, elderly gamekeeper who had scared the hell out of us. We kept the tarp over the number on our motorboat, and, giggling uncontrollably, puttered off into the safety of distance.

It was our baptism under fire. Like soldiers, some survive the test, Mr. Webb, and some don't. I'm the only veteran left.

That night we named the site of our first sortie Poacher's Point. The

next day (I believe in quick counterattacks, Mr. Webb), I named a neigh-boring area, just as rich in ducks, Poacher's Island.

That was the beginning. Since then I have learned a few finer points about poaching. Do not poach on weekends. Other hunters might see you and follow, and I for one don't like poachers following me into a poach. Also, gamekeepers are active on weekends. Poach during the week, early in the morning, late at night. Pick up your empty shells. Littering isn't nice, and neither is evidence of your dirty work. Poach on miserable days, when the gamekeepers will be warming their toes.

Make quick sorties, in and out. Don't go too deep into enemy territory. I made this mistake one afternoon and walked more than one hundred yards into a bay. On the other side, about four hundred yards distant, materializing out of the swamp, was a duck boat and a man dressed in green. He was using a long pole to glide the boat toward me. My eyes bugged. God but he looked like a giant—an evil swamp spirit. Where the hell did he come from? I about-faced and surged toward shore, but have you ever tried to move fast in chest waders when the water is up to your belly button and your feet are mired to the knees in muck? I should have died of a heart attack, and not from fright. The gamekeeper caught me fifty yards from safety.

"Now don't you feel silly hunting in here?" he asked. I'm sure he was snickering to himself, because I almost jumped out of the muck; I didn't expect him to catch up so fast. He sure can pole a boat a lot quicker than a mired poacher can run to shore. And he was right. I sure did feel silly.

"Yeah!" I gasped. "But there ain't any ducks out there," and I pointed my gun toward where we riff-raff have to hunt—outside the signs. "Well, there ain't no ducks in here either," he said.

He was awful nice about it, a real gentleman. I walked to shore friendly-like and promised myself never to poach no more, no sir.

Well, when I was fifty yards on my side of the No Trespassing signs, and after I had regained my breath, my wits, and my courage, I turned around, looked toward Poacher's Island, and said to myself, "Dummy! Don't go so deep. Be quick. Foxes don't hang around in the chicken yard waiting for the farmer."

And no ducks? Let me tell you, Mr. Webb, two of the few doubles I ever downed were finessed while poaching on your land—a pair of gadwalls and a pair of ringnecks that were flaring in a heavy wind. They were the nicest shots I have ever made.

Some of my prettiest moments have also been there—all alone except for that eerie feeling that you are being watched. Then the sun, all bronzed and serene, goes under in New York state and flights of blacks, between six and a dozen birds in each, cross the reddened sky, with flashes of precision flying. In the distance a large flock of Canada geese heads south, bobbing up and down in awkward flight. The honking floats lightly to me in the wind. One night, when I was a bit late in getting out (damn engine wouldn't start and I thought I would become a permanent resident of Poacher's Island), a line of snow geese came over my head with a murmur of wind in their wings, sliding through the moonlit air in a wildly sensuous motion, smooth and silky white and wild as Diana. They landed not far away, and the night, lit up with a bright moon, was absolutely still except for the lap of water against my waders and the knock of an oar against my boat.

Mr. Webb, it sure is fun and soul-filling, even though I know you don't like it, for I found one of your handwritten messages stuck on a fence post. As I recall, it said,

> Keep out or beware of the consequences! You know who we mean!
> S. R. Webb

Well, I sure know whom you mean. I was going to frame that note, but unfortunately, that afternoon, while poaching, I overswung on a black and I landed flat on my back in the swamp with my gun pointing toward heaven and water gurgling in my waders. Your note got soaked and so did I. That night I cussed you, and the ducks, and duck hunting and poaching.

I was thinking about us one day while trout fishing, Mr. Webb, in reverie so to speak. The law does give you the right to keep people off your land. But the spirit of adventure and danger will always call people like me to try their luck, evading gamekeepers and poaching a succulent black duck or two. You and I, Mr. Webb, are acting out our roles in history. Our lives have perhaps a touch of Shakespearean predestination in the drama of mankind.

On a more practical matter, Mr. Webb, have you ever eaten black duck that has been poached? There's no finer-tasting bird in the world, particularly if it's been summering on your property. Anyway, here's the recipe for Peter's Poached Duck:

Poach a duck or two, preferably blacks that were raised on land guarded by gamekeepers. This adds zest to the flavor, but do not get caught poaching the ducks, as that makes the meat taste a bit like crow. To remove any guilt-ridden flavor, shoot the duck in legal season, in legal hours, and fortify yourself with a duck stamp and license. Shoot only ducks within a twenty-five- to thirty-yard range. (I use a twelve-gauge Francotte with twenty-six-inch modified and improved barrels.)

Take the ducks home and carefully pluck before cleansing. I prefer to use a hot water and paraffin mixture to completely remove all regular feathers and pin feathers. Then clean the bird and remove the head, feet and wings.

Make a pot of wild rice. Let cool. Mix with one cup chopped onions, the juice from three oranges, salt, pepper, oregano, and two spoonfuls of marmalade. Stuff the mixture into the duck. Place the duck in a roasting pan. Baste with fresh orange juice mixed with Grand Marnier, and leave the orange rinds in the pan. Cook for fifteen to twenty minutes at four hundred degrees or until the breast is pink, as in rare steak. Add to the drippings in the pan one jigger of Grand Marnier, a spoonful of mustard, and a spoonful of marmalade. Warm and serve as sauce with the duck. To accompany the duck, French-cut string beans mixed with sautéed mushrooms and almonds and simmered in heavy cream are quite adequate. For wine I find a Burgundy goes best—a Volnay or Pommard.

Mr. Webb, there is hardly a finer eating duck than the black, and if it's poached on posted property there is added a quintessence of fine flavor that is really savored only by the poacher.

The Suicide

The woodcock hunting is wicked good in Belmont, a small village just north of Weston, southeast of Rutland. This hilly and mostly forested region was originally populated with wood choppers, a couple of sawmills, and a toy factory. Woods were cleared and the land turned into pastures and mowings. Farms thrived and then, in the twentieth century, many withered to foundations and the fields were invaded by scrub brush, then alders.

Alders grow in moist soil and attract angleworms, which the woodcock, that worm sucker, feeds on. Surprisingly, these migratory game birds are recognized as the most delicate of wild fowl. There are more than thirty-one woodcock recipes in the *Larousse Gastronomique*.

In the fall of 1990 my nephew, my Brittany Val, and I were hunting a strip of alders bordered by a gravel pit on one side, by Route 155, the high-way that cuts below the town on its way from Weston to East Wallingford. On the far end is a cornfield that had recently been chopped. We had shot a few birds and were walking the edge of the field when I noticed drill holes punctured in the dirt, made by woodcock as they probed for worms with their long bills. We hunted the woods that skirted this field, and followed it down a hill to an old dirt road and a bridge that crossed a brook and led to hayfields that were still mowed. On the west side stood another swath of alders that were separated from the field by a stone wall, and we set the dog in, fought our way through the brush. It was so thick the branches kept knocking my hat off. The alders were gnarly with age, and when that happens, the woodcock shy away. I think maybe the acid-ity of the trees sends the worms looking for sweeter soil. We put up two birds; Val flushed one wild. Forty years ago, I thought, this cover was prob-ably a hayfield.

I glimpsed, through a tangle of branches, a patch of bright yellow. It was tape, about waist high, stretched between some alders, an ironwood tree, and the trunk of a very large white pine. It formed a triangle, about twenty feet long on each side.

On the tape was printed CRIME SCENE, DO NOT CROSS.

"What the hell?" I said to myself, standing at the point of the triangle marked by the ironwood, about ten inches in diameter. It had smooth skin and it appeared to be blackened by fire. There was matted ground cover. About eighteen feet in front of the tree was a large pine. I estimated its trunk to be thirty-six inches in diameter.

We walked out of the cover, and when we were on the highway I stopped a man on a tractor, asked him what the tape was for.

"Guy burned himself up with gasoline."

The next day I went back and photographed the tape and trees that encompassed this suicide scene. It was about a half mile from the bridge and, walking across the hayfield to the alders, I could see the pine that rose like a ship's mast above the alders. It had been there a long time. *Why did this man kill himself with that tree in front of him?*

It was a fall day, not too cold, cloudy bright. As I stood there, camera on tripod, I looked around. I saw three trees (eventually I counted four) that had bulbous growths on their trunks. No trees or plants grew in front of the pine. It was very quiet; the light was dull, the air was limpid; no birds sang, the absence of wind flattened the scene into silence. My instinct as a hunter told me these woods were barren of all wildlife. I felt something else too, an almost imperceptible quivering that made me uneasy. I folded up the tripod, and when I crossed the stone fence into the brightness of the hayfield, I felt this tension and sense of unease dissipate.

I developed the film, filed it, and buried the incident in my mind. Yet . . . every fall during hunting season, with my shotgun cradled in my arm, I visited the site of this man's death. Someone had taken down the tape and rolled it up and left it on the ground. The next year the tape was again circling the trees. The following year, the tape was gone. Someone else, I said to myself, also has an interest in this site. Later I heard from a friend that the person who committed suicide was originally from Belmont . . . that he liked to fish.

For the next decade, at the oddest moments, my mind would form a picture of this man's last moments, of the smoke-blackened tree and the large pine and of a man carrying a gas can walking into that woodcock cover to the base of the big pine. Why would a man walk half a mile into an almost impenetrable mass of alder trees, carrying a gas can, then dowse his body and burn himself to death? I thought of the horror of the gas

exploding and fire searing his body, sucked into his lungs, the pain. Did he pour it on his head? Or on his legs? The scene was scarred into my imagination. For some reason, I thought of myself as him, lying under the tree, looking up at the pine. Who was he? I couldn't envision what he looked like. Did he have brown or blue eyes? Was he bald or gray-haired, was he right- or left-handed, tall or short; did he smile and did he look directly at you? What kind of ice cream did he like? Did he drink? What were his hobbies? How had he lived his life? Was he ever married?

As a journalist my curiosity was aroused by his death but I never considered it a story. Then, when I began compiling this book, I found that my personal life, which I keep out of journalism, does cross into the essays and stories I write. Why had I buried this one? I had a number of friends commit suicide in the 1960s and early '70s, and I try to keep their ghosts out of my mind; maybe that was it. Or maybe it is the old American practice of evading the thoughts of death and the fragility of life. Or the consequences of the choices we make, like lighting a match.

Seventeen years later I visited Belmont on a sharp spring day when the snowbanks beside the roads were punky and patches of snow were clumped on the north side of trees and slopes. Just west of the village center is Star Lake. It was ice covered but the outlet was clear. In the pocket park by the lake canoes sat on platforms. Melting snow exposed a scattering of dog shit. Nearby is the Odd Fellow's Hall, Colfax Lodge Number 21. Across the street are the church and fire station. At the four corners are the library, the historical society museum, and the country store with gas pumps out front and attached post office. Classic, wood-frame architecture marked the town's age; it was founded in 1792. It's a pleasant, compact place to live, I thought. As I walked to the country store an old black Lab took its time moping down the center of the road, past the cemetery and library to, I assume, a meal at the country store.

At the store I inquired if anyone knew about the suicide that happened so long ago. Blank looks. There's been no suicide here, one said. Newcomers have taken over the store and to them the town's oral history is a foreign language. So I walked into the post office and spoke to the postmaster, Jane Hill. Glasses, blond hair, friendly. She knew the history.

"That was George Ellis. His brother is Frank and sister is Bernice. Ben and Agnes were their father and mother. They lived behind this store in a fixed-up horse barn." She gave me the telephone number for Frank. "George wasn't too smart. No, I don't know why he did what he did. He's buried in the cemetery just up the road. So are Agnes and Ben. You'll see a mausoleum. That's not theirs but they are buried just below it."

I walked up to the cemetery, backtracking the black Lab. MECHANIX-VILLE CEMETERY, the sign read, OPEN FROM DAWN TO DUSK. In 1911 the town residents changed the town's name to Belmont and also changed the name of Jackson's Pond to Star Lake. Early gentrification, I thought.

It didn't take long to find the Ellis tombstones on the town side of the cemetery near some broken-down maples that appeared to be near death. In front of his parents' markers was a single stone. Drifted snow half-covered the short monument. I squatted down and scooped it away.

GEORGE H. ELLIS, 1932–1990, it read. Carved above the name was a jumping trout and the outline of mountains.

"Damn," I said to myself, "he did like to fish!" And what was carved on his tombstone sure looked like a brookie, the small native trout caught in the nearby streams and ponds. I knew darn well he fished for those tasty six-inch brookies that lived in the stream crossed by the bridge and the road that led to the hayfield and the big pine.

Belmont is in the township of Mount Holly, so I drove to the town office to look at George's death record. His body was found on June 22, 1990, at 14:15. His estimated death was June 10. His body was taken to Burlington, and an autopsy performed by a Dr. Morrow. George was cremated.

George lay there for ten days after he killed himself. Who found him? His body was not only burned but must have been decomposed. Had animals been dining there? I know there are coyotes in the region. Fox, bear, fisher cats, too, are meat eaters.

Frank Ellis, George's brother, lived in Mendon, a town north of Rutland. I called up the number the postmaster gave me. A woman answered.

"Mrs. Ellis?" I asked.

"Yes."

"I would like to speak to Frank, if he is there."

A pause. "Who is this?"

"You don't know me, but my name is Peter Miller. I came across the place in the woods where Frank's brother committed suicide. I'm a writer and . . ."

"My husband passed away four years ago."

The Belmont postmaster was not up to date on this matter, I thought, and began a verbal tap dance. Mrs. Ellis, Norma, said I could visit.

A simple, neat bungalow on a cul-de-sac off Route 4, not far from the Mendon apple orchards. Norma lives alone. Friendly, and like many people who are older and single, appreciates company. We sat in the living room.

"My husband Frank died of prostate cancer. I met him at a dance in Belmont, but we never lived there. Frank was smarter than his brother George."

She sat in an easy chair, hands in her lap. Although it was near noon, the room was dark.

"George lived with his father and mother in a fixed-up horse barn. His mother was not educated, and George did not go beyond the eighth grade. He wasn't retarded; he just wasn't smart.

"George and his parents worked for farmer Armstrong. I think he was eighteen or twenty when his mother found a beer in the refrigerator and kicked George out. He was glad to leave and went to Rutland and worked for P. J. Noonan, a tire company. He never married.

"He had a guardian and he wanted to buy a pickup but he said no. This bothered him. He also had a brain tumor and was in the hospital and had another appointment with the doctor."

The heck with the pickup, I thought. The brain tumor would have caught my attention.

"George did not keep the doctor's appointment. Rather, he drove from Rutland to the old road where the brook is. He parked his car, siphoned gas out of it, and walked into the woods.

"Frank said George had built a platform facing the pine tree and lit himself up. He was missing for a week."

"Do you know who found him?" I asked.

"No . . . My husband was pretty upset. George had a checkbook that was in his apartment and they couldn't find it or any money. Two state police detectives investigated. The thought was that maybe there was foul play. George had never been suicidal.

"Some marijuana plants were found deeper in the woods, past the big tree."

Our conversation meandered, but not in a pleasant way. She had a son who died of leukemia. The thought brought her back to her husband's death.

"Frank was in pain from the cancer and on drugs. He hallucinated once and said, 'George wants me to go with him. I said no, I don't want to go.'"

Norma is psychic, she told me, and has seen ghosts that appeared like a black nebulous wave, in her house. She also saw things that would happen to people, sometimes bad, she said.

That was enough for me. I had been psychic at one time and saw things too. It scared the willies out of me. Our conversation wound down, and I thanked her for her time and graciousness.

As I drove home I thought of Norma and Frank and always I came back to George. Who found him in the woods? What was the condition of his body? Did he have a fishing rod with him? Who planted the marijuana? And above all, I wanted to know, is what did that pine tree mean to George and why did he use fire to kill himself? What was he thinking?

Frank would have known the details, and he's gone. I went to the state police barracks in Rutland and was told that the records pertaining to this case would be at their headquarters in Waterbury, where I live. I visited them, and they told me to pay twenty dollars to do a search. I paid in cash. I never heard back and considered my payment a contribution to the state police retirement fund, but I did find that 1990 was the last year the state police filed written records. The computer took over the year after George's death.

I dropped my research for other work, but several months later again tried to acquaint myself with George. I tracked down the State of Vermont recordkeeper—another dead end. Those old records, he told me, reports written by hand or typed, had been destroyed.

I felt like my shoelaces were untied and I couldn't reach them, but I made some progress. Dennis Devereux lives in Belmont and had been a state representative. His father had run the country store and renovated the old barn as an apartment for the Ellis family.

"Ag never went past the fourth grade," he told me. He was referring to George's mother Agnes. "She did baby-sitting, cleaned houses, odd jobs."

"George was called Bung. He drank some and was not smart. They have an older sister in Florida. Neither boy liked her.

"Ray Bana farmed that land and owned it, where the suicide took place. Ellis's mother was a Johnson before she married and lived three-quarters of a mile from the suicide.

"We used to take picnics down by the stream and the bridge," said Dennis. "It was an old bridge and my mother would not cross it."

Bung. Where did he get that nickname?

May 20, 2007, was the last time I visited George's suicide site. This time I took a camera. It was a Sunday afternoon, cloudy, spitting rain and raw. I took a photograph of the road sign. It is now called Scampsville Road, so named for a small settlement where, one day, long ago, an old lady found some trespassers on her property and said, "Scamps! Get off my land!"

The road is nothing more than two ruts in mud and ends at the bridge about three hundred yards away through a tunnel of trees. The bridge had been repaired by the Vermont Association of Snow Travelers and is part of their trail system.

This time I looked carefully at the stream. George probably fished under the bridge, where there was shade, and also downstream, where there was a small hole and falls. He would have used a fly rod to dangle worms and not scare the trout. The brook was less than ten feet wide. George would have been lucky to catch a trout over seven inches.

Six maples, some so old they have collapsed, line the road leading up to the pasture. To the right at the edge of the field, no longer mowed, is a tangle of brambles and scrub brush and one lilac bush. Partially covered on the edge is the foundation for the old home, a layering of field stones. The land was sold to the government as a CCC project in the 1930s. Herb Harris and his family lived there. Adjacent to it was a poured concrete foundation and I guessed it was a small barn for Jersey cows. Deep in the thickets, very well hidden, is the skeleton of a 1930-something car, its wheels half buried. Engine, radiator cap, steering wheel, hubcaps, everything of value had been ripped off. You would never see that car if you didn't force your way into the brush.

From the corner of the barn foundation, to the northwest, about one hundred fifty yards away, the big pine tree lorded it over the alders.

George Tarbell, who used to be Belmont's road commissioner, knew George: "I used to hay that field next to where George was found. I remember in the late 1940s George and I fertilized it with horse manure. There were lots of horses used for twitching out the logs. One fellow had eighty of them. He lived up on the mountain.

"We worked for Bill Moulton, who leased the land for haying. He milked eighty cows at one time.

"I think a boy and his father found George. They were hunting. Think they had a dog."

There was a dog, but no hunters. If that was true, they were hunting out of season. I had called the *Rutland Herald*'s librarian to locate an article about the suicide but I was not allowed in the archives and the archivist said he would look and get back to me. He never did. I then talked to Paul Carson, the state librarian in Montpelier. They have the *Rutland Herald* on microfilm. He found a clipping about the suicide and faxed it to me. It was not hunters or marijuana planters who found the body but Vermont state troopers and a state police dog borrowed from Connecticut. The dog found George's body in less than half a day. That was on June 22. The body was very badly decomposed. With the help of the personnel director for the state police I finally found the investigating officers; both had retired. One had moved to Florida. The dispatcher for the Rutland barracks called the other officer, who still lived in the Rutland area, and related my request for an interview. He refused to talk about it. "Maggots" was his only comment. That was enough for me. I decided not to pursue any further the finding of George's body.

The police used dental records to identify the body, but they knew it was George, for his car, a 1980 white Citation, was parked by the bridge. People had seen it there but thought it was someone who was fishing. Chances are, if they looked, there was a fishing pole in the car. Or did George first go fishing and have the pole with him? Local lore is that George first fished the stream before he went into the woods, gas can in hand.

I walked along the field to a point opposite the big pine. It was mid-spring; weeds were dormant, leaves had not budded. Marsh marigolds were in bloom in the ditch and skunk cabbage was growing near George's tree. I found what I was looking for, an opening in the stone wall opposite the pine tree. Was it for logging, or a hay road? George certainly was familiar with it. I walked in a large circle around the pine tree but could not find any signs of the road or where it went. I did find a crumpled Budweiser beer can that looked like it had been riddled with bird shot. I put it in my pocket. If there was marijuana growing deeper in the woods, it had nothing to do with George, I thought. Many times I have found a couple of marijuana plants growing in Vermont woods. I came back to the suicide site. The burn marks were no longer on the ironwood tree. I peered down at the site where George had lain and there was a turd, about nine inches long. Bear scat, I thought, made last fall. Later, when I examined the beer can, I found it was not birdshot that punctured the can but teeth marks. Several of the holes were a quarter-inch wide. Only a bear would have such large teeth, been that thirsty and frustrated to crunch a crumpled Budweiser can.

I squatted down with my back to the tree which once was scarred with burn marks and where George had struck his last match (had he ever smoked?) and looked up at the pine, so strong and permanent, rising tall among the brush and alders and junk wood that surrounded it.

If he built a platform to lay on, was he emulating the way American Indians would lay out their dead? People of India also cremate their dead, placing the body on a bed of wood next to a river and burning it, cracking open the skull. The parts of the body left unburned float downstream. I had seen it.

Why fire? Was it a cleansing act? Or was it because he had a brain tumor?

Death by fire. The late David Halberstam, the *New York Times* reporter, author, and Pulitzer Prize winner, saw the self-immolation of the Buddhist monk Thich Quang Duc that took place in 1963 on a city road in Saigon. Thich was protesting the Diem government and their slights to Buddhists. Halberstam wrote,

> Flames were coming from a human being; his body was slowly withering and shriveling up, his head blackening and charring. In the air was the smell of burning human flesh; human beings burn surprisingly quickly. Behind me I could hear the sobbing of the Vietnamese who were now gathering. I was too shocked to cry, too confused to take notes or ask questions, too bewildered to even think.

This public immolation led to the downfall of the Diem regime in that year and helped form American opinion against the Vietnam War. It, along with the photo of the young Vietnamese girl, nude, running and screaming after being napalmed, did much to turn us against our government.

Yet in these woods, this very hidden spot, where I squatted, George lit himself up and no one watched. There was no message, just a painful transition.

I'll never know much about George. I will never know what that tree meant to him. Did he lunch here while resting horses, did he have picnics here with his family, or was there a secret liaison that no one ever imagined? Did he play in the cool shadow of the pine and climb the tree when he was young?

I mourn for George, this man I never met and who had a tumor growing under his skull and who picked such a hard way to go. I still don't know what he looked like.

Dear Folks at Orvis Repair

This story was originally published with a photograph of the snake in *Gray's Sporting Journal* in 1987. Readers pointed out that my rattlesnake was actually a king snake. That didn't at all influence the amount of adrenalin that was released.

Dear Folks at Orvis Repair,

Enclosed is my eight-foot, six-weight Orvis Spring Creek carbon fiber rod, which has given me excellent service over the past six years.

Please note that it is no longer an eight-foot rod; rather, it is a seven-foot, eight-inch rod. Four inches are missing from the tip. Two inches broke off initially, I broke off two additional inches to test the elasticity at the tip. Please let me explain how the original two inches broke off.

It was the last day in June of this year that my friends and I were floating the Jefferson River in Montana, from Cardwell to Sappington Bridge. Bob Butler of Headwaters Anglers was our guide for the day. He led us through some fecund rapids where we pulled out sleek browns with firm yellow bellies and bright orange spots. We were using spuddlers and Mickey Finns, which the trout seemed to dislike immensely, for they hit viciously. Occasionally we could see a long deep shadow—the type that sears the gut—follow the streamer as we stripped it in. These reminded me of the barracuda shadows I'd seen in the Caribbean, for they too would stop a certain distance from the boat, watching and waiting, not striking, then disappearing back to wherever they go to think about what the hell is going on. These behemoth trout of the Jefferson usually don't show their snouts until the fall, but this year the river was low and comparatively clear for June. Like a barracuda, they often stopped and looked. We didn't catch one.

We did pull out respectable fish from under overhung banks and from rocks not more than an inch from the shore. It was a sunshiny day with a suspicious looking sheen of clouds to the west, which decided not to attack us. By noon the weather turned hot and still. An occasional breath of desert air desiccated our bodies.

By one the fish called it quits and retired for a nap. We lazed down the river, watching maliciously as Bob rowed. Then we donned life jackets and jumped into the river, and floated downstream on our backs, gazing up toward the endless sky, thinking of not much at all. It was a beautiful, lazy, placid, trout-producing float. After our swim, my friend Matt dozed as he sprawled spread-eagled over the bow of the boat. It was an unusually pleasant day for him for he had, for once, hooked bigger fish than I. Bob offered me a lunch of Fig Newtons smeared with peanut butter. It was your typical, easy-does-it-let-it-all-hang-out, Montana type of float.

We did get into an anglers' argument with Bob, who originally came from New York, but now has a Montana accent and uses colorful metaphors in his speech, which he must find effective in dealings with his clients. He called my rod, my Orvis, an "Effete Eastern Fairy Wand," and plugged his Western pole, which was stiff as a spanner wrench. I think he called it a Sage. Well, we argued back and forth about accuracy, resiliency, and things like that. Bob had to agree that I did catch a number of fish without any problem, except for the time I hooked a branch and had to break off. The leader didn't break, as I held the rod straight at the attached fly, and the current moved the boat downstream, proving once again that immutable force will quickly uncover the weakest link. In this case it was not my leader knot that snapped loose but my fly line, about ten feet from the butt. It was a two-day-old Cortland. Matt guffawed and accused me of stepping on it with my stream cleats, which I will now admit was true.

The rod, though, your Orvis eight-foot rod, was completely undamaged, as it should be for any fisherman who knows how to break off from a moving boat. The danger is that the fly will release and snap right back into your face, lodging securely in your forehead or cheek. This is why eastern fisherman should wear cowboy hats.

I had another loaded reel and was none the worse for wear, except when I thought of what I had just spent on that Cortland.

We floated early into our takeout. It was still and baking hot, which did not dim the enthusiasm of the Jefferson Mosquito Squadron, Sappington Bridge Wing, which gave us a voracious welcome. We beached our McKenzie neatly and headed for our camper, Stone Fly II. Still on the river, in another boat, were our friends, led by Chief Crazy Rod, who has a habit of ordering the guide to beach the boat so he can walk the rapids and blanket bomb the stream with his casts. It takes a long time to finish a float when Chief Crazy Rod is in command. I have heard guides complain that they would like overtime when our leader is aboard.

As I abandoned the shore and mosquitoes for the camper, I noticed some slob had kept four fish and gutted them on the bank, leaving the mud-coated entrails scummed along the shore. Under a nearby bridge was the last hurrah of what appeared to be a raccoon. Only its fur remained. He was so far gone that he didn't even smell. Probably the mosquitoes had carried away the carcass.

We lay down in the camper, not talking, saturating our mummified bodies with Diet Cokes. Matt found on the table a FedEx package addressed to him, which our friendly outfitter at Headwaters Anglers delivered when the transfer was made. So here on the Jefferson, miles from nowhere, without a contrail in the sky and only mosquitoes for company, Matt read a contract that, if he signed it, would give him a chunk of a ritzy Connecticut suburban town. Matt comes to Montana to escape double-A profile stress, but it follows him like a mountain lion stalking a calf. He attacks back with the telephone. Matt showed me the contract.

"Five million!" I yelped, looking at the contract. Suddenly I felt guilty. "I think I'd better go out and take some photographs," I said. "Might make fifty dollars."

Matt released his fat-cat smirk. "It's only money."

"Yeah, I know," and snapped the door open and shut and raced through the mosquito squadron.

I had noticed, three hundred yards up the pebble road on the right, a sloping hayfield where large round swirls of hay had been stacked by some behemoth machine. I thought it would make a good stock picture that my agent might be able to sell for the annual report of some agricultural company like John Deere, or *The Hay Rancher's Quarterly*. Something like that.

I was dressed as I had fished—no shirt, Russell running shorts, and flip-flops made in Taiwan. I walked up the gravel road with my Orvis eight-foot fishing rod in one hand and my Nikon hung around my neck.

Why bring the rod, you ask? Well, there was an uncut hayfield in front of me and I was going to walk through it and swish the rod in front to wake up any snakes that might be in my path. But the more I looked at the hayfield, the more I decided I would skirt it. I walked farther up the road and hip-hopped over a barbed-wire fence. (Yeah, I know I was trespassing and that Westerners prefer to hog-tie Easterners for committing such a dastardly act, but it's ingrained. My mother used to say that I was trespassing when I was born.)

Each hay bale was about four feet in diameter and was stacked in a fifty-yard row on a freshly cut mowing. They were stacked three high and the light, low in the west, textured the swirls of hay. Behind was nothing but blue sky and a couple clouds trying to catch up with their bigger cousins, which were scudding eastward.

I moved sideways, looking for the best angle, then backed into another barbed-wire fence. I needed more distance from my subject in order to make a flattened, graphic shot, so I hopped that fence and with rod held vertically in my left hand, along with my Nikon, which now was an extension of my eye. While moving back, I looked around, first seeing sparse vegetation, a few prairie gopher holes, no snakes, and then no vegetation. I made little side steps as I looked through my viewfinder to work in one of the small clouds behind the haystack so it floated as a sort of apostrophe over the stacked circles of hay. The sidelight gave the hay a three-dimensional look. So what if it wasn't downtown New Canaan? I was creating something—fifty bucks worth of creation.

It was then that I heard a sort of "burrrp," which made me unglue my eye from the Nikon and glance at the ground. What I saw was my toes and flip-flops, my knee, and part of my shorts. Also included in my vision, a few inches from the flip-flops, was a very thick, long, oval, stretched-out, shiny presence with a sort of checked pattern on it. In fact, I noticed scales as my eye wandered up to the end of this presence that was nearest to me. There I saw a head, shaped triangular, about six inches up from the ground and about six inches from my calf. It was not looking at my calf but looking up at me, as I looked down on it. Its eyes were shiny. I think it was as surprised as I was. I had flip-flop-sneaked, in my short side steps, right into the snake's bailiwick and he didn't like it.

Now, if you were dressed in thin Russell shorts, Taiwanese flip-flops, and no shirt, what would you do when you came face-to-face with a rattlesnake that was practically kissing your knee? And what would you do if you were an effete eastern fly angler from Vermont with a fairy wand in his hand looking at the first rattlesnake you have ever seen in your fifty years on Earth?

I did not think of my nakedness, nor of the fact that when facing a rattlesnake one is supposed to move slowly, so as not to bump into the rattlesnake's buddy, as they like to travel in pairs. I imagine I was impressed that this snake was about as long as I am tall and thick as a boa constrictor. What I knew was that I ought not be standing where I was standing.

Adrenalin is a wonderful drug. It can be very rejuvenating as it sharpens reflexes and loosens joints. Now I can't exactly explain what happened next or how I accomplished it, but somehow I used my Orvis eight-foot Spring Creek fishing rod and vaulted over that rattlesnake. That's correct. I vaulted at least six feet in the air and landed eight feet away, on my back, did a somersault and sprang to a crouch, facing the snake, camera and rod held in front as weapons, wishing they were my two Parker shotguns.

To tell the truth I vaulted so fast that I jumped out of my flip-flops. Ever see those photographs of a pair of shoes in the middle of the highway where a person was hit by a car and that was all that was left? Well . . .

Now I was down to my shorts and my two weapons as I faced the rattle-snake, who had moved about six feet from my flip-flops toward me and was coiled, and his mean-looking head was giving me the eye. He was then about eight feet away. I believe I moved backward.

I was not about to move closer, then the fear struck me that another snake was nearby and I eyeballed the environment around my naked feet. Nothing but prairie-gopher holes.

Did you know that rattlesnakes love prairie-gopher villages? They love to slink down the holes and disengage their jaws and trap a prairie gopher in a back room and strike him with their fangs and poison him to death and swallow him whole. You didn't know that? I didn't either.

I circled around that rattler as fast as I could to where my flip-flops were planted; for some reason I felt very vulnerable without my flip-flops. I remembered, suddenly, that I was a photographer; a journalist who had been in tight places before, so I snapped pictures of the snake. I thought I snapped a dozen but I shot only one; I guess you could say I caught Rattlesnake Fever.

The snake, after I resoled my feet with the flip-flops, slinked down to where I pole-vaulted, where all the gopher holes were. He then raised his

head above the thin sage, gave me a sidelong glance of disdain, stuck out his tongue, and slithered into a gopher hole. He was so thick he filled the whole hole. I could think only of how evilly sinister, sensuous, and, yes, sexual this snake was as he went deeper and disappeared from sight.

Then I got the shakes—post-adrenalin attack, you know. This had happened before, after an avalanche whopped me, and another time when I fell off a cliff, and the time I bluffed the two New York City muggers. I went back to the camper where my friends laughed at me and said I had a great imagination and so what's another rattlesnake?

It was then that I noticed that the tip of my Orvis Spring Creek eight-foot six-weight rod was minus two inches of the tip. That was when I broke off the extra two inches to test the strength of the tip. Your rod must have been reinforced with adrenalin when I needed it most. Perhaps I was light on my feet.

What I would like to do is offer to you a testimonial that Orvis rods are perfectly adaptable for pole-vaulting over rattlesnakes. They are light, give good leverage and height, and get you away from the evil shivers with great elasticity. I recommend the Orvis rods for this safety procedure and I believe that the Western Series nine-foot for seven- and eight-weight rods would be even more handy for rattlesnake pole-vaulting, at least as far as distance and height are concerned. Now I did break the tip, but I do believe I did that after the pole vault when I did the somersault on the ground.

Don't ever let anyone tell you or any customer that an Orvis is an Eastern Effete Fairy Wand.

Please repair the tip or replace it and return the rod. I understand that you have a guarantee for repairing rods not broken in dog-fights or car doors but broken while being used in a legitimate fashion. I feel that rattle-snake pole-vaulting is a legitimate use for an Orvis rod, if you happen to have one handy.

Sincerely,
Peter M. Miller

Dear Mr. Miller:

We are in receipt of your eight-foot graphite rod which is in need of repair. As you know, Orvis guarantees their rods against faulty workmanship and defective materials.

The broken or affected section does not appear to be a result of defective materials or workmanship, but in view of your valued patronage, I have taken the liberty of reducing the attached estimate by 20%. We will return your rod on or before the date indicated on the estimate.

If you feel we have made an error in our evaluation, please call or write so we may assure your satisfaction.

Thank you for your patience and understanding in this matter.

Sincerely yours,
Greg Comar
Technical Director
The Orvis Company

Skiing on the Bromley Patrol

First published in *Vermont Magazine*, Winter, 2008

In the 1950s and early 1960s the game, if you loved to ski and were broke, and we Vermonters all were, was how to ski at the local area and not pay. It never occurred to us to cheat, that wasn't the style of our generation, so we followed another route.

The first was to offer your body as a packer. Many of the resorts did not have grooming machines, or if they did, they couldn't operate on the steep pitches. So after a snowfall our job was to pack the trails on skis. We formed a line and sidestepped up and down the trail. For that we received one or two day passes. This worked well but we didn't always have a big dump of snow, although more of it fell back then.

The next move, and much more guaranteed to keep us on the slopes, was to be a volunteer ski patroller. This required a first-aid course and often, but sometimes not, membership in the National Ski Patrol. I skied at Big Bromley near Manchester and once I made the list, as it was called, I was in for lots of skiing, but it was first come, first ski, and Spud Harrington, the head of the patrol at that time, would sign up the first twenty or so volunteers. If you were late, and the list was full, you were out of luck.

It was very good duty. We skied all day, except when we responded to an accident. We reported to the patrol shack at the top of the mountain, and each time we were assigned a different trail. We were yo-yos on the slope. The paid patrol did the dispatching, when they were not playing cribbage. We would close and open trails and take down bodies and bring up toboggans. There was one downer, and that was to be assigned all day to Little Bromley. That was a rope tow on a beginner's slope that had a vertical drop of about fifty feet. It eventually got its come-uppance as the hill was bulldozed flat and is now a parking lot.

Then of course you could become a paid patrolman, if you didn't have to go to school and could hack the very low pay. I did that too.

In the early fifties I was a volunteer, and then, in the late fifties, after my military service, a professional patrolman. We didn't have radios, so every trail was patrolled regularly and we would call up on crank phones located strategically around the mountain when we found an injury. We skied our heads off. We wore black ski pants and black nylon parkas with red crosses sewn on them. We must have been sinister looking on cold days when we wore black masks.

On spring days when the snow was firm there was not much to do except ski. One warm day a pretty woman was riding the J bar on the side of the mountain and somehow she messed up getting off the lift. The end of the J bar hooked under her sweater and stripped it up to her neck and left her dangling after the safety trip wire was released. She was not hurt, and when we released her onto the snow, she fell on her back, skis apart, brassiere showing. She smiled.

"Hanky Panky, anyone?"

On a snowy day we would have sometimes more than twenty bodies to bring down the mountain. Our first aid was rudimentary. In the early fifties, when I was a volunteer, we used a toboggan with a short heavy rope tied in a knot on the front, and a long rope on the rear. One patrolman held up the front of the toboggan and snowplowed down the mountain, and if the toboggan moved too fast, he would throw the knotted rope

under the toboggan to slow it down. The patroller on the back acted as a stabilizer, holding on to the rope, which was about eight feet long, to keep the toboggan from sliding sideways and also to act as a drag, by either snowplowing or side-slipping. We strapped our casualties tightly on the toboggan and took off . . . pretty fast sometimes.

Once on the West Meadow we had strapped on an injured woman, I think she sprained her ankle, and headed down. Well, there was this big patch of ice and the fellow on the back fell down and let go of the rope. He shouldn't have done that. The toboggan slipped sideways, I caught an edge and fell and let go of the toboggan. I shouldn't have done that.

So we were lying there, after sliding off the ice, and watched the toboggan, with the woman securely strapped in, head helter-skelter down the mountain. All by her lonesome.

"EEEEEEEK!" she was screaming.

We were horrified. If the toboggan went down to where the trail narrowed, there were some big trees to smash into. We watched, too frozen to move. I can't remember anyone else on the slope on this wretched afternoon, which was lucky.

Fortunately, the toboggan veered to the left, hit some snow, and bounded lickety-split off the trail into snow drifted deep before some small spruces. There was an explosion of snow, the toboggan went upright like a jumping trout, and then fell silently. The EEEEKing stopped. We scrambled to the toboggan, which was face up, and there was the woman, white-faced and silent as death. She had big eyes.

"Hey, you're okay, just one of those things, we'll have you down in a jiffy." She didn't say a word. I think fear had paralyzed her tongue.

We skied down with that poor woman strapped in the toboggan right smartly to the patrol room, opened the door, dragged the toboggan in, and ran out before anyone noticed us, disappearing up the mountain. We kept a very low profile. We never heard a word about that incident, neither from the head of the ski patrol nor the woman.

In 1959, after I returned from the army, I was hired as a professional patroller at Bromley. As I recall, the pay was about sixty dollars a week. There were improvements. The toboggan now had welded onto it two upright pieces of iron bar on the front that were waist high. Then two more iron bars were welded to that at a right angle so the patrolman could stand between them and use them to guide the toboggan, or put pressure on it to slow it down. Attached to the right handle was a lever for a brake that was on the rear of the toboggan. One man could handle this toboggan.

It was springtime, the snow was soft, and this kid had broken his leg on Pabst Blue Ribbon, an expert trail. There were lots of bumps and the head of the ski patrol, named appropriately Ski, asked me to check for any serious dips in the trail before he brought the kid down on this newfangled first-aid toboggan. I found nothing too deep, so Ski started down, toboggan trailing behind. Up and down he went over the bumps until he hit one steep one. It wasn't too bad but the handlebars he was holding onto were too long. They dug into the upcoming mogul and Ski and the toboggan did a flip. It was spectacular. Ski got up swearing, and we turned over the toboggan. There was this kid, still safely strapped in with a splint on his leg. He had dark hair, a glint in his eyes, and a big smile.

"What a trip!" he said.

I loved that kid and that was the last year I ever patrolled.

Spring Skiing

First published in *Ski Magazine* in the 1980s

When the sun rises well above treeline, and the sugar clouds are lazing overhead, and the sap surges through the maple trees—in Vermont that's the beginning of spring.

My juices flow at the same time, because the same conditions that produce fancy maple syrup—cold nights, warming days, a deep mantle of snow—make the sweetest skiing of all.

Yet how odd it is that skiers will flock together for George's birthday, crowding the slopes and liftlines—then, like lemmings, drive or fly back to their urban nests, stash their skis, and get out tennis racquets, halyards, or lawn mowers.

"Those crazy turkeys," said my friend Jake, as we rode up the double chair on a lazy spring day in April. A few hundred of us had the mountain to ourselves. "When it's cold and miserable as a snake's belly, those zonkers pound up and down the slopes. Now we have the best of everything—real good skiing, the finest corn of the season, lots of sun—and they take off. They must have big holes in their brains."

There are two kinds of snow that turn on my skiing—the freshly fallen powder of winter and the corn of spring. They are equally enjoyable, but corn snow has the edge, for it can be skied over and over, whereas once the powder is cut the thrill is gone.

Have you ever skied fine corn snow that has settled and frozen, then thawed several times so the surface becomes billions of kernels of frozen ice, several millimeters in diameter and about two inches deep, lying on a frozen base? There is lyricism to a slope of corn snow, and it is difficult to make a mistake. Your body and skis flow with motion and grace down the mountain. Add to that warm weather and you sing over the snow. You can sing anywhere on the slope—down the trails where the bumps are the biggest of the season, or in the woods, making a slalom course out of the trees. You can ski the steepest chutes on the mountain—they won't

avalanche when the corn is ripe. You lean off the mountain, into space, over your skis, turn, set—the skis bite into the corn, then you lift into your next turn. It's like high diving, only under control.

In spring, the skies are bluer. You can feel the sweetness in the wind and smell the freshening of the trees. Down jackets are packed away and out come bikinis, shorts and T-shirts, blossoming like alpine spring flowers. Picnics spread out over the mountain. Jugs of wine are carried to very high places and emptied. Muscles grow relaxed and loose, the mind becomes easy, the smile natural. Warmth spreads quickly from skier to skier.

Memories of spring skiing stay with me because for some reason I learn more about me that time of year. I was camping on Mount Washington and skiing Tuckerman's in mid-April. A close friend and I had climbed Hillman's Highway and skied Oakes Gulf under bluebird skies. Tired but loose, we sat on the front of the lean-to enjoying an after-dinner drink of rum and tea when the northern lights flickered on. Ribbons of green flashed over the peaks, shimmering. Magenta-colored spotlights streaked over the dark white of the mountain, silhouetting the spruces. We watched in awe and later talked about our lives. That evening, both of us made decisions. Ray quit his job in New Jersey and moved to the mountains; I decided it was time to leave the mountains and find a career in the city.

The next day we skied the Headwall, then climbed high above the Left Gully and, with our guts clenched, we skied the steepest chute on the mountain—straight down, nonstop, the corn spraying and wetting our bare legs as we linked turns, catching the rhythm of the descent. Both of our lives took different directions from this week of skiing and our friendship grew stronger as our outlook on the important things in life took a slight bend inward.

A dozen years later, Ray was dead, killed in a car accident. I was recently divorced, had lost my home, and had watched the collapse of my business. A Pilatus had just dropped me, along with some new friends, high on a glacier in France. It was the first week in April and the valleys, hidden under mist, were green. It was quiet, with just a whisper of wind. We skied down a steep wall and then hit the corn snow. We rode it down the hill for over eight miles, making long, graceful swings, letting gravity do all the work. We stopped only to eat an orange and drink some cold white wine.

The flow of this spring run wiped a lot of the sludge out of my body—the messiness and hurt of the recent past. "What the hell," I said to myself, riding over the corn on this French mountain. "What the hell," and I started to laugh as we swung down a small couloir onto a steep pitch and then into a wide slope. An hour later, over a *pastis*, I formulated a new philosophy: always look ahead during the run, for the next slope could be the best yet, and the best runs come at the end of the season, when the sun is warming and the sap is flowing.

The Haute Route

On January 6, 1985, I turned fifty-one, the same age as my father when he died in a sanitarium. Alcoholism killed him. He lost his job, his family, and his self-respect. I thought of that often as I grew up.

There are a number of ways to recall a sad death, or to mark a half-century of life. I'm a skier, shaped on the slopes of Vermont, fine-tuned in the West and Europe, and I decided to ski the Haute Route, from Chamonix, France, where I was living at the time, to Zermatt, Switzerland, with my daughter Hilary, then twenty-three.

Anyone who has done the seventy-six kilometer Haute Route knows it as a high mountain trek of incredible panoramic alpine views, entirely unpopulated except for tiny groups of skiers. It is also a series of corn snow runs of glorious lightness, sometimes steep where each turn is a free fall. Sunlight sparkles on snow as you climb using skins, sliding one ski in front of the other, over and over. God, you think you'll never get to the summit, but you do and it's worth it. Of anything the Haute Route is, it's about being so aware of yourself—surrounded by snow-covered Alps, you taste the air, feel the sun, have joyful descents. It's about being free, and alive.

Yes there are squalls, and snowstorms and whiteouts and ice, and occasional danger and . . . the unexpected.

On the third night we stayed at a mountain hut in Switzerland. We had four in our group. Ahead of us were three parties of seven each, German, French, and Swedish.

We were the last group to leave in the morning and crossed a long flat to an abrupt hill shaped like a loaf of bread. The way the tracks criss-crossed it you knew it was steep. The other groups were ahead of us, the lead one just beginning the climb. The sky was glazed flat with clouds, so different from the warm spring of yesterday. It had abruptly turned cold, and I had to change from gloves to mittens. The soft snow was icing up. The guides ahead of us turned their groups back and skied down to the hut to wait for better weather. Not Jorge, the only Puerto Rican ski guide in the world. He urged us on. Halfway up the hill, which was steep, the corn turned to crust. Then a thick freezing fog settled over us. Jorge was in a hurry to reach the plateau above this climb. We were crossing a steep pitch and I knew one mistake, one fall, and you would slide down and over the cliff to the river below, which we could hear roaring. This either-or choice brings intense concentration to how you move your skis. I remembered the time I first skied the steeps on the Headwall at Tuckerman's, in New Hampshire, and fear and vertigo sent me down the length of the bowl. I overcame that fear on the second run. That was more than twenty-five years ago. I had no fear, just the sense that I was not going to make a mistake. I remember the care I made in kick-turning on the switchback. I had couteaux and skins on my skis and I planted them firmly. Hilary and Jorge were fine on their cross-country skis with skins. They were above me. Jorge was yelling encouragement and telling me to hurry. It was a fight against nasty weather.

When we reached the top plateau the fog was so thick you could hardly see the tips of your skis. Jorge had his altimeter and map out and was comparing altitude readings when a gust of wind snatched the map out of his hands and it disappeared into the fog. Jorge, ever cool, said, "No problem, I remember the altimeter reading. No problem!"

We searched for the track that would take us off this small plateau.

I went in one direction and could see the snow stop; my skis dangled in space. I backed up. Jorge was still searching with his altimeter when Hilary yelled out, "I see piss tracks!"

She had found the trail. We roped together, jumped down a three-foot ledge, and skied below the fog into hazy sun. It was warmer on this side. The jewel blue of the glacier bumped out of the snow and the slope became steep. We unroped and skied down on corn snow, lifting the tails high so as not to trip, free-falling fifteen feet, setting the platform and doing it again. I remember smiling. I was free, exhilarated.

We didn't finish the trip. Bad weather set in at the next hut and wouldn't let up, so we skied down the valley and took a train back to Chamonix. Hilary stayed a few days and we skied Argentière before she left for home.

I returned to Vermont in early summer, but it was not until January that I could keep the promise I made to myself, to visit my father's grave in Bound Brook, New Jersey. The tombstone is a large loaf of pink granite set in a corner plot my grandmother bought in 1929, a month after the death of her husband. On it is carved a lily and the name MILLER. Two granite vases filled with soil sit on each side of it. In front, marked by small granite tablets, are three graves. My grandfather's lies in the middle. To the right, as you face the tombstone, is my grandmother's. To the left is my father's. His stone says, simply, LLOYD S. MILLER, 1899–1951. He died in March, eleven days before his fifty-second birthday.

Oak leaves, blown from the tree that stands on the street side of the cemetery fence, lay glued on the grayish-green grass. It was a cloudy, raw day, one week after my fifty-second birthday.

The grave register says that my father died in Hamilton Township, Mercer County, New Jersey, of cerebral hemorrhage. What it doesn't say is that he drank himself to death.

I have a picture of our family, taken by Bachrach, of my father, mother, brother, sister, and myself seated in front of the living-room fireplace in the farmhouse in which we lived, ten miles east of the graveyard. I was the youngest, the baby in my mother's lap, who looked dumbfounded at the camera. It must have been about 1935. My mother, in a long dress, is beautiful. Standing, but leaning almost protectively against the antique chair my mother is sitting in, is my father. His dress is impeccable, his black hair, parted in the middle, is brushed back close to his head. He is as handsome as my mother is beautiful.

My father was a bond salesman for Salomon Brothers and Hutzler on Wall Street. I vaguely remember hearing that in the early 1940s he made thirty or forty thousand dollars, which was a large sum for those days. His father had been a very successful banker, and my father was trying to live up to that reputation. He had the proper schooling for it—Lawrenceville Preparatory, then Princeton.

We lived on a small, gentleman's farm, in a colonial house with a screened-in porch. In the front was a garden where, on summer mornings, my father would pick a flower—he favored carnations—which he stuck in his lapel. He wore dark business suits and a black homburg and rode the train from the North Branch station to Hoboken, and then he took a ferry to Manhattan. The moaning of the train whistle, late at night, when I lay in bed, comforted and stirred me as it echoed up the valley.

I don't remember when my father started to drink. I do remember find-

(Photograph by Buchrach)

ing a bottle of whiskey hidden under a sofa pillow when I was looking for change that fell out of pockets. I found another under the oats in the feed bin in the barn. My brother and I, as a prank, nailed down the lid, which was pried open when we looked the next morning.

One evening my father stumbled drunkenly into the living room and had a fierce fight with my mother. I looked on silently, open-mouthed. I used to take drives with him and he would park at the Elbow Inn. I waited in the car, mesmerized by the neon signs, while my father drank.

"You know, he was a horrible drunk," my sister said to me. My brother and sister do not remember him favorably. I do, perhaps because I was so young. I remember the time he took me fishing at Swartzwood Lake and the early frosted mornings in November, when we waited for hunting season to start. Lady, my father's English setter, whined and fretted, as I did, until my father said, "It's time." I followed behind him and his hunting partners, without a gun. Even so, my heart sang.

I also remember the day that I came back from Camp Echo Hill, a summer day lightened by a soft breeze, when my mother told me we were moving to Connecticut. It was exciting for me, this unexpected adventure, until I learned that my father was not coming with us. The car was packed, my mother, brother, and sister in it, waiting for me. I remember crying as I walked rapidly around the large lawn, flipping my penknife into the ground. My father followed me. I can't remember what he said as he put his hand on my shoulder, but there were tears in his eyes too. When we drove away, my father stood in the center of the lawn looking toward the pasture, his back to us. He wore a yellow, open-necked, short-sleeved shirt and tan pants and held his hands on his hips. I was eight.

I visited him every so often on the New Jersey farm, which had turned lifeless, and at Cape Cod, where my grandmother had a house. There I met his mistress and played Chinese checkers with her.

Salomon Brothers fired my father for his drinking. The farm was sold, and he moved in with his mother, who could afford to support him. There was hatred in my father's family, hatred of my mother for divorcing him. They hated us, too. My mother felt it, my sister and brother never wanted to see or visit my father. But I did.

I liked my father. He was many things that I am not. He was always courteous and polite. He was gentle. He dressed beautifully and I admired that, for I was nothing but a farm rat of a kid. I liked walking through the woods with him and driving in his convertible Chevrolet. I had a dream, when I was young, of taking him to a lake and living in a cabin where we would fish and chop wood together and he wouldn't need to drink.

Loss. I missed, as I grew up, having a father to talk to, about careers, jobs, about marriage, about all those little hints that can take so many years to acquire, and I missed the quiet companionship of taking a hunting or fishing trip together. But because of that loss I grew up stronger and more independent, perhaps more than I should have.

I saw what too much money could do to people, and subconsciously I am frightened of money, so I continually complain about never having any. I did not want anything to do with banking or business, so I became a photographer and writer.

I promised myself that my children would never suffer a divorce and of course that happened, to my children and me, when my oldest was eight. I came to know what my father felt, that day he stood on the lawn in his yellow shirt, when I was eight. I think of the deep sadness we both experienced at losing a family. It's as if we had failed so quickly in life.

At the time of my divorce I had no job. And like him, I took solace in drinking, although I must admit I did it with much more exuberance.

My father's shadow seems to walk with me, sometimes as a warning. After a couple of years, I pulled myself together. I started a successful career of freelancing. I saw my daughters regularly until my ex-wife took them to live in England.

In the fifty-first year of my life, at the same age at which my father died, his memory fluttered in my memory, the memory of what his last year must have been like.

I thought of his life, and the life he gave me, while I photographed the Valley of the Moon, in the middle of the Atacama Desert in Chile, as the desert blushed red in the afterglow of the sunset, and overhead the sky blackened and the stars lighted up with fierce brightness. I thought of him while fly-fishing the Madison River in Montana, and landing a 20-inch brown as a rainbow arched over the valley. And I thought of him while I was skiing the Haute Route with Hilary. I thought of him as Hilary and I hugged each other for warmth and assurance on that snow-blown, foggy plateau, the wind frostbiting our faces, our guide as lost as we were.

I want to leave something more than my father did. Perhaps, though, what I leave is that which my father left me. His shadow walks within my shadow and my shadow, for better, I hope, than worse, will walk within the shadows of my children.

I Ski Alone

Originally published in *Ski Vermont*, Winter, 2004

Well, not always. I do ski with friends and family now and then, but I prefer to ski with me and my shadow. Fast! And on long skis!

I never really thought about this until one day when I was skiing with some friends in their sixties—around my age—all veteran skiers. We were skiing the Hayride on Mount Mansfield, over fresh snow under a cerulean sky. There was a bite in the air, sun-warmth on the cheeks, the kind of day when your skis wag their tails and say, "Hey, let's go! Let me loose, I'm raring to slide!"

The group skied one hundred vertical yards, stopped, jawed for about five minutes, then skied another short section and pulled over to the curb. God, I knew why my skis were frustrated and it didn't take long before I said the hell with my companions and pointed my skis downhill, doing long, linked turns. While they were still jabbering I was riding back up the quad as the mountain's gleaming white trails slipped under my ski tips. I skied alone for the rest of the day. Had a helluva time.

Next year I will be seventy, and I have been skiing seriously for fifty-seven years. I've raced. I've climbed Tuckerman's Ravine and, the first time I did it, was scared out of my wits and egg-beatered the whole length. Never did take a formal lesson. Learned to ski and photograph carrying a heavy pack, usually on one shoulder, which is why I walk funny. Through the years I skied on four continents, but most of all on every ski hill in Vermont, including the Morgan Hill rope tow in Weston (RIP); Bromley, where I ski patrolled; and my nearby favorites: Mount Mansfield and Glen Ellen, which is now called Sugarbush North.

I wouldn't say I'm a good skier, but I know how to stand on my skis. I don't carve turns; I prefer long GS turns . . . I go fast into the turn on the side of the trail, unweight both skis, turn and shift my weight to the tails of the skis, then move it forward to the downhill ski, edge and cut across and down the trail and do the next turn . . . let the mountain and gravity do the work. It's a technique similar to snowboarding, but I learned it in the French Alps and brought it home to the trails of Vermont.

What this technique requires is long skis, speed, and a fairly empty trail with no or few bumps—a level of grooming that is the panacea for older skiers with shot knees. It is best done in the morning when the trails are freshly groomed and there are few skiers. You don't need much strength. Instead of stopping and waiting, or trying to catch up to your buddies, you feel the wind bite your face, the rhythm of extended turns, weightlessness. Why should I stop and talk when I can see points of light blur-flashing under my skis, or when I'm chasing my shadow down the mountain? This is inward skiing, floating my soul, soaring my consciousness. I don't know how to explain it. More ethereal than sex? You don't get this rush by standing on your skis and chatting.

I don't always ski flat-out. Last winter I stopped halfway down the Nose Dive at Stowe and looked at the frosted chin of Mount Mansfield—a scoop of vanilla ice cream with sprinkles on it peeking through the gray beech trees, some with bear-claw scars climbing the trunks. I must have stared at this scene for ten minutes before I promised myself to come back with a large-format camera and photograph how the mountain and beech

trees flattened themselves into one dimension. Can you imagine me skiing with a group when I either go too fast or else stop to stare at trees for ten minutes?

On another spring day, skiing off-trail, I took a break, pulled a sandwich and red canteen out of the pack before I turned it into a ground pad, plunked myself down, leaned against a birch, and stuck my skis, still attached to my boots, vertically in the snow, swiveling my head toward the sun. As I was munching away a porcupine lumbered into view, passed a couple of yards from me, then climbed a tree and sat on a limb. He looked like he was meditating. It was a private moment for both of us, accompanied by silence.

I ski on a pair of 193 cm Olins that must be fifteen years old. They're my GS skis. Oh, I have one of the first of the parabolic Rossignols, wide enough to use for water skiing and not much longer. They are good in powder and slush. And I also have a newer tapered pair of Heads that I traded some photographs for. They're fashionably short, about seven inches shorter than my Olins. Real easy in powder but when you're cruising . . . it's harder than hell to put your weight back on a pair of skis with hardly any butt. These parabolics are made to carve turns as the ski instructors of America have dictated. Otherwise, when you are going lickety split, skis flat, in a tuck, feeling the wind suck your cheeks and the adrenalin squirting, those short, wide parabolic skis begin to wobble. The skis are alerting my control board: "Danger! Slow down and carve your turns or you're going to crash!"

They say a black Irishman (that's the dominant half of me—stubborn and crowned, when I was younger, with jet-black hair) will drink until he falls on his face. With trails groomed like a race course, a pair of long skis and plenty of room, and no one to slow me down, I can ski until I fall over dead.

When We Were Young and Skiers

First published in *Skiing Magazine*, 2007

Why was skiing so great back fifty years ago? Was it better than now? Let me tell you why.

Skiing was a sport, an adventure, and a social club. We knew everyone on the hill (mine was Big Bromley), from the jack-jumping lift attendants, to the glossy ski school director, Neil Robinson, who showed us how to run gates, to owner Fred Pabst, whose greeting was always by the first name: "Peter (or Jill or John), How the Hell Are You!"

We used 210 cm wood skis and wore comfortable leather boots and skied fast on God-made snow. (Okay, sometimes we skied on grass and ice, but it didn't matter.) We dressed plain and black, and our clothing flapped like a luffing sail when we took it straight. The smells come back—hot ski wax, wet wool, wood smoke. A snowy day turned brilliantly yellow when viewed through oversize army surplus goggles. We ski-packed trails for day passes and volunteered for the patrol. We ski bummed and knew a bunch of ski songs.

Bogner stretch ski pants made the scene—Wow! Along came the sixties and fem lib took hold, so did the birth control pill . . . skiing was sexy. We didn't know how repressed we were, growing up in the fifties. Then the Vietnam War sliced our country apart, which drew us radicals together in our hatred of killing and politicians. We were drug- and booze-loving hedonists. Many of us moved to the drop-out ski capitals of America, Stowe and Aspen.

Growth brought snowmaking, crowded trails, real estate developers, condos, marketing directors, high prices on everything. The sport morphed into an industry . . . cliques of social skiers . . . ski suits with arm pockets for cell phones . . . Daddies spending forty grand to outfit one kid for a year of racing school . . . Hummers . . . Snowboarders! They shred the sides of trails where we hide from the traffic and, when it is not crowded and we want to let it rip, there they are sitting in the middle of a trail under a crest. Numbnuts!

I remember when a day lift ticket at Bromley was $3.50. Now I live near Stowe and a day ticket is $76. I'm a dropout . . . again.

Growing Up with Guns

First Published in the *Stowe Reporter*, 2001

I wouldn't say we were gun crazy or gun nuts, but all my teenage friends owned rifles, shotguns, and often pistols. The years were the late 1940s and early 1950s. We were Burr and Burton high school students in Manchester, Vermont. Most were sons and daughters of local merchants and of farmers from outlying towns that had no high school. Some were people such as myself who lived twenty miles away and boarded at the school.

Among the boys, fun consisted of football, double-dating, fishing, hunting, and shooting. Hunting was the state's unofficial sport, particularly deer hunting. I owned seven rifles, two shotguns, and three pistols. We used them mostly for target shooting and plinking at cans. I worked hard at my marksmanship; during the summer I shot about a thousand rounds of .22 shells a month with my .22 automatic Savage rifle and my pistol. With the rifle I could fire seventeen rounds as fast as I could pull the trigger.

I became a good shot. I taught myself to hit the bull's-eye at fifty yards, and then I became a good enough marksman to drive the tacks holding the target. During the summer we shot crows and woodchucks, and in the fall we hunted squirrels, rabbits, and partridge. Deer season opened the second Saturday of November, but most of us were not good enough woodsmen to knock down a buck.

Sometimes a group of us would gather on weekends with our pistols and rifles for target practice. One of my shooting buddies would hold a cigarette in his mouth and, from about fifteen paces, I would chip it down with five shots from my .22 automatic Savage rifle, to an inch from his lips. He never budged and I never missed. Sometimes a gang of us would point our pistols and rifles at a can and blaze away in unison. It was our way of recycling. In the fall we took out the shotguns for partridge shooting.

Once, at high school, a classmate brought in a .45 Colt automatic that had belonged to his father. It was a heavy clunker of a pistol with a large

bore. After classes we took it out in front of the school where there were large maples, and he loaded it and handed it to me. I picked out a mark on a tree and shot. The gun bucked like a bull and I missed by six inches. I couldn't understand why, for I was very accurate with my Ruger .22 automatic pistol.

In my sophomore year I broke my ankle playing football and was on crutches for six weeks. I was then living in my mother's apartment at the school. (She was a teacher, but fortunately, I did not have her for any classes.) I kept my .22 there and when deer season opened, as I was still on crutches, I slung the rifle over my shoulder (my 30-30 Winchester did not have a sling) and hobbled into the woods. I saw only does, which were illegal to shoot. At the end of the season I followed the practice of many unsuccessful Vermont hunters: I shot my rifle into the air until it was empty. Then I hobbled back to school.

One spring day I was fishing and, as usual, I carried my pistol, one of the first Ruger automatics. The fishing was good, so I forgot about shooting. Somewhere along the bank, I dropped the pistol. I reported it to the police, but thought I would never see it again.

About three weeks later, a Vermont state trooper walked into the Burr and Burton study hall and asked for me. The teacher called out my name and told me to come to his desk, which I did with quite a bit of anxiety. The officer gave me a big smile. Without saying a word, he plunked down on the desk the pistol I had lost, and walked out.

I later traded that pistol for a Smith and Wesson K22 revolver and bought a fast-draw belt. I had that in our dormitory and often, when I wasn't practicing holding the pistol still while looking in a mirror, I practiced with a friend. He held a book in his hand. When he dropped it I would draw the unloaded revolver and dry-fire. I could get off two snaps before the book hit the floor. Before we played this game we each checked the cylinder to make sure it was empty.

The fast draw didn't work so well in the field when the revolver was loaded. I surprised a woodchuck in a pasture and, as he ran across the field, I did a quick draw and pulled the trigger a bit too fast. The bullet went out the end of the holster and into my Levis. I was shaking as I pulled down my pants. There was a little red line along my thigh and two new holes in my jeans—one blackened, where the bullet entered, and another where it exited. Two weeks later I sold the revolver and the quick-draw holster. Within a year I would be shooting with a camera.

I imagine our parents and teachers would have been horrified at the games we teenagers played with our rifles and pistols, but we were part of an outdoor culture, and almost every home in Vermont had a couple of guns in a closet. We all learned to shoot before we were teenagers. We became good shots and good hunters.

It never entered our minds to use one of our guns to kill a teacher or a schoolmate, or any human being, or to ever fire a gun in anger. What we worried about was accidentally shooting ourselves in the foot. I came closest.

The Dropout Capital of the East, 1965–1975

First published in the *Stowe Reporter*, 1999

What a wonderful fortress Stowe was in those years that straddled the Vietnam War. On the other side of the mountains were Johnson, Nixon, Kissinger, McNamara, body counts, napalm, corporate life, Madison Avenue, riots, suburbia, and the towns, states, families, lost loves, court fights, broken marriages, and promising careers many of us left and wished to block out forever. We were tired of our country lying to us but worst of all we feared, as Pogo said, that the enemy was us. Our panacea—or perhaps our limbo—was Stowe, a sandbox filled with snow. Here we could deconstruct ourselves. Yeahhhh.

Coupon clippers or broke as Jesus, we stuck together. We hummed along with Joan Baez when they tore old Dixie down, although we lived in one of the whitest communities in America. We were our own American pie. We loved Muhammad Ali because of his big mouth and buzzing fists, but most of all because of his stand against Vietnam.

We mowed lawns, painted houses, pumped out septic tanks, tended bar, waited tables, and cleaned homes. We skied and taught skiing and skinny-dipped and hiked and fished and hunted. We partied. Oh my, we partied. Stowe had voted wet, and Ken Strong and Ted Ross opened the Shed. On the first night, the shelf holding the liquor fell down. One afternoon Ted McKay took his drill to a swollen thumbnail he banged with a hammer and blood squirted over the bar. Jim Jackson came in with a pistol and shot the clock off the wall. We stumbled down drunk so much that the local cop would hang out near the Shed not to arrest us but to drive us home. Drugs. Did we inhale? You bet!

The pill and fem lib linchpinned the era. *To the Shed and then to bed and you didn't know whose.* Sex was fun! It was as much a sport as skiing. There were even scorekeepers. Was it Dapper who drove around so early in the morning to check out whose car was at the wrong house? Down in Warren a local pilot would take off at dawn and when he found the wrong cars paired off, he'd buzz the house. It seemed like half of Stowe couples were dozy-doing around someone else's mate.

In the winter we skied. In the fall we hunted ducks and woodcock and grouse and went to the girly shows at the Essex County and Tunbridge World's Fairs. We celebrated Thanksgivings where as many as thirty sat down for multiple turkey dinners and all the fixings, brought by couples, single women, and single men, and often cooked by Ted Ross at Jim Jackson's house.

Every summer Sunday, when the weather was sunny, we played slow-pitch softball behind the elementary school. Our teams were made up on the spot, and our uniforms were what we had on, usually cut-offs. I usually played barefoot, and from the way it hurt for three weeks, I apparently broke a toe sliding into third.

About the same time that the last farm on the Mountain Road went to auction, my marriage closed down too. Poke Slayton, our sheriff, walked into the dining room of our Moscow home, said "Sorry," then handed a writ. My wife was hiding over by the stove; it was divorce papers and she hadn't told me.

That was that. I went up to the Shed to cry for my family and myself. In those days if you were male and married with children, you lost everything, even if your wife sucked baby blood.

So I lost my family, my house, and all the possessions my wife coveted. My job evaporated, so I was penniless and under court order to pay alimony and child support. In need of a place to sleep, I moved to an unheated attic in Colbyville and immediately came down with pneumonia.

I joined the sexual liberation with a vengeance, coaxed by a bunch of women. My drinking came naturally. We didn't give a damn about much of anything except having a good time and obliterating our libido.

In 1968 I earned seven thousand dollars as a freelance photographer and writer. Out of that came about twenty-five hundred in alimony and child support. When my friends or I were broke, we went to Kermit Spaulding at the Union Bank and asked for a loan of five hundred or a thousand dollars. No problem. No forms to fill. No one ever thought of defaulting. Kermit just passed over the money.

There was a dark side. Most of us were well educated; in my case I gave up one of the best journalism jobs in America to drop out. We purged our dreams and hopes, but they burned holes in our psyches. In too short a period six friends committed suicide. I devised a suicide stress graph of one to nine that factored in everything from too much thinking to broken marriages, lost jobs, family pressures, finances, crippled egos, alcohol, and general mental nausea. When I hit the nine level, I decided booze and sex was a more efficient antidote than a shotgun blast to the head.

None of us came to Stowe to make money, to find a career, or to be responsible, but there were forces at work that were ending this blip in our lives. Vermont was changing. Farmers were forced to replace hemlock barn floors with cement, and to add milk coolers. Many farmers had no choice but to sell out to the developers.

The interstate cleaved our state and halved driving times from cities, so carpetbaggers arrived. New ski areas proliferated and then expanded. A-frames and cookie-cutting faux Austrian chalets displayed the new bad taste. The first Democratic governor in Vermont of the century was elected, the state legislature was reapportioned, and the rural small towns lost their equality. IBM moved to Burlington and brought with it suburbanization. The girly shows at the county fairs became politically incorrect.

Worse, people moved to Vermont to make money. Time-share condos popped up like cornfields. Sharp-tongued lawyers and real estate agents cloned themselves. Before this change, there had been no pecking order. To be chic at this time was to drive a two-hundred dollar woodchuck-mobile, bought from the Wolcott used-car lot. We patched these junks with duct tape. We did not covet fancy houses or bikes or affluent friends. But now cliques began to take over the hen house. Princesses, matrons, the sailing crowd, the cocktail circuit, the entrepreneurs, the ski-industry reps, they all searched out their own stoop.

Stowe was mutating into a commercial venture; the Mountain Road was being stripped, the quality of shops lowered itself to bus mentality. Tourism became a science and visitors a statistic. New people came to Stowe and discovered how quaint it was, how fresh, how amusing, how it needed a bigger police department.

We dropouts became flotsam as the state created and enhanced repressive taxes.

Costs of living, from groceries to gas and fuel oil to electricity, were higher than in most other states, but wages were low. To survive in Vermont we had to work several jobs with no time to look back. More people were fishing for a mate with a financial pedigree; it was the only hope for some. A few escaped to responsible jobs or set up a small business; others moved to the city or out west. I returned to New York City and reinvented myself, then moved to France, and returned to Vermont in the late 1980s, to take responsibility for the little talent I have.

I'm still here, closing up over a half-century of existing in Vermont. I see bleakness in the homogenization of the state. I hurt when I look at the mountains that too often have come down with tract-mansion acne. I see how the 1960s bent some of my friends and killed a few. But I still stumble over beauty in sun-brushed snow, and am awed when I find a mowing gilded by late October light

I'm from Vermont, I do what I want, but it just ain't as easy.

Nothing Hardly Ever Happens in Colbyville, Vermont

Colbyville, 1970

My typewriter sits on a small stand under a picture window in my apartment's living room. Every morning I sit at this typewriter and write. Or try to write, for sometimes the words don't come. Then I stare out the window.

Directly below is a small patch of lawn with my vegetable garden squatting in the corner. Behind the garden is an old barn with weathered boards. My neighbor to the north, Esther Truax, owns the barn. The annual upheaval of frost is slowly crumbling the foundation. To the left of the barn is a dirt road that curls up a steep hill. On the left side, at the beginning of the hill, is an old frame house with a long addition attached to its side. The house is painted yellow with white trim outlining the twelve windows that stare back at me. There are also two dormers sticking through the roof. The place is called Aylward's Nursing Home, although Aylward no longer owns it. Locals call Aylward's a halfway house, a home-away-from-home for some of the patients at the Waterbury State Hospital, which is about a mile and a half down the road. The hospital farms the patients to Aylward's, and the owner is paid for bedding and feeding them.

Every so often a bus drives up the dirt road. The halfway patients climb in, just like schoolchildren, and they are driven to the hospital. They are never gone for more than half a day, then the bus comes back and the patients file off and disappear into Aylward's. The bus is painted blue.

The main amusement for these halfway folks seems to be walking, and sometimes jogging, down the dirt road, past the barn and the empty barnyard, past my small vegetable garden, tangled with weeds. I don't like to pick weeds, and the garden seems to grow just as well, especially the zucchini. I eat zucchini in salads, or fried, boiled, mixed with cheese, in omelets, and in spaghetti sauce. By late summer I detest zucchini.

Sometimes the halfwayers stop by the garden to watch the weeds and the zucchini grow, but usually they continue past my house to Bissette's Market. Bissette's, which is no longer owned by Bissette, is a Mom-and-Pop store on the main road that is open all hours and is run by—who else but Mom and Pop. Their names are Frank and Helen Kilkenny. There my halfway neighbors buy Cokes and ice-cream cones. They buy Cokes and ice-cream cones all day long and walk up and down the road. All day long.

Actually, they don't really walk; they shuffle, stride, or jog. Loose arms swing forward and backward, almost in a jerking motion, completely out of synch with their gait, which is heel first, hard, and then arms swinging to catch up with the stride. The body agitates forward, and then the process is repeated.

"It's because of the Thorazine they are given to calm them down," an old-time local told me. "What they're doing is the Thorazine Shuffle."

Whether or not Thorazine causes the Shuffle, they all do it; the redheaded woman who likes her hair done in a butch, the fat blond boy who actually does the Thorazine Shuffle-Run with a grin on his face and a wave to everyone—he seems to enjoy his fix most of all. Ben is a gentle bald man who smiles at the world, or what he perceives the world to be, as he jounces back and forth. He wears a gold watch chain that hangs in a semicircle from his belt to his pocket. He picks pails of blackberries, during the season, and sells them for two dollars a pail. Mary is a kind woman who walks with more dignity than the rest. When she was younger, she traveled as a tourist through Europe. Then there is Ebenezer, who has been shuffling back and forth in front of my window longer than any of the others. I call him Ebenezer, but perhaps his real name is Ethan Frome. He has high cheekbones, a large, aquiline Yankee nose, and he never smiles—the epitome of the moss-back, rock-ribbed Vermonter who had it harder than anybody before the downstaters discovered skiing and cheap real estate.

He marches down the dirt road to the main road, about faces, and marches back, to the cadence of the Thorazine Shuffle. Some young neighbors across the road call him Touch 'n' Go, for as soon as his foot touches the asphalt on the main road, he turns around and goes back to the halfway house. He never smiles, he never says anything, and I have never seen him suck on an orange-pineapple ice-cream cone or swig from a Coke bottle. Whenever I pass him on the road, to get my Coke or ice cream fix, he stares at me, then through me, with a look as stark and cold as a wet spring night. It is a look of fear, suspicion, abandoned, crumbling farmhouses and old cellar holes. Suspenders hold up his pants.

Every so often the orange and white rescue wagon drives up to Aylward's, backs in behind the building, then leaves. The siren is always off. A new patient arrives or perhaps an old patient leaves. Alive, dead, strapped down, I never know. I turn back to my typewriter.

Directly across the street is another rambling frame house, painted white. Neil and Devaney live there, young refugees from Massachusetts who are homesteading in Vermont. He makes his living as a heating engineer, and works at a drawing board in a little shack he built outside of their home. It is surrounded by a woodpile, and is heated by a small potbelly stove. Neil and Devaney are, at heart, farmers. When they arrived in Vermont, they bought some chicks and raised them in a crate outside Neil's work shack. Then they added rabbits to the chicks, sheep to the rabbits, geese to the sheep, and so on. Their animal house multiplied and soon they made an arrangement with Esther to use part of her barn. The barnyard, which, as I mentioned, is directly in front of my picture window, which is over my desk, suddenly was populated with chickens and geese and several mallards, four sheep and a Shetland pony called Dusty, a black and white sow called Pig, the rabbits, and Neil and Devaney, who appeared every morning, buckets in hand, to feed and water their menagerie.

During the day the pony and the sheep worked the pasture behind the barn. The geese often escaped from the yard, for Neil never did learn how to build a barnyard fence, and they would parade single file, the ducks following, up to the halfway house, passing the Thorazine Shuffle folks heading to Bissette's for a pistachio cone and a Coke. Last summer pistachio was their big favorite. The summer before that was orange-pineapple. Sometimes the geese would hiss and chase one of the patients, who would holler, run, then laugh. Soon, the patients were stopping by the barnyard to talk to the animals, particularly the old sow, which they were most affectionate to, as it lay on its side, caked with mud. The sow smiled at everybody.

The inertia of writer's block, indolence, and daydreaming became a treat. The halfway people shuffled down the road, while the geese waddled up the road. Back and forth they would go. And I would watch.

The chickens stayed in the yard with only an occasional foray into my garden or across the road. One day I counted forty-four of them. They were mostly Rhode Island Reds, but there were two Crested Polish chickens, all black with a funny crown of feathers shading their heads. There were also two Arucana hens, who laid green eggs. Scurrying about this bunch were about a half dozen Bantams. Servicing the hens were one Polish rooster, one Arucana, one Bantam, and two Rhode Island Reds. One of the Rhode Island roosters was medium sized and a bit nervous. The other was a huge bird with fallen waddles. I called him King, for he ruled the roost.

The Polish and the Arucana roosters had a poor sex life. There evidently was some discrimination against them. Although they made it regularly with their own kind, they never got it on with the Bantam or Rhode Island hens, which were the barnyard WASPs. Occasionally, the Polish rooster would chase one of the Rhode Island hens, and then a bigger hen would turn and chase him. The Arucana was the least active of these studs. Maybe he was a closet hen. King, of course, chased all the hens, and for that matter, all the roosters too. King serviced his harem at least a dozen times and maybe more. He would chase a hen down, running in circles, flap onto the hen's back, fasten his talons into her tail end while pecking hard at her head and holding on, squashing the hen to the ground as he gave it to her. When he released the hen, he strutted and crowed while the poor hen dashed to the safety of her own sex.

The smaller Rhode Island rooster had to grab his tail on the run, for the King was always after him. This rooster was a real milquetoast. Two hens were having a snit and were jumping, flapping their wings and snipping at each other, as females will do to straighten out the pecking order. The rooster ran circles around the flapping hens, as if to say, like a hen-pecked husband, "Now, now, girls. Please!"

The Bantam rooster was the most highly sexed. He was a gorgeous bird, and he knew it, with his red, russet, and brown colors and neat, sleek feathers. He was the fastest bird in the yard, and was always chasing the hens lickety-split, while King was always chasing him, trying to protect his harem. I watched the Bantam run down a Rhode Island hen, pounce on top and attack, but it was frustrating for him because he was too short for the Rhode Islands, and they would shake him off.

The King had caught that Bantam rooster only once, by cornering him in a large feed can. There was a horrible squawking, and the poor Bantam flew out of the can, feathers badly ruffled and dignity ruptured. The King dug his spurs in deeply.

All the hens were being laid so much that their feathers were worn off above their tails where the roosters latched on with their claws.

The old sow slept through most of this barnyard sex. Sometimes the geese would parade into the pen, single file, do a few left turns, and parade out, the mallards following. Dusty, the pony, pranced in twice a day, kicked at a few chickens, let fly at the sow, which squealed, and bewildered the sheep as he pranced out of the yard and up to the pasture.

One morning, while typing an article, I looked out the window and focused my eyes on the barnyard scene. There was a white pig mounted on the sow. "God Almighty!" I yelped and ran downstairs, grabbed my camera, and went out to photograph this open-air sex. Neil and Dev were watching the action.

"Boy, he sure is giving it to her," said Dev. "But he's sort of small, don't you think?"

"He'll make it," said Neil, nodding his head. "Got the boar from the pig butcher who lives up the hill."

Compared to the sow the boar was scrawny. Thin, white, with narrow little pink eyes, it took a whiff of the sow and was on her at once, grunting. The sow squealed and shook him off, but the boar mounted her again. His rod was thin and corkscrew-shaped. "Looks like an efficient tool," I remarked.

The halfway folks joined us. Some of them cheered, and some looked on a bit dumbfounded, and I began to wonder how long they had been mixed up. Meanwhile, King was again chasing the Bantam who had just mounted King's favorite, the hen with the most feathers missing from her back. The sex-crazed roosters paid no attention to the sex-starved boar, and the sheep seemed to care less.

The white pig soon lost its uniqueness, and I went back to my typing. I was on the phone to an editor, discussing some story or query I had, and looked out the window for respite. My eyes focused on the barnyard.

"Jeeesus!" I said. "The pig is fucking the sheep! I gotta go!"

I crashed down the stairs, laughing madly, picked up the camera, ran out to the barnyard, and snapped away. The pig was really giving it to the

sheep. It was one of those long, slow sex acts—no hurry in the world to get it off. The boar looked at me with a sidelong glance as he pumped away. He had a sly smile on his face. The sheep put up with it until the poor animal fell to its knees from the weight of the pig. I kicked the pig off. "Enough is enough, you lecher!" I yelled. The sheep waddled away and the boar went in search of the sow. I went back to my typewriter. I forgot which editor I was talking to, and I never heard back from her.

Later in the week, I again was daydreaming out the window. Ebenezer was marching down the road. The redhead with the butch was sucking on a cone, doing a pretty good shuffle up the road. Following her were the four white geese and the mallard ducks.

A few of the hens had left the barnyard and, as chickens will do, were crossing the road. Suddenly, one of the mallards back-webbed it, scuttled up to a hen, and mounted her. This cross-breed sex thing was getting old hat. I went back to writing.

Neil and Devaney's barnyard sideshow was expanding rapidly, so Neil offered to buy the barn from Esther. They didn't agree on a price, and one thing led to another until the widow evicted the pig, the pony, the four sheep, the geese, the ducks, chickens, and rabbits, and with it all the fornication I had grown so fond of watching over my typewriter.

Now when I look up I see an empty barnyard. The pig man came down with his bathtub and hot water and butchered the sow. The halfway residents still do the Thorazine Shuffle up and down the road. Occasionally, a tractor winds up the road, or the UPS truck, or some motorcyclists gunning their engines. Neil and Devaney have divorced. Esther sold the barn to the Kilkenny's, who tore it down to move it to a nearby town and rebuild it into a home.

Eventually, the halfway house was sold, the fire department burned it down, and a chocolate factory took its place.

Outside of watching the zucchini grow, nothing much at all happens anymore outside my picture window in Colbyville, Vermont.

The Jeep

First published in the *Stowe Reporter*, 2001

A couple of months ago I was visiting with George Woodard, one of my Waterbury neighbors better known for his acting and wit than as an organic dairy farmer. He glanced at my Jeep Cherokee.

"Bit rusted, ain't it?"

My Jeep has skin cancer. There is rust around the front window, which leaks. Rust in the doors ate away one of the hinges so it won't shut without a strong shove. I can kick the bottom of the doors and bits of rusted metal fall off. My Jeep's cancer goes deep. The rear bumper's supports have been eaten away, and I can punch a screwdriver through the floor. Still, this car has heart. The engine runs perfectly; the transmission is fine. Yes, there is a hole in the manifold, and the gas tank leaks if you fill it more than halfway. I ran through one drive, had it replaced, and now this one kicks when I throw it into gear and drive over twenty miles per hour.

"I'm proud of that car, George. I bought it in 1989. It now has 201,000 miles on it . . . but you know . . . they won't let me into Stowe anymore."

George mused on that.

"You can drive roundabout through Worcester when you want to go to Morrisville. Bit longer, but they won't hassle you. They don't have politically correct police in that town. Don't think they have any cops at all."

But then Eddie, my mechanic, put his foot down after the last oil change.

"You got to June 30 to drive that car, for I'm not inspecting it no more. No sir. I'd get fined more than you if you were pulled over. Peter, that car is a mess!"

"But the engine runs fine, and you just put in that rebuilt starter motor."

"I ain't inspecting it. That's it!"

In the old days I could have duct-taped the car and got away with it. That was before the car dealers, the state, and the auto-repair shops saw a way to make money from over-salting roads and toughening the inspection regulations.

My old Jeep was with me in 1990 when I drove around the state finishing the *Vermont People* book. From 1993 to 1995 it led my 1968 Airstream forty thousand miles from Montana and North Dakota to the Texas Panhandle as I photographed and researched *People of the Great Plains*. It carried me on hunting and photography forays over Vermont roads that were so rough I got stuck four times—twice in mud, twice in snow. The marshals in New York City hijacked the car a couple of times because I didn't pay parking tickets, and I had to fork over ransom in parts of Brooklyn I don't ever want to see again. Lately that old Jeep has taken me around to photograph farm women for my next book project.

No more. A couple of weeks ago I bought a Jeep Grand Cherokee Limited Edition V8 from a fellow in Burlington who never drove the car on a dirt road. A new one costs $37,000. I bought mine for $11,250. Impeccable shape. 79,000 miles. Vintage 1995.

The car has air-conditioning, something new to me. There is a CD player, and digital readouts that spell out how many miles to the next service, when the gas tank is empty, and what mileage I get to the gallon when I'm driving five miles an hour uphill behind a leaf peeper. I now know that Stowe is north of Waterbury, because there is also a digital compass. The seats are covered with leather and are electrically set for the most comfortable position. There is an automatic shift, which I had used before only in rental cars. With the ease of a floating thistle, the V8 pulls my Airstream, which I will be living in this summer as I finish my farm women book. Oh yes. There is an analog cell phone, but I don't have anybody to call except the weather report.

However, this vehicle is a bit of a phony. This SUV is so fancy no sport (save for me) would want to drive it off-road. It has less space than my '89 Jeep, so it doesn't really have much utility. It is a vehicle of excess driven by certain people as an extension of their perceived status.

Yes, I am allowed to drive into Stowe again. I fit right in with the retired CEOs who drive their V8 Grand Cherokees (thirty-seven thousand dollars) to Lackey's to pick up the *Wall Street Journal*, and with soccer moms who drop off their kids at the playing fields with their Chevy Suburbans (forty-thousand dollars). A wild Indian driver once drove me

through the Bad Lands in Pine Tree Reservation in a Suburban. He was checking for cattle. There were no roads, and there were many mud holes. That's what the Suburban was designed for.

Politically correct dinner-party-giving thirty-year-olds without much to do drive their Range Rovers to the Harvest Market to purchase lemon-curd tarts. The minimalists, who would have a Mondrian and an Eames chair in their room if they knew what they were, drive Mercedes ML 320s (forty-four thousand dollars) when they go to the Helen Day opening shows. Mothers with babies drive their Lincoln Navigators (fifty thousand dollars) to the Little River access to cross-country ski, pulling their *enfant terrible* in canopy-covered, high-tech sleds. They like to sport Nantucket parking lot stickers on their windshields. I've seen only one Hummer in Stowe, buzzing along on SUV Alley, the road that leads past the Percy Farm, and the teahouse in the sheep pasture, into Sterling Valley.

I used to be proud and defiant when I drove to Stowe in my rusted-out '89 Jeep. Now, I feel, I feel . . . embarrassed. Have I become one of them? Have I, too, lost my soul? Can I live with honesty and integrity anymore? My bank account says yes. My Jeep Limited Edition says no.

Anyone want to buy a Jeep Grand Cherokee 1989 with a rebuilt starter,

good tires, and could be tinkered with to pass inspection? Only $300.
Comes with a 201,000-mile pedigree.

I sold the '89 Jeep for two hundred dollars. In 2008, the '95 Jeep, after
161,000 miles, gave up. You can have it for five hundred. I bought
on Ebay, just before the gas soared, a 2005 Jeep Grand Cherokee
Trail model. Holds all my camera gear, can pull my Airstream, but
I'm thinking of mothballing it and buying a 1980s Citroën Deux
Chevaux.

On Being a Woodchuck

First Published in the *Stowe Reporter*, 1996

Many people are not familiar with the different meanings Vermonters have for the word *woodchuck*. Let me explain.

A woodchuck, in the original meaning of the word, is a rodent; *Marmota monax* is its Latin classification. It is also known as a groundhog, a marmot, and a whistle-pig.

The Vermont woodchuck, animal species, has reddish-brown hair, lives in pastures, whistles at the approach of strangers, and is a good digger. It lives in dens at the end of tunnels. Its front porch is a mound of dirt surrounding the hole leading to its den. Nearby is another hole with no dirt around it. This is an escape route, or "hidey hole," as some Vermonters call it. The woodchuck hibernates from late November to late March and never, in Vermont, appears on Groundhog Day.

A woodchuck can eat a quarter ton of hay a year and that is one reason farmers have antipathy for the animal. Also, a cow can break a leg in the woodchuck's hole.

The late Boots Cornell of Morrisville was probably the greatest wood-chuck hunter in the world. In his lifetime he killed over fifteen thousand woodchucks and should be in the *Guinness Book of World Records*. He kept a notebook in which he recorded his annual kills.

The Vermont woodchuck, human species, has some similar traits. It prefers to live away from people and would hibernate if it could. The definition, in the past, for a Vermont woodchuck was a person born in Vermont, and it was a term of pride, if not endearment.

The term has been sullied in recent years by flatlanders who have imported themselves into the state with an attitude. They think of wood-chucks as rednecks, which displays their ignorance of semantic nuances. A redneck does not have the wit, intelligence, or humor of a woodchuck, and although there are certainly rednecks living in Vermont, many of them are from out-of-state.

A *woodcharles*, and we have a few of them, is a new flatlander who is educated in the right schools, is too erudite for Vermont, and is way to the left as an environmentalist. They usually don't deer hunt and they have a trust fund.

Now a *glitterchuck* is a native Vermonter gone yuppie (marpy—"middle-aged rural yuppie"—would be a better word, although both words are obsolete). Usually they are real estate agents or contractors who cater to the woodcharleses, who always overspend on land and houses.

A glitterchuck can also be an out-of-stater who dresses like a Vermont woodchuck and is very aggressive in trying to make as much money as possible from whomever they come into contact with. They wish they had a trust fund, and they are not to be trusted.

The days of woodchuckery are rapidly passing, since the state began mandating woodcharles-ism. For instance, a true woodchuck owned a woodchuckmobile, a vehicle bought for a couple hundred bucks from a junkyard and held together with duct tape until it no longer ran, when it was recycled back to the junkyard for a similar vehicle.

Then auto junkyards were forced to build fences to hide their vehicles from the public, prodded by glitterchucks, who ran car dealerships.

Woodcharleses who became legislators mandated that duct-taped cars could not pass inspection. They did this at about the same time that they outlawed the town dump.

To "woodchuck it" was an honorable way of repairing something so that it worked as long as it did not look pretty. Again duct tape, the twentieth century's answer to baling wire, was usually called upon to repair lamps that were falling apart, to hold together not only cars but loose gunstocks, to wrap on heels to prevent blisters with new boots, to close drafts around doors and windows.

Stowe has few woodchucks, but those who remain are stubborn hold-outs. A new animal, it appears, has moved into Stowe. It is the fisher cat, a predator that feeds on woodchucks and hedgehogs (porcupines), which they eviscerate and eat inside out. They also have a taste for house cats, and if yours has disappeared, this is probably why.

Fisher cats, human species, assassinate verbally their opponents on school boards and town committees and, if they are developers, they use their politically connected cronies to push through their plans. They like sprawl and take delight in cutting up pastures into housing lots. Money and power is their game and they sometimes have matriculated from the town booster variety of glitterchuck. This nasty animal is replacing the woodchuck, esteemed for years as a friendly neighbor who likes to whistle on a fine summer afternoon. So goes the neighborhood.

Take Back Vermont

First published in the *Stowe Reporter*, 2000

It really caught my attention. TAKE BACK VERMONT, hand-painted in white, stretched for at least thirty feet across a red barn squatting a few feet off Route 25 near Waits River. To the right of the sign was a sliding door that framed a tractor; on the left was a pasture. The farther east I drove, the more signs I saw. This was early September.

"Hmmm, that's an interesting idea," I thought to myself. "Take the legislature from the urban areas and give it back to the small towns. Take back Vermont from sprawl and developers and tract mansions and make it affordable for Vermonters. Take back our state from the tenured bureaucrats, too many of whom are dictatorial in regulating. Roll back our taxes so we can afford Vermont."

I stopped at a country store for a sandwich, and at the counter someone was buying a six-pack of Tunbridge Ale. I commented that I had never heard of it, and the storeowner told me some lesbians ran the small brewery.

"This fall they're making a beer called Vermont Pride," she said. "The profits go to some transsexual group. That beer isn't going to be sold in my store! See the sign on my lawn?" She pointed next door to her home. TAKE BACK VERMONT, the sign said. The woman had moved here from New Jersey.

I hadn't thought too much about the civil unions law. The state Supreme Court ruled that gays had civil and constitutional rights, so the legislature followed through with the new law, which was simply a legal device to give people of the same sex most of the rights that married couples have.

"Well," I said to myself. "It gives them the right to divorce." I imagine there are civil divorces, but most of the divorces I was familiar with, including my own, were anything but civil. As half of the straight marriages end in divorce, how will gay unions fare? The lawyers must be rubbing their hands.

Now the Vermont civil unions law had become international news.

Feature articles appeared in the *Economist* and the *New York Times*. Holland had legalized gay marriages. The outcome of the election for Vermont governor appeared to depend upon who is for and who is against gays. The election might affect the tone of America's tolerance for equal rights under the law throughout our country.

Governor Dean signed the bill into law, and Ruth Dwyer (his Republican opponent) led the pack against it. (Dwyer called Dean a radical liberal. Although since that time Dean has gained a national reputation for liberal views on some issues, at that time he was governing Vermont as a conservative Democrat. By comparison, Dwyer's rhetoric put her just to the right of Mussolini.)

I have heard of a Vermonter who drove to Montana and was asked to leave a small town because he was from that state that passed a gay law. Another was refused booking on a big-game hunt because he was from the state that supported homosexuals. In Stowe I heard that motel bookings were down because of backlash to the civil unions law. Yet outside of the gossip, all it boils down to is that the Bill of Rights and the Constitution give gays, blacks, Native Americans, Nisei, Mayflowers, and even graduates of Ivy League prep schools the same legal rights. Anything else is discrimination, intolerance, or bigotry, call it what you will.

Despite its liberal image, Vermont has a long rap sheet on intolerance. The Ku Klux Klan was very active in this state before World War II but, since Vermont was white as Ivory Soap, they didn't have blacks to bash around, so they picked on the Catholics. When my mother, Mary Mitchell Miller, brought our family to Weston in 1947, the local postmaster invited her to tea. They got along well until the postmaster leaned over and confided, "Mary, six months ago we got rid of the last Jewish family, and six weeks ago the only Catholic family left town."

"How nice, Ray, " answered my mother. "Now you have four more." She went on to bring in the Benedictines, who started the Weston Priory, which is now well known throughout the country. It remains a vibrant feature of Weston, while my mother and the postmaster have both long since passed away.

In the 1970s I was talking with a bunch of Vermonters and one mentioned how we have to watch out for "niggers, Jews, 'n' cum'nists." I asked him if he ever met a "Jew," a "nigger," or a "cum'nist."

"Huh!" He whipped around and squared his shoulders. "Whaddya mean by that? Huh? Whaddya mean?"

Many of the prestigious ski lodges in Vermont—in Manchester and Stowe—had a discrimination policy against Jews. One leading lodge in Stowe kept a list of the racial backgrounds of its guests. Some lodge owners asked drop-ins point blank if they were Jewish, and if they answered yes, they were asked to go elsewhere.

The most interesting story about this period of Stowe history I heard over dinner in New York City in the 1980s. Susan Schwartz, a handsome, raven-haired woman, recounted how she took a week's vacation at a Stowe lodge just off the Mountain Road. She found, upon her arrival, that Jews were not welcome. She said nothing until the end of the week, when the other guests elected her Ski Princess of the Week. She got up in front of the guests and thanked them gracefully and with a smile said: "I want to thank you all and wish to let you know that not only am I now your Ski Princess, I am also a Jewish Princess."

Gays will have their rights, eventually. But as we learned from the civil rights movement in the sixties, it will take a generation before any real progress is made.

Same-Sex Union and Dog Ownership

By Ted Ross

My friend Ted Ross penned this in 2000 when Vermont legalized civil unions. His column, and my response, appeared in the *Vermont Eagle*. and later in *Stick Season Grouse*, a book by Ted Ross published in 2004.

Vermont has been catapulted to worldwide prominence by a historic, so the framers say, piece of legislation signed into law by Governor Dean. Granted, he signed it with as little fanfare as possible, fearing backlash in November. But it was difficult to downplay, even though he was in his office during the signing and afterward, mumbling platitudes to the press. Every major network was there, capturing footage of triumphant same-sex couples embracing.

I hope I'm wrong. I don't see any reprisals in November, though polls show the bill highly out of favor with the Vermont voters who elected the legislators to represent them. Some of these lawmakers were bold enough to say they didn't care what their constituents felt, they were going to support what they felt was right. They deserve to be pilloried by the members of the communities who elected them, but I bet these arrogant clowns will escape all punishment.

In the meantime states that do not have laws on the books defining marriage as being "between one man and one woman" are hastening to do so . . . too late. Vermont will lead the way. Once these causes célèbres get momentum, the US Constitution itself is swept aside, not just some puny state measure that is easily repealed. Even the Vermont House attempted to hedge by granting civil-union, not marriage, licenses. The ink was barely dry from the governor's pen when it became obvious how long this would last. A matched pair of gravel-voiced lesbian activists who were instrumental in moving matters through the courts referred to the bill as a first step toward marriage, honoring their twenty-seven-year commitment. The old gals seemed nice enough, enjoying handholding on their farm for the cameras.

Vermont's image to this day among the totally uninformed is—what, conservative, Republican, Yankee? Well, not anymore, and not since the sixties, when almost as a lark the state elected a Democrat governor. Unheard of. He was a prodigious drinker and party man who was known to fall down stairs on at least one occasion into a press conference. He was fun, charismatic (never forgot a face or a name), and though he did not bring sweeping change, Vermont as a one-party state was past. Then the hippies and liberals with a mission visited and, unfortunately, stayed. In the year 2000, our one congressman is a former hippie from Brooklyn who ran as a socialist independent for his fourth term. Our senators are two dinosaurs, the Republican more liberal than the Democrat. The bureaucracy of our state government has swollen to double since the current governor came to office. The Republican Party is in such disarray that a joke candidate ran in the US Senate primary in 1998, an eighty-year-old farmer who did not even vote for himself.

Of course, anyone opposing same-sex marriage or, for that matter, any affirmative-action program on moral or religious grounds is despised and ridiculed as a mean-spirited cad. The press joined the fray, and even one's own children—poorly schooled in a failed liberal education system, but well indoctrinated in classes that show documentaries like *Heather Has Two Moms*. People are scared.

Okay, they win, but fair is fair. I want to legally marry my German short-hair, Mildred. Same-sex marriages, why not mixed species? The unisexers state that it is discriminatory not to recognize love and commitment. I love my hunting dog and she loves me unconditionally, which is more than I've had out of marriage and other relationships with humans. Of course, I didn't deserve such devotion, but Mildred neither knows nor cares. Panda, an English springer spaniel who shared my life for fifteen years, would have married me at the drop of a hat, and she was an open field-trial champion. She did get cranky and used to leave the room if I mixed a third martini. Divorce? Never! If one thinks a 50-percent divorce rate amongst hetero couples is high, wait until the courts clog with same-sex divorce, in spite of their mantras about commitment.

My dog union is just the tip of the iceberg. All pets should qualify—Mrs. O'Leary and her cow, Tarzan and his favorite ape—the opportunities are endless. My dogs sleep on my bed, not in it, and besides, most married couples eventually stop having "meaningful sex" anyway. Those who talk about great home sex are lying. Bill and Hillary stopped having relations a dozen years ago according to his testimony, and they are icons. If I were so inclined I could marry my dog in Vermont and move to a state like Missouri, which has no laws against sodomy, with liberal psychiatrists and their lawyers fighting to keep it so on the basis that it provides relief for psychotics if the animal is consenting. These are strange times, Mama . . . strange times indeed.

The obvious extension of all this is allowing same-sex marriage to mixed species. To this I answered absolutely not! What, is our society, perverted?

A Rebuttal: Pure, Crass Canine Prejudice

By Peter Miller

I have known Mr. Ross for years. He calls me a flaming liberal and I call him a redneck conservative, but I am shocked, absolutely shocked, that Mr.

Ross will marry Mildred, a bitch he picked up in Texas a few years ago, and not his stalwart male companion of the last fifteen years, Tweed IV. Tweed is his favorite springer spaniel, and many times I have caught him kissing the dog. I know that both Tweed and Mildred share Mr. Ross's bed.

Mr. Ross implies that Mildred could sleep under the covers if he decides to let her, but he didn't mention what Mildred thought of the idea. What kind of marriage does this dog owner propose with Mildred? A nonconsummated platonic marriage? And if that is so, why won't he marry his male companion, Tweed, who has been such a faithful companion and a good hunter?

The reason is just plain prejudice. Mr. Ross is against same-sex marriages or mixed-species same-sex civil unions. I know his heart lies with Tweed; their love and affection for each other is boundless. Like many conservatives, Mr. Ross follows the politically correct social mantra instead of allowing his libido to have some say in the matter. Mr. Ross is not in the closet, but he is in the doghouse when it comes to canines.

Civil unions give legality to same-sex "marriage" and, as Mr. Ross implies, this can lead to legal dissolution, which is divorce. The lawyers will soon be burnishing their skills in civil-union splits as they anticipate further financial rewards from the emotionally distressed. But who is going to handle dog–human or other mixed-species divorces? Will the animal-rights crowd start hiring and training lawyers and putting judges on retainers? You bet your pooch the human won't get a fair shake. Will there be canine or feline specialists in counseling and divorce? And how will the settlements be configured?

If the present laws are honored, Mildred, if she divorces Mr. Ross, will own half his home. She'll bark Mr. Ross off the premises and show Tweed the door. And can Mildred or Tweed or any same-sex or hetero-sex mixed-species marriage-civil-union partner-husband-wife get restraining orders if his or her mate abuses him or her?

I think, in the case of Mr. Ross, he should be allowed to marry his bitch Mildred and enter into civil union with Tweed, and draw up a prenuptial agreement between the two dogs as long as they are both allowed to sleep on Mr. Ross's bed.

Mountain Ghosts

First published in *Ski Magazine*, 1981

Ghosts, sprites, fairies, succubi
Wraiths, phantasms, banshees, incubi
Haunters of the present, victims of the past . . .
"No such thing!" doubters exclaim.
Hah! They do . . . Yes, they do . . .

A great many ghosts seem to be alive and well in Vermont. They are found on the mountains, in the cabins, ski lodges, and hotels. They jounce through the woods, turn off lights and snow guns, and ski down mountains, looking, searching . . . but for what?

Some skiers swear that they have seen the old J bar at Bromley clanking up the mountain with the last owner, Fred Pabst, yelling out, "Hey! Godammit, how the hell are ya?"

Forget the yarns above. More than likely, they are just stories from a lively mind. Here are some real stories, laced with facts and history about ghosts that reside in ski country.

Nobody knows exactly who Emily was or where she lived. But the best guess is that she lived in Stowe Hollow, across the valley from Mount Mansfield, in the first half of the nineteenth century. On the day before her marriage, she was walking down a dirt road when she was startled by a draft of runaway horses bearing down on her. Emily quickly ran to the side of the bridge she was about to cross, lost her footing, and fell into the stream below. She was killed by the fall.

Her swain, whose name has not been remembered, was grief-stricken to the extent that the next day he jumped off the bridge and killed himself.

The covered bridge in Stowe Hollow is known locally as Emily's Bridge. Teenagers, for generations, have taken rides up to the bridge to park, neck, and be scared out of their wits. Cars and some people claim to have been scratched. Those who have been there have heard the clatter of hoofs rattle across the bridge, followed by a scream echoing from the stream and a pulsating blob of ectoplasm.

Ed Rhodes is a Stowe native whose family goes back to the first days of the town, in the eighteenth century. He is interested in digging up the past and checking out esoteric facts.

"I really don't believe Emily fell off that bridge," said Rhodes. "I went up there and looked around, and it's not a long fall and it's not a steep pitch.

"The bridge crosses Gold Brook (gold has been found in the streambed, which is another mystifying story), and back in the last century there were two covered bridges over that brook. The lower bridge was taken down and replaced with a cement structure. There is a very steep and dangerous drop from that bridge to the river.

"I believe Emily and her husband-to-be met their fate at the lower covered bridge," said Ed. "Later, Emily's ghost moved up to the covered bridge that is still standing."

A friend told me this story: "One night, during the summer, a friend and I wanted to track a thunderstorm across Stowe. We were in the car and we followed the downpour and lightning as it moved through town and into Stowe Hollow. We were in the center of the storm and parked in Emily's Bridge, watching and listening to the storm.

"Suddenly, right next to my window, I saw a pulsating greenish-white light. It was just inches outside the car door. The hairs went straight on the back of my head. I knew it was Emily, but my friend had never heard of the ghost. Suddenly, he shouted, 'Let's get out of here!'

"At the same time I saw the light, my friend recounted—after he calmed down—that he had heard a hollow-sounding voice, a woman's voice, pleading to him 'Help me, help me!'"

Emily has a ghostly neighbor, Cora, who sometimes appears about five miles down the road in an old farmhouse on Route 100, about a mile north of Waterbury Center. The ghost of Cora is an elderly woman with gray hair tied in a bun. She has a narrow pinched face and wears a long

gray dress with an apron. She is thin and holds herself very erect, especially when she is sitting.

Cora must have lived in the upstairs bedroom that faces south. A springer spaniel who lived in the house would never go into that room. Even after it was freshly made, the bed in the room would often have a depression in it, as if someone had been sleeping there. The doors in the house would open and shut at odd times, the stairs would creak, and items seemed to move themselves around the kitchen.

Cora is a docile ghost, and the couple that lived in the house got along just fine with her. But then, one night, the mistress of the house asked her husband for a divorce. She had a secret boyfriend and had made plans to run away the next day. The husband was shocked, but the next day—a Sunday—was even more shocking. When the two were out of the house, pretending all was normal at a volleyball game, the house caught on fire. There was extensive damage, and it delayed the woman of the house from running away—for at least a few months.

Although some people, such as the fire marshal, believed it was faulty wiring or a stove that was left on, others believe that Cora, showing her displeasure at disharmony, set the blaze.

Cora remained after the fire. This writer saw her when he was replacing furniture in the den. She was sitting on a sofa, staring at me as if to say, "It's about time you put this room back in order!"

"I see you Cora," I yelled, and stabbed a finger at her, and then she disappeared.

That winter, Cora appeared in the hallway and was seen by skiers who had rented for the winter. One saw her in the mirror while he was shaving.

A builder who worked on the house and has an interest in ghostly history did some research and found that Cora lived during the last century and that, mysteriously, her death certificate was ripped out of the town records.

Ed Rhodes had heard some of this story from the branch of his family that lived in Waterbury.

"I'm not sure what house," he recalled, "but back in the last century a daughter did her mother in with a hatchet. I'm not sure whether it was that farmhouse or one just up the road. The daughter was put into the Waterbury Mental Hospital, where I understand she died."

This writer believes that Cora is the mother, who was so saddened by the tragedy in her family that she is trying her best to share her spirit with a happy household. Now, however, there are no more families for Cora to mingle with, and she might have left her home sometime after the fire and divorce. The house was sold after the divorce and completely renovated into an Italian restaurant called La Tregora (now renamed Michael's On The Hill), which is not really in Cora's style. In the manager's office there is an old picture of a farming couple standing on the front lawn of the house. Could the woman be Cora? Although she is dressed in the fashion of Cora, she looks too robust, although maybe a century of ghosting slims you down.

Bailey Rawson is known as the founder of Rawsonville, Vermont, and his graveyard is a fenced-off plot opposite his former home at the fork of Routes 30 and 100, several miles from Stratton Mountain. Few know that Bailey still makes his home in that house, rather than under his tombstone. The building has been a lodge, a real estate office, and a ski rental. Although some past residents of the house laugh at the idea of ghosts, others tighten up when the subject is broached. One old-timer, who lives in Rawsonville and who is related to the departed Bailey, would not talk about the ghost.

"I know about it," he said, as if he just swallowed a glass of vinegar, "and what I know ain't good, and I ain't talkin' to nobody about that ghost or that house!"

In the late sixties, the lodge was known as The Top's House and was run by a young couple. They had some bad luck. Her horse went berserk when she was riding it, and it threw her, stomped her, and broke her back. She was layed up for six months on a backboard.

After recovery, her Newfoundland dog, an affectionate pet, came into the house one day and ripped open her head. She struggled out of the house, a complete bloody mess, and leaned on the car horn until help came. She needed one hundred stitches and almost died.

This was never actually blamed on the ghost of Bailey Rawson, but hold on for a minute . . .

A group of skiers from Connecticut rented the house and Nick Cippolino, of Greenwich, drove up to open the house for the season. When he walked upstairs he saw a short stout guy with a gimp in his leg hurrying down the hall.

"Hey!" yelled Nick, who was brought up on the streets of New York and still carries a piece, "Whatcha doin' here?" He chased the short stout guy, who ran into the bathroom and closed the door. Nick ripped the door open and went inside. No one was there.

Nick inquired around town about this intruder and described him. "Oh," said one native, "that's Bailey Rawson. He's been dead for years."

Bailey liked the bathroom, particularly the modern fixtures. One night Nick, his girlfriend Sherry, and other friends were sleeping downstairs when at about four in the morning they heard the upstairs shower running and someone walking around. No one had left his or her bed that night.

Later, Nick, to demonstrate the existence of the ghost to his friends, banged the kitchen table three times and yelled, "Bailey Rawson, if you're here, pound back three times."

"Bong! Bong! Bong!" the cellar pipes answered, as if someone was banging them in the cellar. The friend and his girlfriend immediately left the house.

"Bailey Rawson would put up with people for only so long," remembered Nick, "then he wanted to get rid of them. And he sure is mean to animals."

Sherry was walking their dog one night on the walk-around porch (since taken down) when she heard a car coming but could see no lights. Her dog was suddenly not beside her but in the middle of the road. The car passed and she found the dog 150 feet away, unconscious, obviously hit, and apparently by the car. The dog had a concussion and was a nervous wreck.

"It was like I blacked out and the dog was physically thrown in the road," said Sherry. In another instance the dog was somehow transported from a high-fenced pen to the other side of the road. A Jeep was run off the road by another mystery car, which loomed in front of them with no lights.

The Bailey Rawson home sat empty and for sale. The basement is filled with water. Although there is no head, the pipes still creak and clank at night, as this writer found out last winter.

Bailey Rawson, if you ever see him, is a short guy, muscular, with a limp in his right foot. He leans toward the right when he walks, and is known to be a very mean ghost.

———————————

Update, 2008: The house has since been completely renovated and turned into a store and is supposedly ghost-free.

———————————

Fleas

My friend Ted Ross has a few travel companions he is never without. The first are his two springer spaniels, Arrow and Barney. The second is his continually replenished bottle of gin. Neither is more important than the other, although I have never seen Ted kiss his gin bottle. Neither have I seen him suck on it. Rather, he prefers his gin shaken with a bit of vermouth and served, with two olives, in an oversized martini glass—which is refilled about four times every evening. Amazingly, this gin-guzzler rises every morning without a hangover and his good humor and wit intact.

So, yes, I am used to Ted arriving at my house in his beat-up Texan truck, now scoured robin's egg bleached blue, with two hundred thousand miles driven on it between Texas—where he quail hunts in the winter, Hollowville, New York—where he has a home he just reverse-mortgaged ("I have no kids and I need the money and so what?"), my home in Vermont, and a fishing lodge camp he established in Nova Scotia. In the back of the truck, when he pulls into my driveway, are two dog pens, a bag of dog food, his hunting clothes, a sheathed Holland and Holland over-and-under 20-gauge shotgun, a gallon of cheap sherry, a duffel bag of clothes, and that box that contains his gin, vermouth, and maybe a wild turkey or some pheasants he has collected from guiding at a hunting club near Hollowville. In his heyday Ted was a salesman, a tennis and ski instructor, squash player, piano player, and . . . he had a listing in the Social Register. Now he has personality and physical characteristics that are absolutely Falstaffian.

Ted sleeps in my spare bedroom with his two dogs. Sometimes the dogs are stretched out on an old sleeping bag spread out next to the bed; sometimes they are sprawled on the bed, sandwiching Ted. He stays for a couple of days, and if it is hunting season, we'll go out with his two dogs in search of woodcock, a pastime we have enjoyed together for over forty years.

We catch up on stories. We don't discuss politics, because his philosophy is in tune with Attila the Hun and mine is more Don Quixote on a liberal quest. When he hits the threshold, which is often three martinis and a half bottle of wine, his face turns redder than normal, his jowls enlarge, he squints, shakes his head from side to side, blinks furiously, and reminisces about wonderful hunts and wonderful springers he has owned. "God, but we have lived in the best of times," he'll say.

I agree and remind him that his liver must be blacker than licorice pills and that one day he will explode from the alcohol he consumes. He claims that the juniper berries in the gin keep him healthy. Then he shrugs.

"I drink, therefore I am."

Ted's visit in the fall of 2006 was special. Very special.

He stayed for a few days, we did some hunting, and he left for home. Two days later my daughter Dodie and her partner Fred arrived from England and took over Ted's bedroom. They own a Mexican restaurant in London and she imports chilies from Mexico. Ted is an excellent chef when he is sober but by the time he is ready to serve the meal he is potted, and that's often how the meal tastes. Dodie, on the other hand, is a superb chef. So we were eating well, doing some hiking and general leaf peeping.

The day after they arrived, Dodie came up to me and said, "Dad, I'm scratching at lot."

"Fleas!" said Fred, who was scratching even more.

"TED AND HIS DOGS," they said in unison.

I immediately drove to the hardware store with Dodie and went to the flea-buster shelf. I was checking out the products when Dodie looked at me and said: "DAD, THERE'S A FLEA ON YOUR CHEEK!"

I bought two cans of flea spray and went home and sprayed the floor in their bedroom, then hit the hallway, bathroom, living room, and myself. I was scratching too.

Fred and Dodie flew back to London.

She called when they arrived home.

"Dad, Fred scratched all the way home on the airplane. My ferrets have fleas. They never had fleas! Doesn't Ted use Frontline?"

My God, I thought, are the international flea police going to pester my daughter and me? This might become a global incident. I went online to find out about fleas. Between 1347 and 1350 bubonic plague, the Black Death, killed two hundred million people throughout the world, and mostly in Europe and Merrie England. The cause? The oriental rat flea carried on the back of the black rat.

Was this the beginning of a modern-day pandemic?

No, the cat flea was the culprit in America. No pandemic, just itching, pain, frustration, paranoia, and the sense of being diseased and living in a diseased house.

What I found out was that when Ted departed, with dogs, they left behind fleas. A female flea, that parasitic, warm-blooded, blood-slurping animal with saws and sucking mouth parts can lay twenty eggs after one blood meal. It doesn't take too long for ten female fleas to create a quarter million offspring in various stages of their lives—egg, larva, pupa, and imago. The last two bite. I was flea infested. My house was flea infected. And I was the only blood meal.

I am not sure whether fleas are epicures or gourmands. They do not bite my daughter. They loved to suck on Fred's blood, and they really love me. We must be three-star destinations.

The first night I spent scratching. Welts grew on my ankles, calves, and arms. A semicircle of bites decorated my anklebone. I bought anti-itch cream and a gallon of flea spray and sprayed the sleeping bag and floor and bed. There was an old pine floor in the guest room—I renamed it the Flea Room—and I flooded the spray into the cracks between the boards.

The fleas then invaded my bedroom. I bought flea bombs and bombed bedrooms, hallway, living room, kitchen, and bathroom. Then I sealed doors and left the house for a couple of hours.

When I returned I checked the rooms. I got down on all fours and inspected the floor. I saw a little black speck and touched it, and it jumped a couple of inches. I took out the vacuum cleaner, put some mothballs in the bag, and vacuumed the floor and the cracks. I did the same to the rug in my bedroom. I did this in the morning and the night. I washed all my clothes and bedding every morning. Then I held the drier filter to the light and, yep, fleas were embedded in the screen.

I started inspection tours wearing a T-shirt, underpants, and a pair of long, bright-yellow soccer socks. I walked into the Flea Room, sat on the bed, and looked at my socks. Soon black specks were climbing up! I vacuumed again, bought another gallon of spray, and pumped it into the cracks.

I removed the bed, an Ikea futon on a wood frame, and moved it outdoors, flea-busted it, and sold it. I took the sleeping bag and any movable rugs and hung them from the deck railing.

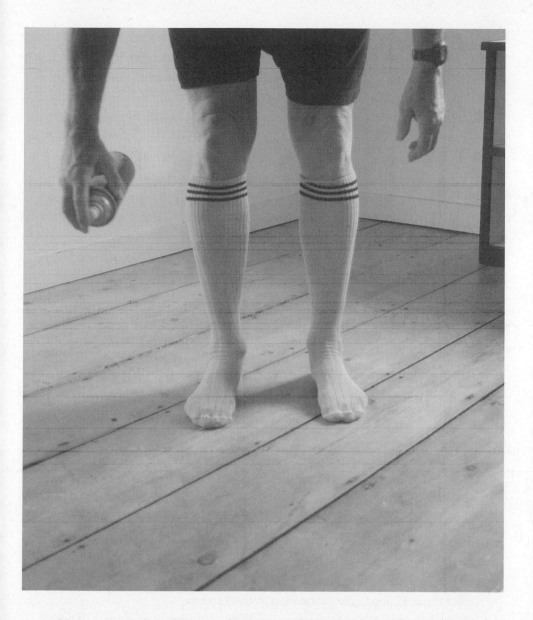

However, I still had those suckers in my bedroom. I ripped up the wall-to-wall carpeting and carved it into strips and took it to the dump. I moved into an empty room and slept under a clean blanket.

It was now a week since Dodie left. I washed everything once a day and inspected the drier filter; it always had fleas in it. My yellow socks, when I sat in the living room or in the bedroom, had these little black specks climbing up them, a Delta Force.

I could not sleep without coating my itching legs with salve and, finally, calamine lotion. I became depressed and didn't want to see anyone. (Well, what would you think if you found me walking around all day in my underpants, bent double and inspecting at close range my yellow soccer socks?) I vacuumed and bombed and sprayed, and I still found them climbing up my yellow socks.

Fleas are jumpers and climbers. An eighth-inch-long flea can jump seven inches high and thirteen inches forward. Just imagine if they were two or three inches long, all with saws and sucking tubes and antenna that could read the carbon dioxide we animals exhale and awaken to attack from feeling motion or heat? I had forty bites on one leg. With each bite the flea injected an anticoagulant and some of their blood. What if forty three-inch fleas attacked me? What if billions of them formed a global army? All of us humans would be sucked dry and dead and then what would those fleas do?

I called an exterminator. "I'll get rid of them," he said. "I always do and I guarantee that. You have to leave the house for a day. Seventy-five dollars a room."

He arrived with his gear. I vacated the premise and hid in the woods. When I returned I called him up. He said, "Don't worry, you're flea-free."

I did the yellow-sock check in the Flea Room, sitting on the bed I had moved in there from my bedroom. Within two minutes black specks were charging up my calf. I screamed in anguish and called the exterminator.

"That's impossible," he said.

"You want to look at my new bites?"

"I'll have to call the state. There must be a new breed."

Again he arrived to re-do his thing. I put the socks in the washer, dressed, and left.

Again I went through the yellow-sock test. More troops, just hatched, were assaulting my kneecaps. AAARRGH!

I did some analytical thinking. These fleas are breeding in the cracks between the floorboards and maybe the flea poison isn't getting down to them. I had a brilliant idea. I put on my pants and drove to the hardware store. I bought a couple of cans of polyurethane. I went back to my house, changed back into underpants and yellow soccer socks, and literally poured polyurethane into the cracks. I then bombed the room, closed all the doors, and opened the windows. It was turning cold, and I kept the room shut for a month. I bought scatter rugs to go over the floor cracks near the bed. I bought a new bed. I called a rug cleaner to clean my remaining rugs.

The last flea I saw jumped on my hand while I was reading in the living room. I sprayed the floor, the chair and everything else, threw my clothes into the washer, and jumped in a very hot bath. I vacuumed every floor crack. I scattered mothballs on the floor.

Six weeks after the first flea bit Fred, my home was flea-clear. My bites healed. I washed and put away the yellow socks, although every time I look at them I itch.

Needless to say, I let Ted have it when I saw him next. He only uses cell phones and cancels the numbers when he moves and so it is hard to reach him. He is penurious when it comes to living expenses, and he doesn't like unpleasant calls.

"Don't you use Frontline on your dogs?"

"It's expensive. Well, I did check the dogs, and they were covered with fleas. I could feel them crawling on me at night, but they never bit me!"

"Probably because of your gin-soaked blood," I said.

He laughed. "Another good reason to drink."

He wrote me a check for three hundred dollars, about half of what it cost, including new rugs, and then looked at me seriously.

"You know, a dog would have collected those fleas. You ought to have one. I know where you can get a Brittany spaniel for very little."

Ted still visits and arrives with his springers and his Gordon's or Fleischman gin. He brought a peace offering of a wild turkey he shot. His dogs are clipped well, and he uses Frontline.

I know now if fleas go on steroids, the human race is doomed.

Fred Tuttle, 1919–2003

Fred Tuttle—dairy farmer, actor, politician, and Vermont's most beloved citizen—died of a heart attack on October 4 in Tunbridge, Vermont. He was eighty-four.

Fred starred in the 1996 film *Man with a Plan*, written and directed by his neighbor, John O'Brien. It was a spoof on politics and became a cult film.

Two years later Fred ran for real against Jack McMullen in the Republican primary for US Senate and won. Fred then endorsed the Democratic candidate, Senator Patrick Leahy, and retired to his hillside home.

The following appeared in several Vermont newspapers shortly after Fred's funeral. I photographed and interviewed Fred and his father, Joe, and both appear side by side in my book *Vermont People*.

It was one of those soft, Indian summer days. The early morning fog lifted to bare blue-hazed mountains under a sky unblemished with clouds. The temperature climbed slowly into the high seventies, but the shade was fresh as springwater. It was a day to live easy, but this Thursday, the ninth day of October, Vermont's most benevolent and beautiful month, was Fred Tuttle's funeral.

I had put on my only suit, which I hadn't worn for a decade, my black shoes, a pale pink shirt, and a muted paisley tie left over from a time past. Tunbridge, Fred's hometown, is about forty miles from Colbyville. I drove to Randolph and took the shortcut, over the mountain, past some rolling fields of cornstalks being chopped into silage, then into the woods and down past a landscape of farms into Tunbridge.

The Tunbridge Congregational Church with its simple steeple punctuates the center of town. The interior was plain with graceful discipline. Judy Lewis—it's always a woman at these funerals—was playing the organ that had a deep voice that was constant, solemn but respectful, as attendants ushered in the mourners. On the left aisle were seated friends of Fred. Among them was Senator Patrick Leahy, who defeated Fred in the 1987 Senatorial campaign. (Well, Fred, after he won the Republican primary, deferred to the Democratic senator, on the advice of his wife Dottie: *"There is no way you are going to Washington!"* she once screamed at him when he was toying with the idea as we sat at the dining room table. He gave me a sly smile and I could see he liked, in his own way, to have Dottie lecture him.) Also seated in the church, in the pew in front of Senator Leahy, was John O'Brien, who had the brilliance to recognize that his neighbor down the road was just the right person to star in his film *Man with a Plan*. Next to him was Jack Rowell, associate producer of *Man with a Plan*, woodchuck photographer and fly fisherman, whose photographs sparkle with warmth and humor, and who traveled and documented Fred's years as a performance artist.

Filling the right side of the aisle were members of the family. There were more elderly women then men; their husbands had already died. A few men had the bronzed healthy look of farmers who spent the last month on their tractors, haying and chopping. Others were white-faced, their bodies crumpled, waiting out their time, and they walked with difficulty. A few wore open-collar shirts with suspenders, as Fred had dressed. One elderly man had on high patent-leather shoes; the creases in the toe of the shoe were coated with dust collected during years in a closet. Two wore mismatched coats and trousers. In the front row were Fred's wife Dottie and Fred's children, one of them adopted, some direct descendents, but all part of the fabric of the Tuttle family that is thick in these parts. In 1798 the first Tuttles settled in Tunbridge. In 1872 Fred Herman Tuttle, Fred's grandfather, bought the Tuttle hillside farm, which remains in the family. Two hundred and five years is sure enough time to spread the Tuttle roots.

Fred had two great moments in his eighty-four-year life. The first was as a soldier in World War II. Attached to a combat engineering company, he landed in Normandy on D-Day plus seven and was sent to LeMans when the Germans were just vacating it; Fred could still smell cabbage soup. His unit constructed a bridge in thirty-six hours ("How long does it take them in Vermont to put up a bridge? A year?") but he found time and the directions to visit a house of pleasure. Downstairs he left his helmet and cartridge belt and rifle ("I shouldn't had done that.") and walked upstairs and made love for the first time.

"Guess what, Peter?" He leaned forward, the glint gleamed in his eyes, the famous Tuttle smile began to crease his face, as he held up his hand with the thumb and forefinger about three inches apart. "For one cigarette! That's all! One cigarette!" and he sat back and his face expanded into a huge Cheshire cat smile.

Fred first visited Paris the day after its liberation and was overwhelmed with his reception, so much so that he volunteered to patrol a section of pipeline that lay north of the city and through which flowed fuel for the tanks and trucks on the front line. He was there until the war ended, and his trips to the City of Light were numerous.

"Peter, the Paris women. They were . . . beautiful. Beautiful! There was red carpet on the floor, long bars, they served us drinks, and we sat in sofas. . . . " He was referring to his hangouts on Boulevard Clichy, which he knew as Pigalle.

Fred returned from France not shot at, and having not shot at others, but after seeing too many dead bodies and almost drowning while returning to the States on a troop ship that was caught in a storm. The hold was full of water and Fred kept his head and that of a stowaway dog clear of it. He always liked animals.

When he was discharged Fred rode the train to Randolph, the nearest station to Tunbridge. "There were two pretty women in the station when I got off," remembered Fred, "and they didn't even look at me." That night Fred milked the cows, as he did daily for the next forty years.

David Wolfe, the church's minister, climbed the pulpit and gave a humorous but compassionate portrait of Fred as "perhaps my most reluctant parishioner. . . . " Fred's son recalled his younger years and how his father liked to hunt without killing anything and the importance of Fred as a father. John O'Brien described Fred's natural talent as an actor and mentioned some of the funnier moments he spent with Fred. After years of anonymity and nights and mornings looking at the hind end of cows, days of reaping and sowing and the neverending job of cutting and splitting firewood, Fred savored stardom as he did ice cream.

Forty-five thousand videos of *Man with a Plan*, about a farmer who decided to run for Congress on the slogan, "I've spent my whole life in the barn, now I just want to spend a little time in the House," were sold. Fred's character won by one vote, and stole the hearts of all who saw the movie, whimsical, gently satirical, and so very, very Vermont. Fred became the icon of a Vermont farmer—he had an accent that almost needed translation, an honest mind, and an ability to express himself with as few words as possible, sweetness in his affability. There was no pretense in Fred and he said what he thought. He was just . . . Fred.

At the service Maria Lamson, in a sweet voice, sang "Simple Gifts," and Priscilla Farnham gave a stirring rendition of "Amazing Grace." Fred lay in an open casket at the front of the church. His glasses were in place and he looked peaceful, his eyes closed, as if he were remembering something from the past and might suddenly open them and start telling a story. His hands were clasped, and on his belly lay his cap with FRED spelled on it. (As he said in the movie, it is an acronym: F for friendly, R for renewable, E for extraterrestrial, D for dinky.)

At the end of the service I walked up the aisle to say goodbye to Fred, and I thought of the last time I saw him, a few weeks before. I was camped on his property as I attended the Tunbridge Fair. I brought him a copy of a revised edition of *Vermont People* with photos and stories on him and Joe, his father. When I left Fred he was standing in the doorway in his striped pajamas, hand on the half-opened door, peering out at me, through his thick glasses, like an owl. He flipped his hand up and waggled it in a short wave. It was one of those photographs I never took, but an image that will stay with me all my life.

In 1989 I first met Fred when I came over to photograph his father, Joe, who was then ninety-three. At the same time I photographed Fred as he leaned on his cane and gave me a penetrating glance through his big glasses. We didn't talk much, but he reminded me of Mr. Magoo. His father's photograph and story appeared next year in the book. Every so often I would visit Tunbridge and drop in to see Fred and Joe. After Joe died, I visited with Fred and Dottie.

When I was updating *Vermont People*, in 1998, I photographed Fred in the same pose as I photographed his father, holding his father's photograph who was holding *his* father's photograph. The photograph was taken

in front of the Tuttle barn that was about to fall down in the movie *Man with a Plan*. Eventually part of it really did fall down and needed to be reconstructed.

John O'Brien asked Fred to run in the GOP primary for US Senate against a Massachusetts millionaire. Fred, never bashful, agreed. His opponent, Jack McMullen, had moved to Vermont because, we assumed, he had political ambitions. Everyone called him a carpetbagger, and the campaign and attendant debates drew howls of laughter and nationwide political coverage. Fred appeared on the *Today* show and shared laughs with Jay Leno. He met beautiful women in Hollywood and New York and kissed them all with the same gusto that he kissed babies while campaigning.

The most famous debate between Tuttle and McMullen hinged on one question Fred asked Jack, and it had nothing to do with politics.

"How many teats does a cow have?"
"Six," answered McMullen.

McMullen lost the election to a farmer who milked by hand, who campaigned with a few dollars, and who won 54 percent of the vote. Tuttle then supported his opponent, Senator Leahy, in the senatorial campaign, and capped his campaign fund at $251—a dollar from each Vermont town. He went over the fund when Vermonters, mostly children, donated $600. His biggest expense was the rental fee of two portable johns at a fund-raising dinner at his farm. At the end of the campaign he donated his "PAC" money to the Lincoln Library, which was damaged by flood, and the Tunbridge Library. Even after endorsing Senator Leahy, he still won 24 percent of the vote.

Fred and Dottie lived in a small white house a few hundred yards from the farm, where his daughter Debra and son-in-law Sean now live. The front door opened into a shed that usually had in the corner a basket of vegetables Fred had pulled from the garden. Another door opened into the kitchen. Dottie kept her house neat and prim, with flowers in the windowsill. The cats had taken over the sofa. The dining room table was in front of the stove and sink. On the table were bottles of pills Fred was taking for his heart, his eyes, his diabetes, his rheumatism. We sat and talked. Fred would fire up his accent, thicker than grade B commercial maple syrup.

"How come people don't visit anymore? I don't know anyone in town. Why does everyone go so fast? Isn't it just a mess in Washington? Look at our taxes; why we used to pay taxes with our maple syrup sales. What's happening to our state, Peter? Everything is going to hell ain't it?"

We digressed on to the origin of the stone huts on his property, which may be Celtic, and moved on to farming.

"I sold the cows in 1984," Fred remembered, looking up at the ceiling. "On Friday they picked up the cows and on Monday I had prostrate surgery. Worst thing can happen to anybody is when they have to sell their cows, you know."

But most of all Fred remembered the political campaign, the interviews and appearances and people he met, and the debates and campaigning he did in the 1998 primary. He peered at me over his glasses, those blue eyes gleamed, and that wide, wide smile lit up as he confided, almost in a whisper, "Peter, you know . . . these have been the happiest years of my life. The happiest!"

At seventy-seven years Fred changed lanes from a retired dairy farmer to a performance artist who crossed the reality barrier to become a politician and Vermont's leading citizen.

This past summer I had a booth at six Vermont county fairs, promoting my books *Vermont People* and *Vermont Farm Women*. I had made a poster of the photograph I used in the book—Fred holding the family photos—and displayed it on an easel. Almost everyone who walked by, it didn't matter which fair, looked at the photos, smiled, and said "Fred! There's Fred!" Then they would ask me how he was. Fred Tuttle is Vermont's most recognizable citizen.

After the funeral service we walked a few yards to the town hall for a reception. On one table were newspaper clippings, posters, old and new family shots, and other mementos of Fred Tuttle as a young man, a soldier, farmer, father, actor, and politician. We sat at long tables. Baloney-and-cheese and egg-salad sandwiches filled a large platter beside bowls and plates of pickles and some dips, squares of Cabot cheese, five flavors of Ben & Jerry's ice cream, and fresh, homemade cookies. A big punch bowl had a label stuck on it that read FRED'S PUNCH; I suspect it was vanilla ice cream, milk, and ginger ale swirled together. We renewed acquaintances and told stories about Fred.

It was a good funeral—Fred had a fast passing after a long life of hard work with all the desserts at the end. He won our hearts and always, when I think of him, I smile and say to myself . . . Frrredddd . . . the word drawn out and flowing as sweet as honey. I enjoyed so much visiting with him, sitting at the table, having a coffee and a chat, listening to Dottie's rants to keep him in control, or going to a nickel-a-plate fundraiser at the Tuttle farm with all his neighbors. Fred was fun. He was witty without knowing it. He had a plastic face and such a glint in his eye. He had no guile. He was, and I say this as a great compliment, a simple Vermonter with a wonderful smile and compelling charisma.

I left the reception early and drove my car through the covered bridge that was rebuilt after the flood, a few years back, had washed it downstream, and headed up the mountain. On the left, not a mile from the bridge and overlooking the valley, is the cemetery where Fred is buried. An iron fence surrounds it. Fred was buried in a private, family burial while we were enjoying the warm afternoon sun and munching baloney sandwiches.

A backhoe sat idle in the cemetery as two men shoveled dirt into Fred's grave. Dottie was then at the reception, seated at a long table with friends and relatives. Debra was just beginning to retain her tears. I wondered, as I drove slowly past the cemetery and up the mountain, on this clear, beautiful Indian summer day, if we were not only burying Fred but also the character that made Vermont what it was, what we have cherished and loved.

Steve Hall, 1902–2008

In 1989 I photographed and interviewed Steve Hall for my book *Vermont People*. She was recognized as the best director of amateur plays in Vermont, performed at the Lamoille County Opera House in Hyde Park. She retired when she was eighty-six, and that was in 1988. I had just read in the papers that she celebrated her one hundred and fifth birthday. I had called her in the past but let time slip by, so much time, without a visit. So I made up for it.

Steve died on March 16, 2008, shortly after I interviewed her. This story appeared in *Vermont Magazine* a month later

Steve lives in a red-frame house at the far end of Main Street in Hyde Park. She and her late husband, Baird, bought it in 1951. I knocked. No reply. I opened the door and walked in. "Steve?" No reply. To the left was the red brocade chair I photographed her in nineteen years ago. Next to it was that peculiar Victorian couch of the same color with backrests humped up on either end, the center a no-man's land. Black-and-white prints and a couple of oils hung on the wall, just as they used to. No change; time warp.

I walked into the sitting room and looked left into the dining area. Steve was sitting there, slumped over, her head flat on the circular dining room table, as if she had passed out. The silence soaked into me; even the old shelf clock in the corner was mute. On the wall behind her were slanting red shelves that held a collection of teapots and cups, a few porcelain figurines, a silver plate with H engraved in the middle of it. Steve's chair faced a picture window that let in the soft afternoon winter light and looked out on a large flat field, snow covered and framed by nearby trees. Four people were moving across the field. On snowshoes or skis? It was too far to tell.

The house was warm. I gently touched Steve's shoulder and said, "Steve?"

Her head snapped up and looked at me. "It's me, Peter. Peter Miller."

"Peter!" She recognized me, or faked it. Steve is quick.

Her face was smaller than the last time I saw her, when she was eighty-six. Her hair was thinner, bobbed in the back. The wrinkles on her face were etched deep, as if into a woodblock. Her upper teeth were worn to the nubs. Her eyes retained a blue, penetrating clarity, as they always have. A fire in them reflected a lively intelligence. The high cheekbones that modeled her face cut an austere but classic curve to her chin. Thin lips, thinner than they were. Her voice was clear, vigorous.

I sat down next to her. We looked at each other.

"I don't have many visitors," she said. "What have you been doing?" No nonsense. Same old Steve.

Steve has a facility to make people talk, to be self-analytical, and I told her things I usually don't talk about, the books I did since I took her photograph that appeared in *Vermont People*. I told her of my Great Plains book and how, traveling through that part of the country, I learned so much about people and myself. I told her of the awards the books received and the recognition I received for them. I said it as a fact; you don't boast to Steve.

"Good for you." Her eyes sparked and she smiled. "Good for you."

"I brought these for you," I said, and put on the table three of my books. "Your story is in *Vermont People*."

"I don't remember that."

I had dropped off a book for her years ago. Her memory had erased those things in her life she did not consider important. When I opened the book to her story she held it a few inches from her face, but I don't think she saw it well.

"Let me read it to you." I paraphrased what I had written.

"You directed your first play in Hyde Park in 1952 and formed the Lamoille County Players with two hundred dollars wrenched out of the local banker with the help of his daughter . . . for thirty-six years you directed plays in the opera house that gained a reputation for being professionally staged, directed, and acted, and your productions turned the head of a visiting New York City drama critic . . . Hey, how about that! You said you did some awful good shows and some flops too.

"You directed the local high school plays and eleven times you and your actors went to the Vermont state play festival and won seven times. You took a losing basketball team and promised them a trophy, turned them into actors, and they won their trophy, acting at the same competition."

"Yes," she closed her eyes and smiled to herself. "I was so proud of that. It was a play by Brecht. Can you imagine that, a basketball team doing Brecht?" Her eyes gleamed. "No, I don't remember which play it was."

I continued. "Steve was known for her imperiousness as a director, and at her retirement party in 1988 she apologized. This is your quote," I said.

" 'Trouble is,' I continued to read, 'I was so concentrated on what was happening on stage that I would forget the actors were real people. They were pieces I was moving around. I had a feeling for composition and I loved to create pictures that would support the idea of the scene. I would also forget to give praise for what was done right.' "

She sat still, as if reflecting on what I said.

"I never did much of anything with my life."

I jumped on her. "How could you say that? You inspired many people to act. You brought art to your community. You were a teacher and fondly remembered. You were so proud of your work with the high school actors. You're very important to this community and you were so important to Baird, your family, and friends."

"I guess I was."

The sun slid to the center of the window and lightened the room. For some reason, I started talking about myself, how I had quit one of the best journalism jobs in America, at *Life*, to return to Vermont. That was over forty years ago.

"Why did you do such a thing?"

"Well, Vermont is good for children, and our kids were very young. I didn't like working for a big corporation. They hemmed you in." I mentioned how, when I was very young, and shy, my happiest moments were alone in the woods.

She nodded. "I understand," And then she said, "You're a little lost now. What are you going to do?" I thought about that and told her about the editor in New York who blasted me for not living up to my talents.

"We all have to live up to the talents given us," I said.

"But," Steve said, "you should go further than that."

This time it was my silence as I went inward.

"I'll never forget Baird," I said laughing. The Halls were responsible for my family moving to Vermont. They were friends of my aunt and uncle and the rest is a long story. I mentioned the first time I watched him back up a car. He had a fused back and could not turn around so, hunched up, he looked in the mirror, put the car in reverse and boomed full speed out of the driveway.

She looked down at her hands.

"When Baird died my whole world turned upside down."

Silence returned and settled in.

"I loved him so. He was wonderful to live with. Every day he was positive. You know he loved writing short stories for magazines? He was very successful."

Another sigh of silence.

"Everyone is gone. I have so few visitors and people to talk to." All the people she grew up with, her friends, her husband, a life of memories, all now a wisp, save for her son Eli. In 1990 there were over thirty-seven thousand people one hundred years old. In 2000 there were over fifty thousand. Old age is not venerated in America, or even respected, as it is in many other cultures. Too many Americans die alone in homes for the aged. Steve is lucky to live at home, and how happy she was to talk to me, to have an honest conversation. A short visit can be such a big gift.

"You and Baird and Corinne and Cally, and myself too," I said, "we have lived in the best of times."

"Yes, you are probably right."

I thought of Steve as the last survivor on a boat lost at sea. Time speeds up as you grow older, then finally, it slows down and seems to almost stop.

"Why have you lived so long?" I asked.

She folded her elegant hands, the skin almost translucent, and locked her eyes, so blue and clear and with that spark of intelligence, into mine, and said, "I don't know."

It's hard to shut off a keen mind.

Colbyville Misanthrope

In 1997, Nelson Brinckerhoff, an elderly and wealthy Stowe resident, died. In his latter years, he counted on members of the Stowe Police Department to do errands for him, and to be his friends. During the last five years of his life, he gave almost five hundred thousand dollars to the Stowe police. This was reported in the *Stowe Reporter* in the February 4, 1999, issue, in an editorial called "Lack of Judgment." Although it was legal for Mr. Brinckerhoff to give, and the Stowe police to receive, the paper considered it poor ethics for this to happen. Be that as it may, I considered the affair to be in the strong tradition of Stowe's resort culture. So I wrote a letter to the *Stowe Reporter* that appeared in the February 11, 1999, issue.

Dear Editor:

I imagine some people are flustered over how a few Stowe policemen made extracurricular money. They shouldn't be, for it isn't against the law and is a Stowe tradition.

Stowe has been known as the Ski Capital of the East. It also is the Dropout Capital of the East. Dropouts come in two varieties—those who have lots of cash or a big trust fund—and those who don't.

Those who don't want a piece of those who do, so this is why Stowe is also known as the Gold Digger's Capital of Vermont (Not the East—you can do a lot better in the Hamptons or Newport).

In the past it worked best for women. Marry a trust funder, divorce, and part with a bigger nest egg than you ever expected. Not so long ago women could do no wrong, according to the divorce courts.

Then came feminism and equal rights, so now if you marry a trust funder and divorce, you get a chunk of it. Works as well for women as for men. This is why more lawyers keep moving into town. They want part of the divorce pie.

The best thing about the Stowe police department's monetary blessing is they didn't have to marry it.

Peter Miller, Colbyville

In the February 25 issue of the *Stowe Reporter*, Nancy Wolfe Stead, in her gossip column "Seen Around the Mountain," wrote the following about my letter or me, I'm not sure which.

> Why is the Misanthrope of Colbyville so unhappy with the women of Stowe? I actually think he has the sociology of Stowe all wrong, a brief and nondefinitive reflection on three decades of marriage-misfires in town leads me to conclude that the women were more often the fleecee, not the fleecer.

Well! What an excuse to smoke up the computer! This is my response.

Who would ever think that Ms. Stead, the *Stowe Reporter* columnist, would write about a person from Colbyville! I would be flattered, if I were interested in social status, even though she did not mention my name. All this came about because of my letter concerning the Stowe habit of gold digging and dropouts.

I have been known as the Mayor of Colbyville, although Route 100 has vivisected my small hamlet. I have been called by much cruder words than what Ms. Stead called me, "The Colbyville Misanthrope."

Misanthrope is a person who hates or scorns mankind. Anyone who has read my writing and seen my photos in *Vermont People* or *People of the Great Plains* knows that I cannot possibly be a misanthrope. Those books honor ordinary people.

Ms. Stead was fishing with the wrong fly. How about "The Misogynist of Colbyville"? A misogynist has a hatred of women. However, Ms. Stead and I were intimately involved with the dropout society of Stowe in the pre-AIDS era, and she knows that is not correct.

Or "The Misogamist of Stowe"? A misogamist has a hatred of marriage. This is closer to the truth. I was married once and divorced in Stowe but, alas, there wasn't any money worth fighting over, so there was no gold digging. I never tried it again.

I have also been known as "The Curmudgeon of Colbyville." A curmudgeon is sometimes known as a crank for saying something that is true, but saying it in a very blunt fashion. Andy Rooney is a nice curmudgeon.

Now Ms. Stead, as women gossip writers tend to do, stood up on the woman's side of the barricade in the gold-digging habit when I was referring to the process, which has benefited both sides. One has to remember that in the old dropout society of Stowe, men and women used the tactics of Clauswitz, Machiavelli, Rasputin, Casanova, Cellini, Kissinger, Smiley, and the KGB in their relationships (and sometimes the Kama Sutra).

One of the truisms in the days before equal divorce sharing was that the diggers knew they could only count on generosity if they had wealthy mates and were divorced. So they did two things. They remained nice and attentive, or they tried to get as much as they could before the divorce. The smartest ones did both. When Ms. Stead says men were the most successful gold diggers, she must mean they were smarter in this type of profession, or that more women than men had a big stash.

Colbyville Curmudgeon, misogynist, misogamist, sociopath, satirist, antipodal chauvinist, aorist, solipsist, whatever. But misanthrope? The books I have written show that word does not fit. Ms. Stead needs a session with her lexicologist.

Later Nancy called me up. "Are you mad at me?" she asked.

"Of course not," I replied. "I like to play with words." What I meant is that fighting with words is fun. And informative.

The Trade Towers

Jamie knocked on the darkroom door. I was making prints for my farm women book. After I hypoed a print I opened the door.

"Something awful has happened," he told me. "An airplane hit one of the Trade Towers."

I went upstairs and sat before the television and watched the Trade Tower burning. Then I saw the other plane hit. Fire, smoke, then the Towers collapsing, as if they were sand castles built too high. I didn't say a word and watched the television for the rest of the day.

As a journalist and photographer, I should have rushed down to Ground Zero to photograph the tragedy. I didn't. I couldn't go down to document this loss; to take glorious, heroic photographs of tragedy, for the destruction of the towers and the death of so many people lay too monstrous in my soul, torturing my psyche.

For seven years, from the late 1970s to the mid 1980s, I lived in Manhattan and photographed the Twin Towers. Winter, summer, spring, fall. At dawn and at dusk. From the plaza below the Trade Towers, looking straight up, from the top looking down at Manhattan glowing with hustle, to the north and the harbor to the south, blue and serene at dusk. I photographed the Towers from the Statue of Liberty, from Brooklyn, from the Empire State Building, and in New Jersey from Liberty State Park, the World War II ammunition loading pier in Bayonne, and from the Colgate building, then a hangout for winos and druggies (I carried a pistol in my camera bag), from Steven's Point and Weehawken, where Burr killed Hamilton in a duel. From that vantage the two towers blended into one.

My favorite spot was at the end of the ammunition pier in Bayonne that extended over a half mile into the harbor, and you could line up the Statue of Liberty between the Trade Towers. I went out there at dawn and watched the sun rise over Manhattan, light changing from gray to blue to pink. Once I stood behind my camera from dawn until midmorning on an

August day that would turn humid-hot and I watched the light change, until a haze of heat whitened the towers. Helicopters, halfway below the towers' summit, buzzed back and forth and nearer to me seagulls glided. The scene was diaphanous, gossamer delicate.

I would return to the pier on afternoons when a northwest front moved into Manhattan, bringing with it a clarity that sparkled, a deep blue sky and puffy clouds. The first day would be pristine, the second day lost a bit of that freshness, the third day turned hazy. I would drive through the Holland Tunnel to Bayonne, hike with a camera pack and tripod to the end of the pier, and set up the camera and wait, and every so often take photographs as the sun slipped overhead to western New Jersey, changing the light and color of lower Manhattan every fifteen minutes. After sunset I would wait until that magical moment when the sky turned a mystical blue and the Towers lit up, blocks of light and form against a backdrop fading from blue to black. Sometimes the full moon would rise over the Brooklyn Bridge and arc over the Towers. It was thrilling to watch the floors light up until the Towers became living, pulsing beings. To me they were vibrant structures of life. They represented what New York stood for—a jolt of wired energy, a tangible power with an intangible force.

The Trade Towers anchored the New York skyline and replaced the Empire State Building as the city's prima donna. At the summer solstice, the sun was far enough north so that, when it set, and if you were standing on the pier in Hoboken, it reflected directly off the Towers, turning them into golden, shimmering mirrors. The Empire State could never do that. The Trade Towers had a beauty that surged through my camera lens, to my eye, my brain, my soul, living within me. It was my sort of high.

For a while I lived at the corner of Spring and Broadway in Soho and bicycled throughout the city. The towers were my geographical index. I would bike serendipitously, looking for photographs, and not paying attention so much to what street I was on as where I was in reference to the towers.

I returned to Vermont in the mid-1980s. In Manhattan the yuppies had moved in and buildings were being converted into coops and I, always subleasing, was kicked from apartment to apartment. Finally the rents climbed so high I said the hell with it. I kept my bicycle in New York, and would drive down, bike the city, a risk sport to me, and continue to visit those secret stashes where I would photograph the Manhattan skyline, and my Trade Towers. No matter how many times I went to a particular vantage point to take photographs, the light on the Towers was always different.

Something shriveled in me on Tuesday, September 11. I couldn't do anything for the rest of the week. I moped in my home. On the weekend I dragged myself out, and with my Airstream in tow, drove to Benson, Vermont, where I photographed Jeanne Bartholomew, a farm woman. It was a subdued day. The interview I had, and the photographs I took, seemed to be a relief for Jeanne and me. Neither of us had much to say about the Towers, and when we did, we didn't look at each other.

I parked my camper in one of their hayfields that had just been mowed. On Saturday night, at dusk, I sat in a chair and watched four deer feeding on the upper edge of the field. It became too dark to see them. Then the stars came out, brilliant sparks on a clear, black night.

Sunday morning in that pasture turned into a brilliant day with a deep blue sky. It was the same weather pattern they had in New York when the planes struck—the type of day I would say to myself, when I lived there and looked at the Towers standing tall above the buildings in Soho, "What a great day to be alive!"

It was so quiet; no commercial or private aircraft were flying in the United States. Not even a wisp of a contrail. The morning sun was bright and dried the dew quickly. A couple of grasshoppers fluttered and whirred. The silence that was in the sky subsumed my soul and a dark void filled me. In midmorning, it was broken by the noise of a jet engine—a National Guard fighter from Burlington, patrolling the perimeter.

I cannot look at any photographs of the Trade Towers destruction, nor can I read about the pain of the rescuers or the survivors. I avert my eyes to these photographs and videos. I think of the people smashed to ashes. I think of the symbol of New York caved in. I think of the beauty in my soul, molded by those photographs of the Towers, which to me were more beautiful than any Vermont scene I ever photographed.

I have not been able to return to New York. The only thing I can do is read the accounts of the victims printed in the *New York Times*, but I never can read more than three before I am crushed by the hope and vibrancy killed on that day.

Something was killed in me. A friend suggested I seek counsel, but I can care for it in my way. I will go back to Manhattan and try to rid myself of this angst. I will visit Ground Zero, and walk the boardwalk at Liberty State Park and visit the ammunition pier, which I hear has been broken in two, and I will go to Hoboken and to Weehawken and to Brooklyn, where I will watch the sun set and where the Brooklyn Bridge and the Trade Towers became silhouetted against the setting sun, only this time there will be a hole in my soul.

What has happened? Is it desecration? Is it a loss of humanity and innocence, of an era in New York when America and I were supremely happy . . . and naive? Or is it a loss of beauty? I don't know. I'll go to New York sometime, but not soon, and try to put this death to rest.

Disappointments

First published in the *Stowe Reporter*, 2003

All in all, I would have to say this was a year of disappointments, intrusions of frustrations, small and large angers, and sadness too, that depleted my energy, my creative response to the world. Some of them are petty; others are, at least to me, apocalyptic. I have to live with these bruises and I hope, as the year turns, I can erase them as easily as I can my old e-mail messages. But it won't be easy.

For instance, I am disappointed in Breyer's strawberry ice cream. It was one of the hidden marvels of mass-distributed frozen products, for it had huge chunks of strawberries suspended throughout. I couldn't find those large chunks in the last two quarts I bought.

I am disappointed in myself, for working harder in my sixty-nine-year life than I ever have, and earning less. Or should I be disappointed that our government is passing laws and regulations to increase the wealth of the top fifth of the population, who control half of all household income, while the poorest fifth (32.9 million) have 3.5 percent of the country's income. The average American CEO earns more in one day than the average worker earns all year.

I am disappointed in the Vermont government, which taxes its citizens so high that businesses are forced to move to other states. Companies do not like to locate here because of tax gouging and permit processes and because our property taxes penalize everyone—rich and poor.

I am also disappointed that the Vermont Agriculture Department, along with the US Department of Agriculture, cares so little about supporting small farms and the fresh, clean food they produce.

I am disappointed in America, which, according to surveys, supports a federal government that advocates first-strike combat (what Germany did in 1939 and Japan did in 1941) and refuses to protect the world environment, and I am disappointed in American citizens who do not

see what these policies will do to our country and the world a decade from now.

I am disappointed, seeing friends and acquaintances become self-absorbed in their attempt to isolate themselves from a world that changes so fast they can't keep up. Or perhaps it is that they know they have no control over the speed of the treadmill.

I am disappointed, watching the evening news on television, which too often passes along the government's press releases. And then, between the anchor's adjectives, I have to bear the pain of watching myriad advertising spots telling me which drug to use to lessen the pain of living in this world, or what to use to mop the floor.

I am disappointed, suffering through such hot summers that I need two air conditioners, and that the climate is changing so quickly that the glacier I skied over, fifteen years ago, to the town of Chamonix, France, now stops dead a couple of miles up the mountain.

I am disappointed to find I have to read a thirty-page book of instructions before I can use a digital camera or telephone, and that I have to refer to the manual constantly, while I miss the photograph or the telephone call. Then I find the gadget is obsolete in eight months and I should buy the newer model.

I am saddened to see the rise of self-entitlement in the younger generation—its lack of ethics, its ego, and its greed—they take whatever they want. They are the offspring of Gekko and Enron.

I am disappointed to see business overcome my creativity, and I feel uneasiness and a shaky nervousness about the direction our country is dragging me.

2008, five years later. It's not so much disappointment these days but despondency over our government, state and federal, that acts as fiefdom for a corporate oligarchy. I feel saddened over the killing and maiming of so many soldiers and Iraqis. For what? I feel frightened that I will no longer be able to afford my monthly expenses, as gas and fuel oil and property taxes skin my income. I feel as many Americans do—powerless to bring our lives and our country back on track.

But . . . we still have Vermont, although damaged and under attack by homogenization. We can find beauty in our environment and we have clean water and fresh air. We have neighbors we cherish. For the most part, we are an honest people, independent and, thank God, a little out of touch with the trendiness we read about in the papers and see on television.

———————

Afterword

Like all Vermont boys brought up in a small village, I loved to ski, fish, hunt, and plink with my .22, but a theft, over half a century ago, pulled me into a career in photography.

I was a shy, black-haired sixteen-year-old living in southern Vermont and attending Burr & Burton Academy when my guns were stolen. My mother gave me $160 from the insurance and so . . . I bought a camera. There was no incentive to do that, for the only photographs my family and friends took were mostly blurry snapshots of each other.

So there I was with an Ikoflex twin-lens reflex that exposed square two-and-a-quarter-inch negatives and no one to teach me or to share the magic created by that gleaming black metal box with silver-colored trim and with blue-coated lenses stuck on it. At that time the only photo school in Vermont was John Doescher's School of Photography in Woodstock, and that was way beyond what I or my mother could afford. I made my own equipment to contact prints and develop my film, and sometimes I splurged at the camera shop where they printed—what else—snapshots. Technically, I made awful photographs, but I seemed to be born with the sense of how to compose them.

Although I recorded school activities, I photographed farmers I knew in Weston, where I lived. In 1947 there were thirteen dairy farms in our village. A few yards down the hill from our home was the farm of Hugh and Rachel Foster. He used a horse to cut his hay. May and Cliff Dutton worked together in the fields they mowed along the West River. She was always in a dress and wore a big smile under cornflower blue eyes. The hay rake she used was taller than she. Across the valley, on a beautiful hillside farm that I could see from our front lawn, Will and Rowena Austin, who were retired from farming, sat in rockers on their front porch. He smoked a pipe and wore a handsome moustache under his milky-blue eyes. She wore long gingham dresses, knit, and laughed wickedly, throwing up her head and exposing her missing front tooth. Then I photographed Art Johnson, who picked up garbage. He lived alone in a small house so run down he shouldn't have to pay taxes. Everyone thought he lisped but he didn't. He spoke in old English, with thees and thous. I must have the only photograph of him.

I walked the mowings and pastures and watched them rake the hay into serpentine winnows and savored the smell of the fresh cut. I had hunted woodchucks in these fields and, after I replaced the rifle with a camera, I returned to photograph what I had sensed rather than seen—the sun slanted on hillsides, and the lone maples these farmers planted in the middle of fields to shade themselves and their horses during lunchtime. I was happy, for I had found beauty—in a person's face and in a hillside scene.

Outside of sports I read, fantasized about sex, and discovered classical music that no one in my family seemed fond of. Here I was, a football player, a ski racer, a hunter, and deep down within me was this hankering for beauty and harmony that glowed and made me smile.

Those three years in Weston laid the foundation for my life. When

I graduated I went to the University of Toronto and joined the camera club, where I first met other photographers and which eventually led to a summer job as an assistant to Yousuf Karsh as he photographed Europe's leading artists. Here's a dumb and naïve country kid lighting cigarettes (my cigarettes, I'll have you know) for Picasso and savoring the powerful tones soaring from Pablo Casals' cello as he played Bach in a deserted chapel. I ate in two- and three-star restaurants and learned what a Champagne sauce tastes like. I did what any Vermont kid would do under the circumstances; I said little, looked sharply, and listened. I was awed by the beauty and humanity of Paris.

The circle continued after I graduated from the university and enlisted in the US Army. I was trained as a Signal Corps photographer. My tour of duty just happened to be Paris (someone is watching over me), where I lived in an apartment in the 9th arrondisement. I spent my free time wandering the city, taking street photographs and visiting museums. I didn't know it, but this foreign culture was shaping what I would become. Forty-three years after my Paris years, the photographs I took and the memories of maturing in a foreign city became a book called *The First Time I Saw Paris*.

When I returned to the States and was discharged from the Army, I decided to quit photography. I wanted to write. I secured a job at *Life* as a reporter and writer. There I worked with the finest photojournalists in the world and learned how to communicate with words and photographs in a well-crafted layout.

I did the unthinkable—quit the best journalism job in America to return to Vermont. You have to understand people like me work on passion and what their gut says, not on common sense or what's in their bank account. I had turned into a creative type, and I needed unfettered internal and external space. I loved the beauty I found on the hillside farms in Vermont, and in the unpretentious openness in a native Vermonter's face. It was and is a beautiful place to raise children. My return to Vermont led to a self-employed career as a freelance photographer, writer, and author of eight books. Vermont was a good place to live for such a career because, at the time, it was very inexpensive and kind to people like me who live financially month-to-month.

I am ordained to photograph people. Perhaps it comes from my overcoming a youthful shyness, or perhaps it is because I was lonely, but I don't think so. I see in faces a history and continuity. The first Vermonters I photographed reflected the toil it took to clear a field into a pasture, or build a stone wall and milk by hand thirty cows 365 days a year.

Then there is the light. If you don't like the weather, wait five minutes and it will create innumerable hues and glows; for some reason sun and clouds and the way the light hits the mountains is a work of art in progress. When clouds hide the light there is a stark, simple strength to Vermont—black-and-white country.

Vermont is known for its color, that week in late May when the pastures are gaudy as green Jello and in October when fall foliage is an overload of eye candy. Lord knows, I have shot enough color in Vermont. But to me, certain places have their color personality. Paris is blue and gold. London is red and black. New York is blue, orange, and red. Vermont's strongest character is the black-and-white of starkness, honesty, simplicity, and dignity. Color is something I find you look at and not into; black-and-white sucks you under the surface to questions, and sometimes revelation.

I took my very first portraits when I was sixteen. Photography gave me nerve to stop the car, when I was driving near Dorset, to photograph a painter who told me he was Luigi Lucioni. He was the only well-known person, outside of Governors Phil Hoff and Howard Dean, I ever photographed in Vermont. I prefer ordinary people. And, although I didn't realize it until this year, the people I photographed were all self-employed, very independent in temperament and not at all perturbed about having their photograph taken.

In 1964 I moved to Moscow, Vermont. It was then I began to cruise the back roads, with Camel's Hump, Mount Mansfield and, yes, the Stowe Community Church giving a sense of place to my photographs. I found old deserted houses, farms and people and events, and of course skiing. I shot color for money, and black-and-white for myself, and I wrote innumerable articles for sport and travel magazines. Many of my photographs have never been printed; they remain in files and I hope, sometime, to print these photographs, for what use is it to have a photograph that does not communicate? There were also stories I wrote that never were published; some of them are in this book.

A divorce forced me to leave Moscow for Colbyville, where I live now. In the early 1980s I returned to New York for five years and recharged my creative life. I came back to the Green Mountains with a fresh eye and found so much change. Tract mansions and developments were scarring the hillsides and obliterating mowings and pastures.

Perhaps this is one reason I published *Vermont People*—so that our rural culture was recognized. The other reason was that a former editor castigated me for taking photos for pay and not taking responsibility for the little talent that I have. This hurt; I take photographs because I am an addict. Too many photographers lift a camera only when they are paid. I turned my editorial eye of reporting and photojournalism toward book projects with a rural theme.

I have secret places to photograph, I admit, but I also search for people to interview, to photograph . . . the Lepine sisters, dairy farmers; Bambi Freeman, an ex-ski bum who has made a difference on her sheep farm; George Woodard, that unusual mixture of farmer and actor and musician; and other people I have just met, such as Carroll Shatney, a ninety-three-year-old farmer who raises Scottish Highlanders, and who once ran a business of finding lost cattle with pit bulls imported from Texas. There are others I have still to photograph, the farmers of French Canadian descent, some who came here to escape the tithing fee in Quebec and who vitalized the communities near the Canadian border. There are the stonecutters of Barre, and those wonderful independent sons-of-guns who log our forests. Often they live in small trailers right at the logging site.

Perhaps it is time for me to retrain my eye to capture the new generation of Vermonters. There is a resurgence in young people, especially women, running small farms, and selling their produce at local, outdoor markets. These low-acreage farmers could use tax incentives from towns and the state but usually they are tax-whacked like the rest of us.

Then there are those who move to Vermont for its social cachet. Hopefully they will learn respect for the land, the nearby mountains and the native Vermonters.

So it is with change; ever evolving. Now I know what has been my thrust—I record the history of the present. And as I grow older, and we face the digital revolution with its bombardment of millions of photographs, and as people read less, I find myself turning more and more to writing.

I Want to Go Home,
Home to Vermont

First published in *People of the Great Plains*, 1996

Buffalo, South Dakota. September 1995.

There has been a change in the weather. The wind that crosses these Plains has gentled and cooled. The sun burnishes the tall grass in this unusually verdant, rainy summer. There is a certain smell in the air and a subtle change in my bones and in the color of the sky. I feel the music of September. For the first time in three months, I am thinking of Vermont.

It is September, and I want to go home.

September in Vermont. A subtle fragrance of drying leaves, grass, and corn chaff floats in the air. This fragrance, intense under the midday sun, is wicked away by the cool nights, and the air becomes as crisp as a morning frost. By noon a languorous haze has softened the edges of fields and hills. At an indiscernible distance a partridge thumps the air with its wings. The beat hesitantly accelerates, holds steady, and then slowly fades. The whine of a corn chopper floats up from the valley, and a yellow school bus climbs a dirt road.

It is time to go home to Vermont.

Time slows in September. I want to amble up the hill to the lone maple and lie under it and watch the sun shimmer gold between the leaves. I want to see the first rock-maple leaves turn red as blood, audacious against the green sugar maples. I want to experience the bite in the first frost and the slow tempo of the color descending the hills. I want to feel the curt winds that blow in so quickly, changing the hazy days to a sharpness that makes my blood surge before Indian summer returns.

I love Vermont in the fall. It is September and I want to go home.

I miss the awe of seeing, so high above, the first geese flying south, their excited conversation trailing behind them. September is a time of contemplation of the year passed, for then begins the season of death and

161

renewal. There is peace in Vermont. A nostalgic feeling wells up in me, a feeling of life lived, loved, and gone. It is a sweet private feeling in this September time.

Oh, I want to go home, home to Vermont.

I miss the coming of bird season, of walking over stone walls and following hidden brooks, the water speckled with sunlight as it flows through alder patches where the woodcock lay. I miss the excitement of seeing my dog on point and the feel of a well-balanced shotgun floating in my arms, following the whistle of woodcock wings. I miss walking up wooded hills to dying apple orchards guarded by brambles, and discovering hidden stone foundations and the mystery of wondering who lived there, who planted the trees and picked the apples, who they loved. I miss the sweet smell of fallen leaves, cured by frost and sun and the private places I have within the woods and mowings of Vermont, hidden so far away. They are my magic.

My blood says, Go home, Peter, you've been away too long. It is September.

That first fragrance of fall flows within me, a scent that is drawing me to Vermont. I want to head my car east. I want to see familiar hills and the steady pace of leaves changing color. I want to be part of this ceremony of life and death, as the season flames before it folds into itself and the land lies bone-clean and neat. I want to blend with Vermont and counterpoint the months. Languorous September. Vibrant, dying, October. Stark November, the land surrendered and at peace, bare and brown, waiting for snow. These are my months.

I have come to love the Plains, but I want to go home. Home to Vermont.

Florence Nightingale

This special edition is printed and distributed by arrangement with the origina-
tors and publishers of Landmark Books, RANDOM HOUSE, Inc., New York, by

E. M. HALE AND COMPANY
EAU CLAIRE, WISCONSIN

FLORENCE NIGHTINGALE

by RUTH FOX HUME

illustrated by ROBERT FRANKENBERG

For P.C.H.

who sat up late with it so many nights

Contents

The Brilliant and Beautiful Miss Nightingale

The beautiful Nightingale sisters were being presented at court. Mrs. Nightingale hoped that the girls were not feeling too nervous, because a girl who was nervous could so easily look awkward. She herself was not entirely calm. Elegant parties in the highest of London society were certainly nothing new to the charming and wealthy lady. But today was different. A mother had every right to feel nervous on a day like this! At the doorway to the Queen's drawing room, she gave Flo and Parthe a last critical glance and waved them in. She was satisfied. They really looked lovely, especially Flo in her new white gown from Paris.

London was a gay city in the spring of 1839.

The newly crowned Queen Victoria was young and still full of fun. She loved parties. The London social season was more exciting than it had been for years.

The Nightingales had been traveling in Europe for eighteen months, while Embley, their beautiful house in the Hampshire countryside, was being remodeled. Mrs. Nightingale was probably glad that the house had not been ready for them when they returned to England. It gave her the whole spring season in which to introduce her girls to London society.

The two Nightingale sisters had unusual first names. They were called Parthenope and Florence, in honor of the Italian cities where they had been born. (Parthenope was the Greek name for Naples.) Mrs. Nightingale loved originality and in naming her daughters she had really outdone herself. Who had ever heard of naming a girl either Parthenope or Florence?

Florence, the younger sister, was the smarter and prettier of the two girls. She was tall and graceful, with large gray eyes and beautiful red-gold hair. She was, to be sure, the more difficult of the two, much more stubborn and headstrong than any young lady of nineteen had any need to be.

For this Mrs. Nightingale blamed Mr. Nightingale. He had taken personal charge of the girls' education. Parthe had never been an enthusiastic student. But Florence simply ate up the Greek and Latin, the German and French, the history and philosophy that her father taught so delightfully. What any girl of her position actually *needed* with all those irregular verbs and dates of battles, Mrs. Nightingale did not know. Florence could have put the time to better use by practicing the piano, the other ladies of the family thought. Her quadrille playing was simply not what it ought to be.

There were other things about her younger daughter that disturbed Mrs. Nightingale. Flo was clearly not contented with the charming life she had been born to lead. She was bored with the ordinary occupations of a lady's day—paying calls, receiving visitors, taking carriage rides, gossiping with friends, arranging flowers, sketching and water-coloring. The European tour at least had been a great help. Flo had been enchanted with everything she saw. She had made a favorable impression on the most brilliant circles of Italy and France. Perhaps now that she was launched into society at home, she would settle down and be more docile.

3

Much as she fretted over her problem child, Mrs. Nightingale had never come close to guessing what really went on in the girl's mind. Like many sensitive children, Florence had always felt "different," somehow set apart from her family and friends. As a small girl she had been so shy that the simple act of eating at the table had been misery. She was certain she would not be able to use her fork the right way. As she grew older the shyness gradually disappeared. It was replaced by a furious dissatisfaction with her life. But what other kind of life *was* there? There was no immediate answer to the question; so Florence escaped into a world of daydreams. It was a sweet, secret world of adventure that she shared with no one.

When she was sixteen years old the hazy dreams of her childhood suddenly came into sharp focus. "On February 7th, 1837," she wrote later, "God spoke to me and called me to His service."

The voice that she heard that winter day was much more real to Florence Nightingale than any of the human voices that surrounded her. For the first time in her young life she felt completely at peace with the world. God had a plan for her after all. She had no idea what it was, but she was perfectly content to wait and see.

She did not, at the time, know how long and tedious the waiting would be.

In September of 1839, the Nightingale family moved into their remodeled home. Mrs. Nightingale was delighted with it. So was Parthe. Flo, as usual, was not reacting properly. The six new bedrooms, the magnificent new carpet in the drawing room, the red damask sofas, and tapestry-covered chairs all left her unmoved. Now that the excitement of the European tour and the London social whirl was over, her life had settled back into its polite and dismal routine.

Her relations with her mother and sister grew worse with every month that passed. Whatever she did seemed to annoy them. The things she did not do annoyed them even more. Fortunately for Florence she had a favorite aunt, her father's sister Mai, who took her away from Embley as often as she was allowed to go visiting. Aunt Mai understood Flo as no one else in the family did. She knew that the girl had an unusual mind and was desperate to use it on something solid. In 1840 Aunt Mai took Florence to London to enjoy the festivities celebrating the wedding of the young Queen and the handsome Prince Albert.

While she was there, Florence decided that she would like to study mathematics. She wrote home for permission to take lessons. This simple request created a flurry of emotion at Embley. Mrs. Nightingale easily thought up a pageful of objections. Why mathematics? What possible good would it do her when she was married and running her own household? Where would she have her lessons? Where could a suitable teacher be found, a married man, of course, and preferably a clergyman? Who would chaperon the lessons? Would they not interfere with her sewing and piano lessons?

Aunt Mai acted as go-between and patiently persuaded Mrs. Nightingale to give permission. Thus Florence was introduced to the mysterious world of figures that would one day play so important a part in her life.

As the years went on, Florence became more and more discontented not only with her surroundings but also with herself. Nearly seven years had passed since God had spoken to her. But at twenty-two she was no nearer to knowing what God expected of her than she had been at sixteen. One thing stood between her and God, she decided—worldly vanity. Unless she could overcome her desire to make a name for herself in society, she would never be worthy to do whatever it was God wanted her to do. Yet Florence was now so attractive and so brilliant a young woman that she could hardly help being a great success.

In the spring of 1842, the Nightingales went up to London, as they often did, for a few months of party-going. Florence was greatly relieved. It was much easier to get on with Mama and Parthe when they were not alone together at home. And her own conscience could not be heard quite so clearly in the bustle of the city as in the quiet of the country. In London that year she was more of a success than she had ever been, and she knew it.

She collected new friends. The Prussian ambassador, Chevalier Bunsen, was enchanted with her. "How can any young lady," he asked, "dance so beautifully and yet discuss archaeology and religion so well?" Lord Palmerston, one of the most powerful men in England, frequently entertained the Nightingales. At a Palmerston dinner party that May, they met a young man named Richard Monckton Milnes.

Florence, by this time, had had a number of

serious suitors. But no man she had ever met impressed her as strongly as Richard Monckton Milnes.

They thought alike. Milnes was a philanthropist: he devoted his talents and his money to helping the poor, particularly children who were in trouble with the law. Very few people in those days ever gave a thought to juvenile criminals. He was a poet and a patron of the arts.

Mrs. Nightingale was also impressed. Milnes was heir to a great estate and had a bright political career ahead of him. Soon he was visiting regularly at Embley and at the Nightingale summer home, Lea Hurst. Mrs. Nightingale was delighted. The most eligible bachelor in the whole of England was actually falling in love with Florence.

Only one thing marred Mrs. Nightingale's joy in the courtship of Richard Monckton Milnes—Florence herself. Florence did not seem as enthusiastic as any normal, reasonable girl should be about such a man. Mrs. Nightingale was beside herself. Didn't the foolish girl realize that this year could be the turning point of her life?

The Daughter at Home

In one way Mrs. Nightingale was quite right. The year 1842 *was* a turning-point in Florence's life. But her meeting with Richard Monckton Milnes was not the reason.

In 1842 the long-suffering poor of England were living through the worst hardships they had known for years. Times were bad. Wages were low. Unemployment was widespread. Poverty and hunger stalked through the country. As the Nightingales drove about London, from the hotel to the opera to the next party, Florence became more and more distressed by what she saw from the carriage window. It suddenly seemed to her that half the population of London was either freezing or starving to death.

She found that she could not free her mind

11

from the thought of human misery. Gradually it became clear to her that God's plan for her future had something to do with relieving the sufferings of the wretched.

One day while she was paying a call on the Bunsens, the talk turned to the subject of poverty. "What," she asked the ambassador, "can an individual do to help lift the load of suffering from the helpless of the world?"

In reply to her question, the ambassador told her about the work being done at Kaiserswerth, a little town on the Rhine. There a Lutheran pastor named Fliedner had founded an orphanage and a hospital where Protestant deaconesses were trained to nurse the sick poor. Yet he had begun his work with nothing but a little hut where he and his wife nursed one released prisoner. This, the ambassador told Florence, was the sort of thing that an individual can do when he sets his mind to it.

Florence was moved by the story, but she did not apply it to herself. The idea of nursing had not yet entered her thinking. In her childhood she had, like all little girls, enjoyed taking care of babies, and tending sick animals and dolls. But the picture of Florence Nightingale rushing about bandaging broken-legged dogs and dolls, and dreaming of a career in nursing, is only a part of the Florence Nightingale legend. It is pretty but it is not the whole truth.

Now that she was fully awake to the problems of the poor, Florence found the routine of her life more and more irksome. Mr. Nightingale had a fondness for reading aloud. Every morning he would sit down with his daughters and treat them to the entire issue of the London *Times,* commenting on each bit of news he read. "For Parthe," Florence later wrote, "the morning's reading did not matter. She went on with her drawing. But for me, who had no such cover, the thing was boring to desperation."

Mr. Nightingale also liked to reverse the roles and have the girls read to him. Florence read him page after page of a popular new book, called *The Daughter at Home.* This was an "inspirational" work urging girls who were dissatisfied with their lives to grin and bear it. It was of very little help to Florence.

The only really happy moments during these days of being the daughter-at-home came when she could escape to the cottages of the tenants who lived on her parents' estates. Here for the first time she found herself actually face to face with poverty and misery and disease. She began to worry her mother more and more about help for the poor of the village. Mrs. Nightingale was exasperated. She, too, visited the sick at Embley and Lea Hurst. There was nothing unusual in having the lady of the manor descend on the cottages to do good deeds.

Mrs. Nightingale had always been very generous in giving food and medicine to the tenants.

But she felt that Florence was overdoing things, as she so often did, by actually feeding the food and medicine to the sick herself, by making their beds, by rubbing their backs. It was probably dangerous, it was certainly not ladylike, and it was often inconvenient. It was annoying time after time at Lea Hurst to find Florence missing at the hour of a dinner party and to have to send a servant into the village to find her.

As the years passed, Florence's destiny began to take definite shape in her mind. At last, after eight years of wondering, she knew what she wanted to do with her life. "Since I was twenty-four," she wrote later, "there never was any vagueness in my plans or ideas as to what God's work was for me."

The first person to whom Florence revealed her secret was a visiting American named Dr. Samuel Howe. Dr. Howe and his wife Julia, who would later write "The Battle Hymn of the Republic," toured Europe in June of 1844. Through mutual friends, the Bracebridges, they met the Nightingale family and were asked to stay at Embley. On the first night of their visit Florence went up to Dr. Howe and asked him whether he would meet her in the library the next morning before breakfast.

"Miss Nightingale is a charming young lady," Mrs. Howe said to her husband when they were alone. "Mrs. Bracebridge, if you remember, told us that everyone predicts a brilliant future for her."

"I remember. She also said that Mrs. Nightingale wishes her daughter would be more conventional."

Just how unconventional Miss Nightingale was, Dr. Howe realized the next morning, when he kept the appointment in the library.

"Dr. Howe," Florence said, "do you think it would be unsuitable for a young Englishwoman to devote herself to works of charity in hospitals, as Catholic sisters do? Do you think it would be a dreadful thing?"

Unprepared as he was for such a question from a wealthy English girl, Dr. Howe answered it without hesitation. "My dear Miss Florence," he said, "it would be unusual, and in England whatever is unusual is thought to be unsuitable. But if you have a vocation for that way of life, then go forward. Go on with it, wherever it may lead, and God be with you!"

Florence did not confide in anyone else. She was uncertain of her next step. The mere fact of knowing her vocation did not improve her state of mind. If anything, it made things worse. The year following her interview with Dr. Howe was one of the most depressing she had ever spent.

Yet, although she did not realize it, the pieces were finally beginning to fall into place.

That summer Mr. Nightingale's mother was taken ill. Florence asked to be allowed to nurse her. Since no one could handle the old lady as well as Florence, the rest of the family thought that this was a fine idea. No sooner was her grandmother better than Florence's old nurse, Mrs. Gale, also became ill. Again Florence's serv-

ices were needed. She nursed the faithful old lady until the day she died.

Florence, the family agreed, certainly "had a way" with sick people and was a very handy person to have around in a crisis. But Florence was far from satisfied with herself. To claim, as everyone did, that one learned to nurse the sick by womanly instinct alone was sheer nonsense. As she nursed the two old ladies, she realized more and more how very little she really knew about what she was doing. Later in the year, while she worked among the sick of the village, a daring idea grew in her mind.

In December of 1845 she presented it to her father and mother and sister.

No doubt it would have been more sensible to drop a few hints beforehand to prepare them for the blow, but that was not Florence's way. She announced bluntly that she wished to go to the Salisbury Infirmary for three months to study nursing.

3

Meeting in Rome

If Florence had rolled a keg of gunpowder into the drawing room and lit a match to it, she could hardly have created more of an uproar. For a moment Mrs. Nightingale was too astounded to say anything at all. Mr. Nightingale, after the first clash of argument, was so outraged that he simply removed himself from the scene. He went up to London where he bored his friends for days by lecturing them on the folly and ingratitude of the spoiled modern girl.

Once Mrs. Nightingale had found her voice she used it to full advantage. "You simply want to disgrace yourself and your family with you!" she declared furiously. "If the truth were known, you're probably in love with some low, *vulgar* surgeon, and *that's* why you want to work at the hospital!"

Florence, sick at heart, realized that nothing she could say would change anyone's mind, so she gave up the idea. Her first little bid for freedom had failed. She had never felt more hopelessly trapped by her life.

It is easy, more than a century later, to be critical of Florence's mother and father for acting as they did. The fact is that they had every right to be horrified by Florence's request.

Today the words "nurse" and "hospital" mean something quite different from what they meant in the 1840's. In those days sick people stayed at home, if they were lucky, and either recovered there or died there. Hospitals were for the poor who had no other place to go, and they were disgusting and dangerous places to be. The crowded wards reeked with filth. "Hospital smell," a polite phrase, definitely did *not* mean the smell of disinfectants. The whole idea of antisepsis in hospitals was twenty years away. The operating room was still the scene of real horror, for the American discovery of surgical anaesthesia was not made until the end of 1846.

Even if Florence had been allowed to go to Salisbury Infirmary she would have learned to nurse only by her own observations and efforts. There was no such thing as a school where one learned to be a nurse. The skilled art of nursing as we know it today did not exist. In France nuns served as nurses. But in English hospitals most of those hired to care for the sick were women of low character who had taken the unpleasant job because they could not find work anywhere else. "The nurses are all drunkards," wrote the physician in charge of a London hospital, "and there are but two nurses whom the surgeons can trust to give the patients their medicine." Drunkenness and immorality among nurses were so common that they were simply taken for granted, like hospital smell and cockroaches.

Florence was bitterly disappointed. Mr. and Mrs. Nightingale, with reason, were both puzzled and hurt by her attitude. The household was upset for days. They were intelligent and kindly people, and they felt that any girl in England might envy the life that their daughter was leading. She was beautiful and wealthy, with more education and much more freedom than most unmarried girls of her position. She had her own circle of brilliant friends—statesmen and literary people. What would *they* think of Florence working as a hospital drudge? Parthe summed up the family opinion perfectly when she said, "Why, you might just as well tell us that you want to go to work as a kitchen maid!"

And Florence? "No advantage that I can see," she wrote to her cousin, "comes of my living on, excepting that one becomes less and less of a young lady every year. You will laugh, dear, at the whole plan, I dare say; but no one but the mother of it knows how precious an infant idea becomes . . . I shall never do anything and am worse than dust and nothing . . . Oh, for some strong thing to sweep this loathsome life into the past."

Now Florence turned her energies into another channel. She began to collect information about hospitals and public health. Through her friends in high government positions, she got hold of every report and every document that had ever been printed on the subject in England. She wrote to hospital doctors and directors for facts and figures. From Ambassador Bunsen and other friends she collected the same material on German and French hospitals.

She worked at night. While the rest of the household slept, Florence sat in her bedroom reading reports, comparing figures, drawing up statistical tables. There was an ironic twist to this that she herself could not see at the time. Because she had been forbidden to set foot in a real hospital, Florence Nightingale stayed at home and in her own bedroom began to gather up the knowledge that would one day make her the world's foremost authority on hospitals.

When it was time for breakfast she put away her notebooks and charts, and went downstairs to begin the other half of the double life she was now leading.

Mrs. Nightingale had decided that her younger daughter's strange notions would go away quietly if only Florence had more to occupy her mind. So Florence was put in complete charge of the pantry and of the household equipment. In a great English household of the last century, this was no small task. "I am up to my chin in linen, glass and china," she wrote a friend, "and I am very fond of housekeeping. In this too highly educated, too-little-active age, it is at least a practical application of our theories to something. And yet in the middle of my lists, my green lists, brown lists, red lists, of all my instruments of culinary accomplishment, which I cannot even divine the use of, I cannot help asking in my head, 'Can reasonable people want all this?' . . . 'And a proper stupid answer you'll get,' says the best Versailles [china] service, 'so go and do your accounts. There is one of us cracked.'"

One day in October a new package of books sent by Chevalier Bunsen arrived from Germany. One of them was called *The Year Book of the Institution of Deaconesses at Kaiserswerth.* Florence remembered that the ambassador had once mentioned the hospital on the Rhine where Protestant deaconesses were trained to nurse.

As she read the book, Florence felt as though she were having a vision of the promised land. Here, at last, was the solution to the problem! Her parents had objected to her working in an English hospital because of the low moral tone of the nurses. They could not possibly raise this objection about the hospital at Kaiserswerth. It was a strictly run religious institution.

From that day on, the idea of going to Kaiserswerth obsessed Florence. She pored over the book every night. During the day, when the chatter of the household became more than she could bear, she would slip up to her room to read her precious book for a few happy moments. But how could she get to Kaiserswerth? For the time being she kept the question to herself.

Two years passed. The severe strain under which Florence lived had a serious complication —Richard Monckton Milnes. He had known Florence for five years. He had been courting her for most of them.

Milnes was sympathetic to what little he knew of Florence's dreams. But he was beginning to wonder how much longer he would have to wait for her to make up her mind. A hundred times Florence had been on the point of refusing his proposals once and for all. Instead she put him off with requests for more and more time to think. She knew that marriage had no place in the future she dreamed of for herself. Still she could not bring herself to send Richard away permanently. The reason was simple enough: she was in love with him.

Florence managed to keep going until the end of 1847. But by then she was in a pitiful state of nerves. During the previous year she had become very friendly with Selina Bracebridge, an unusually wise and sympathetic woman. Mrs. Bracebridge and her husband were planning to spend the winter in Rome. They urged the Nightingales to let Florence go with them.

Florence's sad state of health was a good argument, and she was duly packed off to Italy. Mrs. Nightingale doubtless thought that a winter abroad would bring Flo to her senses and improve her health; when she returned, she would get married and settle down.

Mrs. Nightingale would not have been too flattered if she had been around to see how quickly Flo's health improved. Once she was away from home, all of Florence's symptoms disappeared, and for the first time in two years she felt really alive. "Oh how happy I was!" she wrote much later, looking back on that happy winter. "I never enjoyed any time in my life as much as my time in Rome!"

Everything about the city enchanted her. She wrote glowing letters to poor Parthe about the balls she attended, the art galleries and palaces and churches she visited. But her letters carefully avoided mention of her other activities in Rome. She began visiting hospitals and orphanages to study the work done by Catholic sisters. It was a revelation to her. To one of these nuns, Mother

Santa Colomba, Florence confided the story of her struggle for freedom to follow her call. The old Italian woman understood better than anyone had ever done what the young English girl was going through and what obstacles stood in her way. "Take care!" she told Florence. "God calls you

to a very high degree of perfection. If you resist, you will be guilty!"

Rome was full of congenial English visitors that season.

One day as Florence and Selina were out walking they met the Sidney Herberts, a handsome young couple, recently married, who were in Italy on a delayed honeymoon. Liz Herbert and Selina were friends of long standing.

Florence had never met Mr. Herbert, but she had heard a great deal about him. He had until a short time earlier been Secretary at War and he was one of the most brilliant and influential men in England. Introductions were made and the group parted, promising to see each other again in the near future.

As casually as that, Florence and Sidney Herbert saw each other for the first time. Neither of them had any way of knowing how each was to shape the destiny of the other.

Journey to the Rhine

When Florence returned to England, she began to see the Herberts regularly. She and
Liz became firm friends, and Florence soon knew
all the members of the Herbert circle. Most of
these were strong liberals—people who were not
afraid to think about changing the old way of
doing things. They were interested in government
reforms to improve the sad condition of the
poor. Chief among their interests was the need
for reform in hospitals.

Sidney Herbert and his friends gradually realized that the beautiful Miss Nightingale, sheltered
as her life had been, had somehow or other picked
up a phenomenal lot of facts and figures about
hospitals. Sidney Herbert believed that Florence
was meant for something special in life. When she

told him of her great longing to go to Kaiserswerth, he urged her to do it as quickly as possible.

Perhaps, Florence thought, the right time *had* come. There were subtle changes in her family's attitude.

It is easy to see why. For Florence to ask whether she could go to scrub floors in a hospital was one thing. But for Florence's interest in hospitals to win her the respect and interest of the leaders of British government—that was another thing altogether.

Suddenly the way opened before her, as clearly and as painlessly as she could possibly have asked it to do. Or so she thought.

Parthe had the "vapors" continually. She could always produce some kind of ache or pain, and her doctor finally suggested that she take "the cure." This meant going to some fashionable watering place where mineral water and rest were supposed to take care of whatever ailment one had. Mrs. Nightingale decided that the whole family would go to the baths at Carlsbad in Germany and then on to Frankfurt.

Frankfurt was only a short distance from Kaiserswerth. Florence could hardly believe her ears. Surely God had arranged this for her! While the family was visiting friends in Frankfurt, she could go to Kaiserswerth, inspect the hospital, and perhaps take a little training.

Poor Florence! She should have known that nothing would work out for her so easily. In 1848 revolutions broke out all over the continent. Mr. Nightingale, who had not been enthusiastic over the idea of going to Germany, was secretly relieved. The family, he announced, would stay in England and go to Malvern for the cure.

Florence had not told anyone at home about her Kaiserswerth plan. So the family could not understand why a change in watering place had quite such an effect on her. "All that I most wanted to do at Kaiserswerth," she wrote to a friend, "lay for the first time within reach of my mouth, and the ripe plum has dropped." She felt as though Heaven itself were conspiring against her, and once more she was convinced that she was not worthy of God's help in fulfilling His plan for her.

In this dreadful frame of mind, she found herself, as the year passed, escaping into dreams so often and so deeply that she was convinced she was losing her mind. And at this precisely wrong moment something happened that she had been dreading for years. Richard Monckton Milnes, understandably enough, got tired of waiting. He asked for a definite answer. Would she or would she not marry him?

It was the most agonizing decision she would ever be called upon to make. If she refused to marry Milnes, whom she loved, it was only because she felt that marriage would stand in the way of her future. But *what* future? Never in her life did the future seem more empty than it seemed at this moment. Could she really give up her chance of happiness with Richard because of some dream that would surely never come true?

Florence knew in her heart that she could never dedicate herself completely to the work she wanted to do in life if she were married. It was a conviction on which she never changed her mind. But the effort of finally rejecting Milnes was almost more than she could bear. To the bleak misery inside her was added the irritation of her mother and sister. They had had their hearts set on having Richard Monckton Milnes in the family. Oh, why had he fallen in love with the wrong sister! They wept, they pleaded, they argued, they bullied. But Florence hardly heard them. She was consumed with her own grief.

Once again Selina stepped in to rescue her. The Bracebridges were going on a tour of Egypt and Greece. They determined to take Florence with them. Mrs. Nightingale was cool to the idea. Did Florence think that every time she felt too contrary to do her duty as a good daughter she could go running all over Europe as a reward?

Selina could not very well say, "You are driving her to insanity, and it is closer than you think. And I want to get her away from you." But she could argue in less direct ways and she won her point, although there was much grumbling on the part of most Nightingale relatives, down to the last old great-aunt.

Florence was a student of ancient history and archaeology. Ordinarily she would have been enthralled by such a tour as she was soon taking. But this time the change of scene did not work as well as it had the last time. She remained pale and listless, and had no zest at all for the wonderful sights she saw. It was only little, unexpected things that consoled her, like the baby owl that she found in the Parthenon and named Athena.

The wild creature became her pet and rode happily in her pocket wherever she went.

Selina soon realized that the trip was not succeeding in its purpose. She came to a bold decision. There was really only one thing in life that Florence needed, and Selina vowed to herself that Florence would have it. She rerouted their journey so that they would come home through Germany. She and her husband, she decided, would spend a couple of weeks in Dusseldorf. Florence would go to Kaiserswerth. The wrath of the Nightingale family did not frighten Selina in the least. By the time the family discovered her plot, it would be too late to do anything about it.

Poor Florence was so emotionally exhausted by now that for a time even the prospect of Kaiserswerth failed to cheer her. "The habit of living not in the present but in a future of dreams is gradually spreading over my whole existence," she wrote at Dresden. "It is rapidly approaching the state of madness when dreams become realities." Three days later, thinking of Milnes, she wrote, "It seemed to me now as if quiet, with somebody to look for my coming back, was all I wanted."

But in Berlin arrangements were made for Florence to visit the city's charitable institutions. At the first sight of a hospital her spirits revived instantly. By the time she left Berlin for Kaiserswerth, she had overcome the nervous breakdown that threatened her.

And so at last Florence's long journey to the Rhine came to an end, and she saw the place she had kept in her heart for so many years. She stayed two weeks with Pastor Fliedner and his wife, inspecting every detail of hospital life and helping with the orphanage. She left them promising faithfully to return and "feeling so brave as if nothing could ever vex me again."

At the end of August she went home. She had a loving reunion with her family. They were startled but delighted when Athena, the owl, suddenly popped out of Florence's pocket.

They were more startled and not at all delighted when she told them that she had spent two weeks at Kaiserswerth. Yet through their reproaches and tears, Florence felt a sense of serenity that was quite new to her. In May she had reached her thirtieth birthday, and there was a kind of comfort in knowing that she was past that milestone. She had written in her diary, "Today I am thirty —the age Christ began his mission. Now no more childish things!" At home Florence lived surrounded by childish things and childish people. But in her heart she knew that she was no longer one of them and that soon she would be free. It was only a matter of time.

Within a few months of her return she was once again in the depths of despair. She had tried to make up for her long absence by devoting herself to the entertainment of poor Parthe. In her selfish way Parthe was wildly attached to Flo and lived in her younger sister's reflected glory. But Parthe was hard to please. Her fits of vexation and hysterics were far more exhausting to Florence than to herself.

Florence felt her family's disapproval more keenly than ever. A terrible feeling of guilt on their account was added to her own distress. "Oh dear good woman," she wrote about her mother, "when I feel her disappointment in me, it is as if I were going insane." And the cold fear of insanity now hung over night and day. She was terrified when she realized that unless she acted quickly her life would simply go on forever as it was now going. "O weary days, O evenings that seem never to end! For how many long years I have watched that drawing room clock and thought it would never reach the ten! And for twenty or thirty more years to do this!"

No, it was impossible. She would not let it go on. By June of 1851 she had at last realized what had been perfectly clear all along. She would have to make an open break with her family, if necessary. She began to build a wall of steel around her over-tender heart. In the years ahead, she would find that wall useful.

No Other World

Florence had a friend named Elizabeth Black-well who had come from America to study in England. She was a much discussed figure in London society that year. Elizabeth Blackwell was a physician—a real live woman doctor. She had fought a grim battle to get into medical school and become the first woman doctor graduated in the United States. Now she was continuing her studies in St. Bartholomew's Hospital. Who would have thought a woman could ever get even a toe in the door of the venerable old hospital? But Elizabeth had. She too had fought family and tradition, had faced hardship and ridicule. But she had done what she set out to do.

Knowing someone like Dr. Blackwell was good for Florence at that decisive moment of her career.

Whenever Florence was in London she visited Elizabeth's little room near the hospital, and the two would sit before the fireplace and talk for hours about their future plans.

Once Florence brought the American doctor to Embley for a visit. Elizabeth admired the Nightingales' beautiful house.

"Do you know what I always think when I look at that row of windows?" Florence said. "I think how I should turn it into a hospital, and just where I should place the beds."

The two friends tried to figure out some way of combining their work. But there was no way to do it. Florence was still hopelessly entangled at home and seemed unable to free herself. Elizabeth was ready to begin her career. She decided to return to America to practice medicine. The two women wept when they said good-by. Elizabeth wondered in her heart whether her English friend would ever be free to do the work she so desperately wanted to do.

It was shortly after this last meeting that Florence took her first really decisive stand. She firmly announced to the family that she had made all the arrangements to go to Kaiserswerth and study for three months. She did not tell them that if they refused permission she had decided to pack a bag and leave anyway.

Backed to the wall, Mrs. Nightingale gave up the struggle. But she was a poor loser. Grudgingly she agreed that Florence could go, but she herself would arrange the ways and means. She and her daughters would go to Carlsbad, where Parthe could take the cure. Florence could go from there to Kaiserswerth. There was one condition.

The visit was to be kept a strict secret from all friends and relatives of the Nightingales. There were *some* things, Mrs. Nightingale announced, that one preferred to keep to oneself!

The trip to Carlsbad was not a very happy one. On the night before Florence's departure for Kaiserswerth, Parthe staged one last scene to make her sister change her mind. She had violent hysterics and even threw Florence's bracelets in her sister's face when she was offered the use of them for the evening.

But at last Florence escaped and once more saw the place she had come to love so dearly. The three months at Kaiserswerth flew by. "The world here fills my life with interest and strengthens me in body and mind," Florence wrote to her mother in Carlsbad, and then gave a lively description of the day's rigorous schedule. Mrs. Nightingale found it exhausting even to read about such a day!

More horrifying even than Florence's gay account of the rising hour and the peasant food was what she wrote about an amputation, "which I did not mention to Parthe, knowing that she would see no more in my interest in it than the pleasure dirty boys have in playing in the puddles about a butcher's shop."

An amputation! Who had ever heard of a young woman watching such a thing?

Mrs. Nightingale read the rest of the letter in mounting irritation. "I find the deepest interest in everything here, and am so well in body and mind. This is life. Now I know what it is to live and

to love life, and really I should be sorry now to leave life. I know you will be glad to hear this, dearest Mum. God has indeed made life rich in interests and blessings, and I wish for no other earth, no other world but this."

The return to England was not very jolly. Mrs. Nightingale and Parthe were so annoyed with Florence that they would hardly speak to her. Florence, however, was still under the spell of Kaiserswerth and had only one thought in mind. How could she get more training—this time in a large city hospital?

The only large-scale nursing worth studying, she knew, was that done by Catholic sisters. In Paris, two hundred years before, St. Vincent de Paul had founded the great nursing order called the Sisters of Charity. Florence determined to train at their largest hospital, the Maison de la Providence. But how did one go about doing such a thing?

In Rome, four years earlier, she had met Dr. Henry Edward Manning, who was at that time a leading clergyman in the Church of England. He had recently become a Roman Catholic and would one day be a Cardinal. Florence herself felt strongly drawn to the Catholic Church and in 1852 was on the point of entering it. Although she decided not to do so, her strong friendship with Manning continued. She wrote in detail of her difficulties at home, and he answered with sympathetic and helpful advice. Naturally she turned to him with her present problem: how could a Protestant Englishwoman "join" the Sisters of Charity in order to learn nursing?

It was really very simple, said Father Manning, even though it had never been done before. He would simply explain things to the Mother Superior.

Needless to say, Florence's announcement of her new project caused the greatest run on smelling salts that Embley had ever seen. Florence among the Protestant deaconesses at remote little Kaiserswerth had been bad enough. But Florence among the Sisters of Charity in a Paris hospital—it was too much even to discuss!

Exhausting months passed before she could escape. She had planned to study every hospital in Paris and then to enter the Maison de la Providence. There she would undergo the same hospital training that a postulant in the order received.

But her luck was running true to form. The day before her admission to the Sisters' hospital, she received word that her dear grandmother, whom she had once nursed back to health, was dying. She rushed back to England and was able to ease the old lady's last days as no one else could have done.

Florence had no sooner begun repacking her bags when she received an excited letter from Mrs. Sidney Herbert. There was a small private nursing home, Liz wrote, called the Institution for the Care of Sick Gentlewomen in Distressed Circumstances. The board of directors was not satisfied with the way in which the place was being run. The hospital was moving to new quarters, but what it needed most of all was a new superintendent. Lady Canning, a friend of the Herberts, was head of the committee. Liz had recommended Florence for the position. Would she consider it?

Florence had already determined that when she returned from Paris she would not go home. During the long, lonely nights by her grandmother's bed, she had asked herself a hundred times, "But what *will* I do?" Liz's letter was an answer from Heaven. Surely not even her mother could worry about the moral tone of the Institution for the Care of Sick Gentlewomen in Distressed Circumstances.

Mrs. Nightingale could and did, however, raise every other objection she could think of. Florence's long and irritating negotiations with the committee ladies were made to the accompaniment of her mother's arguments and her sister's hysterics.

To her great joy, however, Florence suddenly found herself with a new ally. Mr. Nightingale was a scholarly, peace-loving man. More than anything else in life he wanted to be left alone, to read his books and think his own thoughts. For years he had known that Mrs. Nightingale was acting very badly toward his younger daughter, but he could not face the price he would have to pay for interfering. Now at last he roused himself to action and took Florence's side against the rest of the family. Best of all, he even made her an independent allowance of five hundred pounds a year.

Florence applied for the post and quickly discovered that her years of forced dealings with ladies in society was standing her in good stead. The committee ladies were difficult, to say the least, but she knew how to handle them. "Fashionable asses," she called them, when they were out of earshot. They had to be talked round on several serious points. Was it proper for a young lady of good society to nurse someone of a lower class? Was it fitting for such a person as Miss Nightingale to be present when doctors were examining patients? Florence solemnly promised to hire, at her own expense, an elderly personal attendant and to have her on hand whenever a doctor so much as set foot in the door.

At last everything was arranged. The position was hers (with no salary) and so was full control of the Institution. She could start work in a few months, when the new quarters had been selected.

A few months, Florence thought, would give her just enough time to accomplish her dearest wish of training with the Sisters of Charity. She went back to Paris and at last entered the Maison de la Providence. Two weeks later she was out of it and in bed in her little convent cell, covered with measles. She was understandably furious, particularly since she was convinced that she had already had the disease once.

"For me to come to Paris to have the measles a second time," she wrote to a friend, "is like going to the Grand Desert to die of getting one's feet wet!"

She returned to England in July and went immediately to London. Her family was there, waiting for her. To their consternation she rented a small apartment of her own and moved into it. For the first time in thirty-three years, she was a free agent.

Hospital for
Distressed Gentlewomen

The ladies of the committee had promised to have the new quarters at Number One Harley Street ready for patients by the middle of August. But on her return from Paris Florence found that practically nothing had been done during her absence. The ladies, it is true, had bought two cases of jam from the most expensive shop in London, but they had forgotten to order any brooms or scrubbing brushes.

Flòrence and her faithful Aunt Mai rolled up their sleeves and went to work. "I have had to prepare this immense house for patients in ten days—without a bit of help but only hindrance from my committee," Florence wrote to a friend.

"I have been 'in service' ten days and have had
to furnish an entirely empty house in that time.
We take in patients this Monday and have not
got our workmen out yet. From Committees,

Charity, . . . philanthropy and all deceits of the devil, Good Lord deliver us."

Now that she was actually in control of a hospital, Florence could put into practice the theories that she had been developing for eight years. The committee ladies greeted each letter from the new superintendent with mounting alarm. Some of them already regretted the choice. There had been something romantic in the idea of a young, well-born lady wishing to devote herself to the sick and aged, like a beautiful, ministering angel. But this Miss Nightingale was proving to be more of a whirling dervish than a ministering angel! Was there no end to the woman's energy and odd ideas?

First of all, there was this business of having the hot water *piped* up to each floor. What was the matter with carrying it upstairs in buckets, as it had always been carried? Next she had asked for a "windlass installation" (we would call it a dumbwaiter) for bringing trays of food from the kitchen to the upper floors.

Most amazing of all was the Nightingale mania for bells. She insisted on having bells in each room which, when rung, set off a corresponding bell outside the floor nurse's door. As if this were not enough, she had each of these bells fitted with a valve that flew open when the bell rang and *stayed* open so that the nurse could see at a glance who was calling her!

Thus many of today's most familiar hospital routines were suggested for the first time to the startled committee ladies of the Institution for Distressed Gentlewomen.

But Florence was brimming over with a zest for life that she had never known before. "I am living in an ideal world of lifts, gas, baths and double and single wards," she told her favorite cousin. Not even the committee ladies could dampen her soaring spirits, and she soon had them under control. "When I entered 'into service' here," she wrote her father, "I determined that, happen what would, I *never* would intrigue among the committee. Now I perceive that I do all my business by intrigue. I propose, in private, to A, B, or C, the resolution I think A, B, or C most capable of carrying in Committee, and then leave it to them, and I always win."

There was one group at Harley Street that never from the first moment had any quarrel with Miss Nightingale or with her way of doing things. The patients were devoted to her heart and soul, down to the last Sick Gentlewoman in Distressed Circumstances. Most of these poor ladies were governesses or paid "companions." (In those days it was the only kind of work by which a respectable spinster could earn her living.) When they came to the hospital they were lonely, friendless, and out of work. Most of them knew that there was not one person in the whole world who really cared what happened to them. And then, suddenly, there was Miss Nightingale who, busy though she was, managed to make each poor governess feel like the Queen of England herself! Florence's effect on these women was so great that years later they still wrote her letters full of love and gratitude.

Before many months had passed, the affairs of the Institution were running so smoothly that even the most anti-Nightingale lady of the committee was, as Florence wrote her father, "trumpeting my fame through London."

She began to wish for a greater world to conquer than her little nursing home for genteel women. Once again her interest centered on the large public hospitals, where the real misery of the city was found. She began visiting hospitals regularly and collecting more facts about the dreadful conditions that existed in them.

The more Florence saw, the more convinced she

became that what hospitals needed more than anything else was a whole new concept of nursing and nurses.

Except for a handful of friends like the Herberts, few people shared her opinion. "Really, the nurses are quite good already," Lady Palmerston declared one day when the subject of Miss Nightingale's theories came up for discussion. "Oh, perhaps they *do* drink a little, but after all! How tiresome for the poor creatures to sit up all night!"

This was the typical view of the typical nurse of those not so far-off days.

Florence wanted nothing less than a revolution. Yet she knew that in order to revolutionize nursing she would first have to create an entirely new kind of nurse. And this new nurse would have to learn her profession in an entirely new kind of school—a school of nursing.

But even if such a school existed, where would she find the students to fill it? This was the heart of the problem. Nurses were elderly women of the lowest classes and usually with the lowest character. Nursing as a career for fine upper- and middle-class girls, still young enough to be taught a whole new science? Impossible, unthinkable. It would take at least two generations to overcome the prejudice against nursing.

Yet Florence knew that all over England thousands of girls were starving, as she had once done, for the simple lack of something to do with their lives, something to give them meaning and purpose.

If only there were some way to show the world what real nursing could mean to real suffering—some way to prove what women could do in this man's world if they were only given the chance!

But there was no way to do such a thing, she knew. There would be no dramatic short cut to victory. She would have to fight laboriously for every half-inch of ground she won. Or so she thought.

While Florence rubbed backs in Harley Street, and worked over her accounts with the coal merchant and the butcher, something was happening over a thousand miles away that would soon change the shape of her life. The fact that on November 30, 1853, the Russian fleet sank the Turkish fleet in the Black Sea should not, on the face of it, have had much connection with the affairs of Miss Florence Nightingale. But it did.

7

Trouble in the Crimea

Look at the map on page 57. At the southern end of Russia you will find a peninsula called the Crimea jutting out into the Black Sea. At the southern tip of the Crimea there is a city called Sebastopol. Here, toward the middle of the last century, the Czar of Russia, Nicholas I, built a great naval base. He longed for the day when Russian warships would challenge the sea power of England and France. In order to make Russia a first-class naval power, however, Nicholas knew that he would have to find some way of getting his warships out of the Black Sea and into the Mediterranean.

But how?

To the southwest, across the Black Sea from Sebastopol, is the Turkish city of Istanbul. In

SCENE
OF THE
CRIMEAN WAR

1853 it was still called Constantinople. Waking and sleeping, Nicholas I dreamed of getting his imperial Russian hands on Constantinople. It was not the city itself that he wanted so much as the narrow strip of water that ran past it. This strait was called the Bosporus. The Bosporus was his way, his *only* way, to get out of the Black Sea and into the Mediterranean Sea, where he most wished to be.

And it seemed temptingly easy. The Turkish Empire was weak and corrupt. The Czar himself had described the country as "the sick man of Europe." Other European nations agreed that the "sick man" would soon collapse.

The Crimean crisis arose from a dispute between the Russians and the French over the control of the Holy Places in Palestine. Wishing to extend his power over the dying Turkish Empire, the Czar sent troops into Turkish territory. The Turks, counting on support from the British and French, enthusiastically declared war on Russia.

The British feared a Russian occupation of Constantinople, which meant control over the Bosporus. The thought of Russian warships cruising at will all over the Mediterranean filled the British and French governments with alarm. Gradually the powers drifted into war.

The French and the English were enemies of long standing. Only forty years had passed since the Duke of Wellington had defeated the Grand Army of France and sent Napoleon into exile. But in 1853, when Czar Nicholas finally moved, France and England were driven into an unwilling partnership against him. In March of 1854 they declared war on Russia.

Many important officials in England, including the Queen and the Prince, were not at all sure that declaring war on Russia was either wise or necessary. But the people themselves thought it was a splendid idea, even if they were not entirely clear on just why it had been done. It was much more exciting to talk about the war than to complain about the hard times and the failure of this or that crop. All over England bands were playing and crowds were cheering. This was like the good old days—the days of glory that had led to Waterloo!

On September 14, 1854, English and French troops first landed in the Crimea itself. Six days later they met and defeated the enemy in a fierce battle at the Alma River.

England was caught up in a frenzy of excitement and pride. A national outbreak of speeches and poetry described the glories of the Alma. Few people in England knew how badly planned the battle really was. Fewer people knew that the whole Crimean campaign was a real disaster—a monument to poor leadership and bad management.

"Someone had blundered," Alfred Tennyson wrote later about the most famous incident of the

Crimean War, the ill-fated charge of the Light Brigade. The fact was that someone or other was blundering all through the Crimean War.

The prize blundering, and the most heartbreaking, concerned the sick and wounded of the British army. England had been at peace for forty years. With no wars to think about, the men who

ran the War Office had devoted themselves heart and soul to another pursuit—saving money. In England the budget cuts of forty years showed up only as columns of figures on paper. But in the Crimea, three thousand miles away, they added up to a kind of misery and suffering we can hardly imagine today.

The army was based at Scutari, a small town just across the straits from Constantinople. Between June and September cholera had ravaged the troops much more effectively than the Russians could ever have done. An army hospital had been established at Scutari, but it was filled up with cholera cases even before the battle of the Alma was fought. Knowing what would happen once fighting really began in the Crimea, the Turkish government had presented the British with a huge empty barrack and invited them to use it for a hospital.

By the end of September, the men wounded at the Alma began arriving in Scutari. They were in a pitiable condition, for the British army had been landed in the Crimea without enough transport ships and with hardly any medical supplies. The men wounded there could be given only the most primitive treatment before being shipped back to the hospitals in Scutari. They were lined up on the decks of the few ships available, often with no mattresses and no cover but a ragged blanket. One or two doctors, with no equipment whatsoever, escorted the thousand or more cases packed onto each ship. And these nightmarish voyages across the Black Sea took eight days to three weeks, depending on the weather.

When the men reached Scutari, they were not much better off than they had been in the Crimea. The ghastly condition of the army in the Crimea was more or less taken for granted by the leaders of the army. This was war, after all, and war had always been hell. Old officers, veterans of the Napoleonic wars, could remember much worse conditions and much less medical attention than the men were getting at Scutari. But who in England had complained about the cost of the glorious victories of Nelson and Wellington?

They were right. Not many people in England had complained because not many people in England had known anything but the news of final victory. But now for the first time people in England were learning about the hidden side of war. The whole country began to realize the tragedy that was taking place so far away.

A new figure emerged for the first time during the Crimean War. He is a familiar and respected figure today. In 1854 he was a novelty and a nuisance. He was the war correspondent, the civilian newspaper reporter at the battle front.

The first newspaperman to accompany an army overseas and send back stories to his paper was a spirited Irishman named William Howard Rus-

sell, special correspondent of the London *Times*.
On September 30, the people of England, still
glowing with pride over the victory at the Alma,
read this story with their morning coffee:

"It is with feelings of surprise and anger that
the public will learn that no sufficient preparations
have been made for the proper care of the

wounded. Not only are there not sufficient surgeons—that, it might be argued, was unavoidable;
not only are there no dressers and nurses—that
might be a defect of system for which no one is
to blame; but what will be said when it is known
that there is not even linen to make bandages for
the wounded? . . . Why could this clearly fore-
seen want not have been supplied? Can it be
said that the Battle of the Alma has been an
event to take the world by surprise? Has not the
expedition to the Crimea been the talk of the
last four months? . . . And yet, after the troops
have been six months in the country, there is no
preparation for the commonest surgical operations!
Not only are the men kept, in some cases, for a
week without the hand of a medical man coming
near their wounds; not only are they left to ex-
pire in agony, unheeded and shaken off, though
clutching desperately at the surgeon as he makes
his rounds through the fetid ship; but now, when
they are placed in the spacious building, where
we were led to believe that everything was ready
which could ease their pain, . . . it is found that
the commonest appliances of a workhouse sick
ward are wanting, and that the men must die
through the medical staff of the British army hav-

ing forgotten that old rags are necessary for the dressing of wounds."

Before the readers of the *Times* had recovered from this bombshell, Russell aimed another one. "It is impossible," they read the next day, "for any one to see the melancholy sights of the last few days without feelings of surprise and indignation at the deficiencies of our medical system. The manner in which the sick and wounded are treated is worthy only of savages. . . . Here the French are greatly our superiors. Their medical arrangements are extremely good, their surgeons more numerous, and they have also the help of the Sisters of Charity who have accompanied the expedition in incredible numbers. These devoted women are excellent nurses."

Russell's stories aroused a storm of fury in England. Suddenly the war in the Crimea did not seem quite so glorious. Contributions of money and medical supplies began to pour into the *Times* office. Angry letters filled its columns. Russell's remarks about the French Sisters of Charity had stung the readers sharply. What was the matter with *English* women? Who said they couldn't nurse soldiers just as well as French women?

"Why have *we* no Sisters of Charity?" an outraged reader wrote. "There are numbers of able-bodied and tender-hearted English women who would joyfully and with alacrity go out to devote themselves to nursing the sick and wounded, if they could be associated for that purpose, and placed under proper protection."

If ever a moment in history had been created to fit the destiny of an individual, this moment had been made for Florence Nightingale.

One Person in England

Independently Florence and Sidney Herbert reached exactly the same conclusion. Their letters on the subject crossed in the mail. Sidney Herbert, the Secretary at War, wrote his now famous letter to Florence Nightingale on October 15, 1854.

"Dear Miss Nightingale," he said in part, "You will have seen in the papers that there is a great deficiency of nurses at the Hospital at Scutari.

"The other alleged deficiencies, namely of medical men, lint, sheets, etc., must, if they have really ever existed, have been remedied ere this. . . .

"But the deficiency of female nurses is undoubted, none but male nurses having ever been admitted to military hospitals."

He went on to say that although nurses could not very well accompany the army to the front, there was no reason why they should not serve in the base hospital at Scutari. "I receive numbers of offers from ladies to go out, but they are ladies who have no conception of what an hospital is, nor of the nature of its duties; and they would, when the time came, either recoil from the work or be entirely useless, and consequently —what is worse—entirely in the way. . . .

"There is but one person in England that I know of who would be capable of organising and superintending such a scheme; and I have been several times on the point of asking you hypothetically if, supposing the attempt were made, you would undertake to direct it.

"The selection of the rank and file of nurses will be very difficult: no one knows it better than yourself. The difficulty of finding women equal to a task, after all, full of horrors, and requiring, besides knowledge and goodwill, great energy and great courage, will be great. The task of ruling them and introducing system among them, great; and not the least will be the difficulty of making the whole work smoothly with the medical and military authorities out there. . . .

"My question simply is, Would you listen to the request to go and superintend the whole thing? You would of course have plenary authority over all the nurses, and I think I could secure you the fullest assistance and co-operation from the medical staff, and you would also have an unlimited power of drawing on the Government for whatever you thought requisite for the success of your mission. . . .

"I do not say one word to press you. You are

the only person who can judge for yourself which of conflicting . . . duties is the highest; but I must not conceal from you that I think upon your decision will depend the ultimate success or failure of the plan. Your own personal qualities, your knowledge and your power of administration, and among greater things your rank and position in Society give you advantages in such a work which no other person possesses.

"If this succeeds," he went on, coming to the one argument he knew she could not resist, "an enormous amount of good will be done now . . . and a prejudice will have been broken through, and a precedent established, which will multiply the good to all time."

He ended by assuring Florence that if she agreed to go, the Bracebridges would undoubtedly go with her. "There is one point," he continued delicately, "that I have hardly a right to touch upon, but I know you will pardon me. If you were inclined to undertake this great work, would Mr. and Mrs. Nightingale give their consent? The work would be so national, and the request made to you proceeding from the Government who represent the nation comes at such a moment, that I do not despair of their consent. . . .

"I know that you will come to a wise decision. God grant it may be in accordance with my hopes!"

Florence read this letter with great joy and great surprise. She had already determined to hire a few nurses and go out to Scutari as a private citizen to see what she could do to help. She had written a note to the Herberts to see what they thought of the idea. This was the letter that had crossed Sidney's in the day's mail. But it had never for a moment entered her head that she would be asked to go as the official representative of the British government. She was a woman. Women were simply not sent on government missions by a unanimous vote of the cabinet—at least no woman ever had been. Sidney Herbert's bold action caused a tremendous stir all over England.

Herbert's fears that the other Nightingales might object to the mission turned out to be groundless. They were delighted and not a little awed by the whole idea. "My Love," Parthe wrote, all but twittering, to a girl friend, "Government has asked, I should say entreated Flo to go out and help in the Hospital at Scutari. I am sure you will feel that it is a great and noble work, and that it is a real duty. For there is no one, as they tell her, and I believe truly, who has the knowledge and the zeal necessary to make such a step succeed."

Parthe determined to get in on the excitement. She and her mother hastened to leave Embley and join Florence in London to help her get organized.

Once she knew she was going to Turkey, Florence was determined to waste no time getting there. She set Saturday, October 21, as her sailing date. This gave her exactly six days in which to get ready. The most important and the most discouraging job on the agenda was the recruiting of nurses. Florence herself believed that twenty women would be all she could handle. Sidney Herbert talked her into taking forty. His house in Belgrave Square became the expedition's headquarters, with Selina Bracebridge and three other ladies as recruiting officers. "I wish," one of them wrote to Liz Herbert, "people who may hereafter complain of the women selected could have seen the set we had to choose from. All London was scoured for them. We sent emissaries in every direction to every likely place. . . . We felt ashamed to have in the house such women as came. One alone expressed a wish to go from a good motive. Money was the only inducement."

Florence's heart sank as she looked over the best of the applicants, as weeded out by Selina. The low state of professional nursing had never been brought home to her more clearly. Only fourteen hospital nurses were found who could even be considered for the job. For the rest of the party Florence turned to religious institutions. An Anglican sisterhood, called the Sellonites, sent eight Sisters. St. John's House, another Anglican order, sent six. A Catholic orphanage in Norwood sent five nuns. Five Sisters of Mercy from a convent in Bermondsey were already in Paris, on their way to Scutari. Their bishop had sent them as an independent party of nurses a few days after the *Times*'s account was printed. When they heard that an official government party was being sent, the Sisters waited for it in France.

This made a total of thirty-eight nurses. Mrs. Clark, the faithful housekeeper from Harley Street, announced that she was going along to take care of Miss Nightingale, as she was convinced that no one else could do the job properly. The Bracebridges and one man-of-all-work completed the party. Mr. Bracebridge was the business manager and made all the travel arrangements. He dashed about London in a cab, at the breathtaking speed of ten miles an hour, the cash box firmly clutched under his arm.

Throughout all the hectic preparations needed to transplant forty-three people to Turkey, Florence remained as calm and unruffled as though she were preparing to go to the opera. "No one is so well fitted as she to do such work," wrote the head of her committee ladies. "She has such nerve and skill and is so wise and quiet. Even now she is in no bustle and hurry, though so much is on her hands."

Only once during the hectic week did her ironclad emotions give way. In the excitement at Embley, Mrs. Nightingale and Parthe forgot all about Athena, the owl, and left her locked up in an attic. By the time they were ready to leave for London, poor Athena had died of starvation. When she heard this Florence burst into tears and then excused herself by saying, "Poor little beastie, it was odd how much I loved you!"

Parthe, who told the story later, saw these tears only as a sign of regret for Athena. But there must have been a certain amount of sheer irritation in them. She herself had managed to think of quite a number of things during the past few days. Couldn't Mama and Parthe even remember to feed one little bird?

To everyone's surprise the party was really ready to leave on October 21. The fourteen uniforms for the professional nurses—hastily designed and more hastily made—were not the most glamorous uniforms in the world, but they served their purpose.

Florence's own luggage was austerely simple. She carried only the plainest and most essential clothing, and the smallest possible number of personal possessions. Among these was a small black leather folder containing three pieces of paper. During the previous week she had received hundreds of letters from friends and relatives, peers and clergymen, government officials and well-wishers. She had chosen to carry only three of the letters with her through the war.

The first was from her mother. It was the sort of letter she had wished for many times and never received before now. "God speed you on your errand of mercy, my dearest child. I know He will for He has given you such loving friends and they will be always at your side to help in all your difficulties . . ." At last her work had her mother's blessing.

The second letter was from Father Manning. "God will keep you," he wrote, "and my prayer for you will be that your . . . source of consolation and strength may be the Sacred Heart of our Divine Lord."

The third letter was from Richard Monckton Milnes. "My Dear Friend," he said, "I hear you are going to the East. I am happy it is so for the good you will do there, and hope you may find some satisfaction in it yourself. . . . You can undertake *that,* when you could not undertake me! God bless you, dear friend, wherever you go."

In France the travelers were treated like visiting royalty, or better. No one would take any money from them for anything. Baggage porters, hotel keepers, railroad officials, and restaurant owners vied to smooth the path of the English women—for the French too had loved ones fighting and dying in the Crimea. The fourteen hired nurses were ecstatic over the attention they received. And when Miss Nightingale herself translated menus and served them their dinner in the railroad station, and then bought them each a pair of warm overshoes, they were all but overcome. No one had ever treated them like this before. "It is not people's way with us," one of them sadly explained.

Before leaving London, Florence had called on Dr. Andrew Smith, chief of the medical department of the army. She told him that she had been given funds collected for war relief and asked him what supplies were most needed in Scutari. Dr. Smith solemnly assured her that nothing whatever was needed; every medical supply and comfort was already there in abundance. He wished her well, and added that the presence of a few ladies might be of some consolation to the men. Ladies noticed little things, like a spot on a sheet, that a hospital orderly might overlook.

Florence chose to ignore the good doctor's assurance that everything was splendid in Scutari. At Marseilles she and her Uncle Sam, who had escorted her to France, went shopping. On October 27, when the party sailed for Constantinople, a carload of bales and boxes sailed with them. Florence's sound instincts had never been working more soundly than in the shops and market places of Marseilles.

Their ship was a miserable old tub called the

Vectis. Even for people who enjoyed sea travel, the *Vectis* was a trial—and poor Florence had always loathed sea travel. For nine miserable days the ship creaked and groaned its way through the Mediterranean. Florence was violently seasick. As she lay in her cabin, longing for the sight of land, she looked back with disbelief over the events of the past few days.

Was it possible that less than two weeks ago she had been caring for sick ladies in Harley

Street? And now she was on her way to Turkey and to war. She remembered what Sidney Herbert had said in his letter. "If this succeeds . . . a prejudice will have been broken through, and a precedent established, which will multiply the good to all time."

The clear-sighted statesman had realized from the beginning that if she accomplished her purpose, she would be doing more than relieving the sufferings of the sick and wounded. If she could prove the value of women nurses in military hospitals at the height of a war, she would be proving the value of the nursing profession itself.

But as she lay in the filthy cabin of the *Vectis*, groaning at every pitch and roll of the ship, success seemed most unlikely.

9

Arrival in Scutari

On the morning of November 4, the *Vectis* dropped anchor off Constantinople. The travelers had their first view of the fabled city through heavy rain and thick fog. It looked, Florence wrote her family, "like a washed-out daguerreotype." On the opposite shore they could just make out the outline of a huge yellow building with massive square towers rising at every angle. This was the Turkish barrack, recently declared a hospital. As the nurses gathered on deck ready to be taken ashore, one of them said eagerly, "Oh, Miss Nightingale, when we land don't let there be any red tape delays! Let's get straight to nursing the poor fellows!"

"The strongest," Florence said prophetically, "will be wanted at the washtub!"

There was no real dock at Scutari. The ladies were helped from the ship into small boats and rowed ashore. They were then assisted up a steep hill, almost a cliff, and taken to the hospital. Florence shuddered as she thought of the wounded men who had to be rowed ashore and dragged up that sheer slope.

The party was given a polite welcome and escorted down a huge, echoing corridor to the northwest tower of the building. Then they were left alone to inspect their quarters. It was not an encouraging moment. The space assigned to them, they later learned, was the amount of space usually occupied by three army doctors or one military commandant. There was a large storeroom which would hold the supplies and serve as a kitchen. Three smaller rooms and one large closet opened off it. There was another room higher up in the tower. At the moment it was occupied by a dead Russian general. None of the rooms had any furniture in them, unless one counted the wooden platforms that the Turks used for beds.

Florence looked over these dismal quarters rapidly and then assigned sleeping space. The fourteen hired nurses were put into one room and ten nuns in another. Once the Russian general

83

was removed from his tower, the Protestant Sisters moved in. Florence and Selina took the closet. The remaining room would serve as a sitting room and office. At night it would be a bedroom for the two men of the party, Mr. Bracebridge and the messenger. Mrs. Clark, the housekeeper, would sleep in the kitchen.

The rooms were already inhabited by an assortment of cockroaches, fleas, lice, and rodents of all sizes. At home one did not even mention such creatures in polite society. Here they quickly became a routine part of everyday living.

Whatever dismay Florence might have felt on that first night in Scutari was nothing to what she felt the next day when she saw the rest of the building. She had visited plenty of hospitals in England and France and Germany and Italy. She was accustomed to sights that chilled the blood and turned the stomach. But nothing in her experience had prepared her for the horrors of the Barrack Hospital in Scutari.

It was certainly an impressive sight from the outside. When the British took it over from the Turks, Dr. Menzies, the chief medical officer, declared that a bit of whitewash was all it needed to make it into a hospital. If he had bothered to look beyond the outer walls he would have made an interesting discovery. The imposing structure was built directly over a vast cesspool that had been clogged up and undrained for years. Indescribable fumes rose up through the pipes of open privies and seeped through the wards where the men lay crowded together. There was no attempt at ventilation. And since not one part of the so-called sanitary conveniences worked properly, the rotting floor boards were covered with an oozing slime. "It is impossible," Florence later wrote, "to describe the state of the atmosphere of the Barrack Hospital at night. I have been well acquainted with the dwellings of the worst parts of most of the great cities in Europe, but have never been in any atmosphere which I could compare with it."

As she walked through the foul-smelling wards for the first time, her heart ached for the men who so recently had been marching smartly down the streets of England with the blare of the band and the cheers of the crowd ringing in their ears. How dim these memories must be now!

Most of the men lay on straw-stuffed mattresses, as the supply of beds had run out weeks before. The sheets were made of canvas so coarse that the men begged to be left wrapped up in the filthy blankets in which they had made the voyage from the Crimea.

The men's clothes and bedding were foul. Florence had guessed correctly when she said, "The strongest will be wanted at the washtubs." The number of shirts washed in the whole hospital during the previous month had been six. It was no great loss, Florence soon discovered, that so much went unwashed—for the bedding came back from the laundry crawling with lice. All the washing was done in cold water with no soap. No wonder

87

the men refused to give up their shirts and covers. They said that they preferred to keep their own lice rather than swap with someone else.

The food eaten by these desperately sick men was a scandal. Every morning the assistant surgeon went through the wards with the ward orderlies and made up the diet list. Every item had to be countersigned by the overworked staff surgeon before the orderly could get the uncooked food from the supply officer, or purveyor. When the orderly's meat ration had been weighed out to him, he tied it up with some identifying mark, such as an old pair of scissors or used piece of bandage, and took it to the kitchen. All the cooking for the hospital was done in thirteen copper pots located at one end of the building. As there were no ovens, everything had to be boiled. The meat was never left in the pots long enough to cook properly because the same pots had to be used for making the tea.

When the orderly had claimed his meat, he took it back to the ward and divided it up on his bed. It was doled out strictly according to weight. If a man's portion happened to consist of bone or gristle, that was his bad luck. Cut the meat off the bone before weighing it out? Impossible, Florence was told later, when she suggested this simple remedy. It would take a whole new regulation of the service to get the bones out of the meat.

There were few knives or forks or plates. The men had to tear at the half-cooked meat with their fingers. If a man was too weak to feed himself, he went hungry. Many of the men were on half-diets or "spoon diets." In the regulation book this meant that they were receiving extra foods, like essence of beef, or arrowroot and port wine. But such things existed only on paper in the Barrack Hospital. Men on "spoon diets" were fed some of the greasy water in which the meat had been boiled.

These were some of the conditions that existed in the hospital when Florence Nightingale and her nurses arrived in November of 1854. It was not the fault of any individual doctor or army officer. It was the fault of the whole system by which the army and army hospitals were run. Every phase of army life was hopelessly tangled in red tape. The army doctors spent much more time filling out forms and countersigning requisitions than they did in treating the wounded.

If this mass of paper had actually produced

good, efficient results, there would have been less cause for complaint. But it did not. From top to bottom, the system was so complicated that no one could figure it out. In London departments overlapped and got in each other's way. There was the Secretary *for* War (the Duke of Newcastle) and the Secretary *at* War (Sidney Herbert). Six other departments had a finger in the pie.

In Scutari the same sort of confusion reigned on a smaller scale. The wants of the hospitals were supplied by the Commissary and the Purveyor's office. But no one ever succeeded in figuring out where the duties of one ended and the duties of the other began. Employees of both departments trembled before the army surgeons and lived in fear of somehow overstepping their proper authority. Fear of superior officers and fear of spending money were the twin bugbears of the supply officers. "It is a current joke here," Florence wrote home, "to offer a prize for the discovery of anyone willing to take responsibility." But no one ever had to take responsibility for anything. The system was designed perfectly for the old army game of "passing the buck."

Inefficient though the system was, however, at the first criticism of it hospital officials of *all* departments closed ranks and prepared to resist.

What a blow it had been to the medical officers in Turkey when they heard the unbelievable news! First of all, a civilian newspaper had got the whole country stirred up over things that had been going on in the army since Julius Caesar invaded Britain. Next, the civilian Secretary at War had appointed another civilian to go and meddle in army affairs. And as if that were not enough, he had appointed a *female* civilian. And she had forty other female civilians with her. Women cluttering up an army hospital—it was an outrage! Worse than that, it was an insult! It clearly implied that the army could not take care of its own affairs.

The arrival of the nurses was the talk of the army, from Scutari to Sebastopol. Florence's name alone supplied the officers with material for heavy-footed jokes. They referred to her simply as "the bird." The chief medical officer of the Crimean army, Dr. Hall, summed up the general opinion. "It is very droll," he said between his teeth, when told of Miss Nightingale's appointment. In his heart he did not think there was anything funny about it at all.

Florence herself had expected some opposition from the doctors. She had also decided how to meet it. She would prove to the medical men that she and her companions were not meddling females but well-disciplined nurses who were there to serve the doctors by following their orders. "No matter how much you want to do for the wounded," she told her nurses again and again, "you must never set foot in a ward unless the doctor in charge of it has asked for nurses. And no matter how sensible it may seem to you, never do anything for a patient without the permission of a doctor." It was a galling rule, but she enforced it strictly. Many of the nurses did not understand the need for such strictness, and it made Florence unpopular with them. But this was the least of her worries.

For the first few days after Florence's arrival, the doctors remained cool. Only one important thing was accomplished. The women unpacked the stores bought in Marseilles and set up an extra-diet kitchen. The doctors grudgingly agreed that cooking arrowroot and milk pudding for the sickest men was all right. In fact it was just about all women were good for around a hospital!

The Nightingale Power

Florence's arrival in Scutari had been well timed. In view of what began to happen next, the doctors could no longer hold out against her. On October 25, the Battle of Balaclava had been fought. This was the battle made famous by the light-cavalry brigade that followed the wrong orders and charged straight into the massed Russian artillery. No one in Scutari had realized the full horrors of that battle until transport ships packed with wounded men began to arrive from the Crimea.

All at once the coolness of the medical men vanished. Every available pair of hands was needed. In the horrible confusion of the days that followed, they began to look at the nurses with new feelings. On Thursday, November 10, there were

1015 men in the Barrack Hospital and 650 in the
other hospital. Toward noon of that day a cou-
rier arrived with an urgent message for the chief
medical officer. Dr. Menzies sent for Florence and
told her the news. The enemy had attacked at
Inkerman near Sebastopol, on November 5. In
this battle, fought in fog and darkness, nearly

1800 British soldiers had been wounded. The first transports were just landing. Five hundred men would have to be put somewhere in the Barrack Hospital.

Florence rushed back to the tower to alert the others.

"Five hundred!" one of the nurses gasped. "But—where will we put them?"

"In the empty corridor outside the tower."

"There aren't any more mattresses!"

"We'll have to stuff some sackcloth with chopped straw."

"It will take all day," someone else said. "When are they arriving?"

"In half an hour."

After that no one had time to say anything.

The five hundred mattresses were lined up along the filthy floor of the corridor and squeezed into every corner of the wards. Every ten minutes, it seemed to Florence, an orderly had come rushing up to report that one of the new men was bleeding to death. Then the nurses would run to stuff lint into the wound and wait for someone to find a surgeon.

All day long the wounded men had been carried in. Twenty-four of them, unlucky enough to survive the battle and the stormy crossing of the Black Sea, died as they reached the hospital. The others lay mute and exhausted, waiting to face the surgeons.

In the Barrack Hospital there was no such thing as an operating room or an operating table.

Surgery was performed in the wards, right on the patient's bed. Amputations and the removal of bullets was all the surgery attempted, and most of it was done without anesthetics. Terrible wound infections followed every operation. "Oh, you gentlemen of England," Florence wrote to a doctor friend, "who sit at home in all the well-earned satisfaction of your successful cases, can have little idea from reading the newspapers of the horror and misery (in a military hospital) of operating on these dying, exhausted men. A London hospital is a garden of flowers to it."

The wounded of Inkerman were no sooner settled than a terrible disaster struck the Crimea. A violent hurricane swept out of the Black Sea and across the peninsula. As it passed it sank every ship in the harbor of Balaclava. One of these ships, the *Prince,* had just arrived from England, loaded with every kind of supply. The *Prince* had stopped at Scutari to discharge passengers before crossing to the Crimea. Its desperately needed hospital supplies had not been unloaded, however, because the ship had been packed backwards. The Scutari supplies were buried under tons of ammunition bound for the Crimea. The captain of the ship decided to go on to Balaclava and unload the ammunition first. The hospital supplies could be delivered on the return voyage. In the end, all the supplies lay together at the bottom of the Black Sea.

The loss of the ship was a bitter blow to the men who suffered agonies of cold and hunger before the besieged city of Sebastopol. Even more cruel was the icy winter that now settled in earnest over the Crimea. Freezing winds howled over the men lying half naked in the mud. Not a stick of wood remained to be burned in their campfires.

These gaunt skeletons were more pitiful than the victims of wounds who had come into Scutari earlier. They arrived so filthy and so covered with vermin that they told the nurses to stay away from them.

"My own mother could not touch me," one of them said.

By the end of November, shiploads of dying men were being landed at Scutari. The overworked doctors felt as though they were trying to stem a tidal wave with a cork. The supply department, weak enough under ordinary circumstances, simply fell apart. The hospital officials were faced with a crisis that the regulation book did not cover. They were standing on the brink of chaos—and they knew it.

"I cannot conceive," an eyewitness later wrote, "as I now calmly look back on the first three weeks after the arrival of the wounded from Inkerman, how it could have been possible to have avoided a state of things too disastrous to contemplate, had not Miss Nightingale been there."

But Miss Nightingale *was* there. As the dreadful days passed, it slowly became clear to the hospital officials that she was the one person in Scutari who could stem this tide of disaster.

The purveyor's stores were empty. Miss Nightingale's were not. Against the advice of Dr. Smith in London, she had bought tons of supplies with her from Marseilles. And now she had something even more important than these. She had Mr. Macdonald.

Mr. Macdonald was the man sent by the London *Times* to spend the thousands of pounds collected in the *Times* relief fund. He had arrived in Scutari just before the Nightingale party. The first thing he did was offer his services and his money to the British ambassador, the elegant Lord Stratford de Redcliffe.

Lord Stratford was not in the least enthusiastic. The *Times,* he informed Mr. Macdonald, had been sadly misinformed. The hospitals were well provided with everything they needed. The handsome ambassador was simply quoting what he had been told by the chief medical officer. He had never actually inspected the hospitals himself. The mere thought of it made him ill.

He did have a suggestion to make to Mr. Macdonald, however. Since there was no need for the *Times* fund in the hospitals, might it not be used to build an English church in Turkey?

Mr. Macdonald withdrew, his money still in his pocket. The next person he visited was Miss Nightingale. Did she have any needs that could be filled by the *Times* fund? Yes, Miss Nightingale had said eagerly. Would the *Times* be willing to buy her two hundred scrubbing brushes and some sacking for washing the floors?

Mr. Macdonald immediately put himself and his money completely at the command of Miss Nightingale. She had come to Scutari only as Superintendent of the Female Nursing Establishment. Before she had been there a month, she was, unofficially, the chief supply officer for the hospitals.

"I am a kind of General Dealer," she wrote to Sidney Herbert, "in socks, shirts, knives and forks, wooden spoons, tin baths, . . . towels and soap, small tooth combs, precipitate for destroying lice, scissors, bedpans and stump pillows."

Once the doctors had given up their opposition to her, they went all the way. The magic formula around the hospital became, "Go to Miss Nightingale!" No matter what was needed, Miss Nightingale could somehow supply it. No matter what insoluble problem arose, Miss Nightingale could somehow solve it. The northwest tower became the nerve center of the hospital.

One of the nurses later recalled the day's activities in the tower kitchen. "From this room," she wrote in her memoirs, "we distributed quantities of arrowroot, sago, rice puddings, jelly, beef-tea, and lemonade upon requisitions made by the surgeons. This caused great comings to and fro. Numbers of orderlies were waiting at the door with requisitions. One of the nuns or a lady received them and saw they were signed and countersigned before serving. We used, among ourselves, to call this kitchen the Tower of Babel. In the middle of the day everything and everybody seemed to be there: boxes, parcels, bundles of sheets, shirts, and old linen and flannels, tubs of butter, sugar, bread, kettles, saucepans, heaps of books, and of all kinds of rubbish, besides the diets which were being dispensed. Then the people, ladies, nuns, nurses, orderlies, Turks, Greeks, French and Italian servants, officers and others waiting to see Miss Nightingale; all passing to and fro, all intent upon their own business, and all speaking their own language."

Florence never relaxed her insistence upon following the regulations. When a doctor asked her for something, she would first apply to the purveyor. Only after he had sent back the request stamped "None in store" would she send Mr. Macdonald and his money into Constantinople to buy it. The purveyor complained bitterly that Miss Nightingale would never give him *time* to do anything before rushing off to get it done herself.

Florence was only too well aware of his ideas about time. One day she sent him an order from the staff surgeon for a bale of shirts. It came back stamped "None in store." She marched into his office and announced that 27,000 shirts had been sent from England at her request and that the ship they were on had already landed.

They may have been landed, the purveyor

whined, but he could not release them. Miss Nightingale knew perfectly well that until a board of survey had inspected every shipment of goods from England, he could not release a single item!

"How long will it take the board to inspect this shipment?" she asked calmly.

"Three weeks at the least."

The next day the men who needed the shirts had shirts—courtesy of Miss Nightingale and the London *Times*. She later calculated that she had provided the British army with 50,000 shirts. She did more than supply the clothing: she finally got it washed. The laundry problem had worried her from her first day in the hospital. She solved it by renting a house nearby, buying hot-water boilers with *Times* funds, and hiring soldiers' wives to do the washing.

These wives were another problem. Crushed as she already was with work, Florence could not ignore the pitiful state of the women and children who had foolishly been allowed to go to Turkey with the soldiers. The Crimean campaign was supposed to have been a three-week sightseeing tour. It had not worked out that way at all, and by now the stranded women were in a pathetic state. They were herded together in an airless basement under the Barrack Hospital. Officially, of course, they did not exist. They were nobody's responsibility, and no one in authority cared whether they lived or died.

But Florence did. Fortunately she soon found exactly the right person to take charge of them. This was Lady Alicia Blackwood, who had come to Scutari with her missionary husband. As soon as she arrived she had gone straight to Miss Nightingale to ask what she could do to help.

She was not the first lady who had come around and asked to help. This explained why Florence's lip curled a bit as she answered Lady Alicia's question with one of her own. "Do you really mean what you say?"

"Yes, certainly! Why do you ask?"

"Because I have had several such applications before," Florence said, "and when I suggested work, I found it could not be done, or some excuse was made. It wasn't the sort of thing intended, or it required special suitability, et cetera."

Lady Alicia smiled sympathetically. She too knew the type. "Well, I *am* in earnest. We came out with no other wish than to help where we could."

"Very well, then, you really can help. In this

barrack are now located some two hundred poor women in the most abject misery. They are in rags and are covered with vermin. My heart bleeds for them, but my work is with the soldiers, not with their wives. Will you undertake to look after them?"

Lady Alicia would and did. She put the women to work in the laundry and set them to making bandages. Later she started a school for the children. Mr. Bracebridge helped her by becoming the official food-dispenser for the hungry women. He soon regretted it, for he now had a pack of women and children clamoring outside his door at all hours of the night and day. The Turks twitted him unmercifully about the unusual number of his "wives."

By early December the two hospitals were filled to the last inch of corridor. Yet winter was just beginning and everyone in Scutari knew what must happen before it was over. A letter from Lord Raglan, the commander-in-chief of the army, confirmed these fears. Five hundred more sick and wounded men were on their way, he wrote. And more would follow. The medical officers were aghast. There was no room in the hospital for even five new cases—let alone five hundred!

Florence knew that some kind of bold action would have to be taken. This was not a case of simply moving mattresses closer together and squeezing in the new men. She went to Dr. McGrigor, her staunchest ally among the medical men, and told him her idea.

A wing of the building had been burned out before the British army had taken over the barrack. If it could be repaired, it would provide space for at least a thousand men. And it could easily be repaired by Turkish workmen.

Dr. McGrigor was aghast. Exactly who, he asked Miss Nightingale, was going to pay the wages of these Turkish workmen?

The British ambassador would pay them, Florence announced firmly. Sidney Herbert had told her that Lord Stratford was authorized by the government to spend any amount of money that was necessary. This was surely the time to call upon him and his money!

Dr. McGrigor agreed, although he had serious doubts. This was not the proper, official, *correct* way to do business. Properly, the Chief Medical Officer in the area should write to the Army Medical Service in London. The Director General of the Army Medical Service would then take the matter up with the Horse Guard, and the Horse Guard would, in turn, refer the matter to Ordnance. Ordnance would then petition the Treasury. If the Treasury agreed, the building would then be rebuilt. But that, Dr. McGrigor sadly reflected, would be about a year after Lord Raglan's wounded men arrived.

Miss Nightingale sent an urgent message to Lord Stratford. Lord Stratford replied by sending Lady Stratford to look into the matter. Lady Stratford, who could not bring herself to go inside the hospital, stood in the courtyard, notebook in hand, arranging things with Major Sillery, the military commandant. To Florence's relief and surprise, the work was approved. One hundred and twenty-five Turkish workmen were hired to begin it immediately. A few days later the workmen went out on strike. Florence again got in touch with Lord Stratford. Lord Stratford suddenly decided that he knew nothing at all about the business. Who knows why? Perhaps he did not wish to become involved in a Turkish labor dispute. Lady Stratford announced that she was no longer available for consultation.

And by this time the five hundred new patients were halfway across the Black Sea. Furious and disgusted, Florence went out and hired two hundred other Turks and put them to work. She paid them herself, partly from the *Times* fund and partly from her own money. The work was finished on the day the first of the sick men were landed.

Nothing that Florence had done since her ar-

rival created such a stir as this incident. Old army men groaned in anguish at this new evidence of what they called "the Nightingale power." A gruff colonel in the Crimea wrote indignantly, "Miss Nightingale coolly draws a cheque! Is this the way to manage the finances of a great nation?" His indignation was doubled some weeks later when word reached the Crimea that the government had officially approved Miss Nightingale's forceful action and had refunded every penny she had spent. "Miss Nightingale," he complained, "now queens it with absolute power!"

The men who came from the frozen trenches before Sebastopol felt differently about what she had done. One of them, after he had been washed, shaved, and put into clean clothes and a clean bed, opened his eyes and looked around the ward in surprise. "Am I in the hospital?" he said to the nurse by his bedside. "I thought I must be in Heaven."

Calamity Unparalleled

"There's something I have to say to you, Ma'am!"

Florence looked up from her table. She had snatched a rare moment of leisure to write a letter to Sidney Herbert. "What is it, Mrs. Lawfield?"

"Well, Ma'am, it's just this. I came out here prepared to submit to everything and to be put upon in every way! But—" Mrs. Lawfield paused. She was clearly fighting for the right word.

"Yes? And what's the trouble?" Florence said encouragingly, putting down her pen.

"It's these *caps*, Ma'am!" the nurse finally exploded, pointing a finger at her headgear. "They suits one face and they don't suit another. And they don't suit *mine!* And if I'd *known* about the caps, Ma'am, great as was my desire to come out to nurse at Scutari, I wouldn't have come, Ma'am!"

Florence sighed and picked up her pen. "I'm afraid that's too important a question for me to settle right at the moment, Mrs. Lawfield. Could we discuss it later?"

What to do with five hundred new patients? How to supply all the needs of two hospitals? How to clothe half the British army? These were not the only problems the Superintendent of Nurses was called upon to solve during the terrible days of that winter. There was also the shape of Mrs. Lawfield's face. And there were the hundred other problems that rose every day in dealing with forty women.

Mrs. Lawfield, as it turned out, became a good nurse and even learned to live with her cap. Mrs. Roberts and Mrs. Drake were superb. A few of the other hired nurses were passable, but most of them gave Florence more trouble than they were worth. One had already been sent home as impossible.

The Sellonite Sisters were good nurses, but they tended to grumble about the hardships of hospital life. More serious, some of them bitterly resented Florence's strict regulations about following the doctors' orders. Sister Elizabeth thought, with good reason, that the men should get more to eat. She wrote an angry letter to her family complaining about the medical men. The letter somehow got into the *Times*. The doctors were furious. Even though Sister Elizabeth was sent home, some of the doctors chose to feel that the nurses were all disloyal and critical.

The rest of the party varied. The five nuns from the Norwood orphanage never grumbled about anything, but they had no nursing experience and they did not learn quickly. They were like angels with no hands, Florence thought. The prize members of the group soon proved to be the five Sisters of Mercy from Bermondsey. Their Superior, Mother Mary Clare, whom everyone called "Reverend Mother Bermondsey," was a tower of strength. She was Florence's staunchest friend and supporter in the trouble that lay ahead. Without her Reverend Mother, Florence later wrote, the mission could not possibly have succeeded. Even Mrs. Clark, who had been mightily suspicious at first, finally succumbed to the efficiency and unfailing good humor of the five Bermondsey nuns. "There's no doubt at all," she muttered grudgingly one day, "but that them nuns will get into the Kingdom of Heaven long before any of us!"

Florence had felt from the beginning that forty women were too many for any one person to keep in hand. But she had given in to Sidney Herbert on the point. By mid-December she felt that she was actually beginning to bring some order and unity to the group. What a shock it was, then, to learn one day that a party of forty-seven more nurses had just been sent out from England under the leadership of her friend Mary Stanley.

Sidney Herbert had agreed that *no* extra nurses were to be sent unless Florence herself asked for them. But in England the enthusiasm over the mission was so tremendous that poor Sidney Herbert had finally given way to the pressure and had allowed the second party to go. Worst of all, the new group was told to report not to Miss Nightingale but to Dr. Cumming at the General Hospital. This arrangement might have been made in the foggy belief that it would save Florence some trouble. What it actually did was to cast serious doubts on the full authority she had been promised.

Florence read the news in cold, silent fury. Then she sat down to write Sidney Herbert a blistering letter of protest. Few people have ever been able

to write a more blistering letter than Florence
Nightingale. In it she recalled her original opinion about the desirable number of nurses. "I sac-
rificed my own judgment and went out with forty
females, well knowing that half that number would
be more efficient and less trouble, and that the
difficulty of inducing forty untrained women, in
so extraordinary a position as this (turned loose
among 3000 men) to observe any order . . . would be
Herculean.

"Experience has justified my foreboding. But I
have toiled my way into the confidence of the
medical men. I have, by incessant vigilance, day
and night, introduced something like order into
the disorderly operations of these women. And
the plan may be said to have succeeded in some
measure, *as it stands*. . . .

"At this point of affairs arrives, at *no one's*
requisition, a fresh batch of women, raising our
number to eighty-four. . . .

"The quartering of them *here* is a physical im-
possibility, the employment of them a moral im-
possibility."

She went on in this vein and then added a post-
script which points out for us one of the chief

problems caused by the arrival of the new recruits.

"P.S. Had I had the enormous folly to write at the end of eleven days' experience to require more women, would it not seem that you, as a Statesman, should have said, 'Wait until you can see your way better.' But I made no such request. The proportion of Roman Catholics which is already making an outcry you have raised to 25 in 84. Dr. Menzies has declared that he will have two only in the General Hospital—and I cannot place them here in a greater proportion than I have done without exciting the suspicion of the Medical Men and others."

All during Florence Nightingale's crushing labors in the Crimean War, her work was hampered by bickering among religious groups.

Today we may still see occasional examples of religious prejudice. But fortunately we have nothing that can compare with the violent religious feelings of nineteenth-century England.

Murmurs had already been heard because ten of Florence's party were Roman Catholic nuns. Mary Stanley's party included fifteen more nuns, led by a fiery Irish woman named Mother Bridgeman. There were also Florence's fourteen Anglican Sisters to be considered. The religious feeling was by no means limited to a simple case of Protestant versus Catholic. Within the established Church of England, there was distrust between "high church" and "low church" groups. Protestants outside the Church of England distrusted all of them.

Someone in England now sat down and added up the number of Roman Catholic and high Anglican nurses in the combined parties. Overnight the religious storm was blowing full blast. Angry Presbyterians wrote letters to the newspapers demanding that some Presbyterian nurses be sent immediately. An army chaplain wrote to the War Office and asked for the removal of a nurse who was said to belong to a sect called the Socinians. Another nurse was denounced for circulating "improper books in the wards." She had merely lent a man a copy of *The Christian Year,* by an Anglican writer who leaned in the direction of Rome.

Charges and counter-charges flew back and forth. Catholic nurses were accused of trying to convert Protestant soldiers, and Protestant nurses were accused of trying to convert Catholic soldiers. Angry letters in a newspaper declared that Miss Nightingale herself must be in secret league with Rome. Liz Herbert replied in the same paper that Florence was a member of the Church of England, was "low church" in feeling, and had actually been brought up a Unitarian. This did not convince an Evangelical minister, who wrote back that Miss Nightingale was certainly a secret Roman agent; otherwise why would Catholic nuns have "transferred their allegiance from the Pope of Rome to a Protestant lady?"

Maddening as it all was, the Bermondsey Sisters could not help enjoying this last bit. From then on Sister Mary Gonzaga solemnly referred to Florence as "your Holiness." Florence promptly named the Sister "my Cardinal."

The loyal support of Reverend Mother Bermondsey was doubly useful now that the fierce Mother Bridgeman was in Scutari. The Irish superior refused to acknowledge Florence's authority and would not let her nuns take orders from anyone but herself. Florence privately called her "the Reverend Brickbat."

And all this petty bickering was going on during the ghastly winter days, when dying men were pouring into the hospital by the thousands and

117

the remnant of the British army was freezing in the trenches before Sebastopol.

Eventually Mary Stanley's party was sent to staff newly opened hospitals in nearby Koulali.

Just before Christmas, a small but comforting incident bolstered Florence's morale. A letter came from Windsor Castle to say that "your goodness and self devotion in giving yourself up to the soothing attendance upon these wounded and sick soldiers has been observed by the Queen with sentiments of the highest approval and admiration." The Queen also sent gifts which she asked Florence to distribute to the men. Florence was already overwhelmed with the gifts—some valuable, some useless—that people in England were sending out by the shipload. She had put Selina in charge of this free gift storeroom. Needless to say, regulations demanded a full report on the receipt and final use of every knitted scarf and glass of jelly received.

When the Queen asked Florence for suggestions about other gifts that she might send, Florence thought of something that would mean more to the men than a royal batch of knitted scarves or socks. The army regulations concerning the pay of sick and wounded soldiers had been troubling her

for some time. When a man came into the hospital with battle wounds, the army deducted 4½ pence a day from his pay. But when he came in because of sickness, he lost 9 pence a day. Florence felt that a man half-frozen and half-starved to death in the line of duty deserved as much as a man who had actually stopped a bullet. She had already asked the War Office to make the loss of pay the same for sickness as for wounds, but nothing had been done. Now she asked the Queen to take care of the matter as a gift to the men in her hospitals. The regulation was changed with a promptness that astonished the cautious War Office officials.

As the cruel winter dragged on, the plight of the soldiers before Sebastopol became horrible beyond imagination. A small saving in pay, in case of hospitalization, was a slim consolation. On the 8th of January, it was recorded, the Sixty-third Regiment had seven men fit for active duty. There were already twelve thousand patients in the Scutari hospitals. Exhausted doctors and nurses lived in daily fear of the new shiploads that kept arriving from the Crimea. Then another cholera epidemic struck and the British army, Florence wrote to Sidney Herbert, was plunged into a "calamity unparalleled in the history of calamity."

12

Lady With a Lamp

Florence's activities during these days were staggering. How could any one person do so much? "I work in the wards all day and write all night," she explained grimly, with very little exaggeration. Sidney Herbert had asked her to send him confidential reports on the conditions of the army. She had promised to do so and she knew how important it was to keep the promise. When she had checked her wards for the last time at night, she would go back to her little room and sit in the freezing cold, which she had always hated, writing until her fingers were too stiff to write any more.

She sent Herbert a series of brilliant, fully worked-out schemes for reorganizing the hospitals. She outlined a method for clearing the confusion out of the purveying office. She arranged for a government storehouse to receive all goods sent from England, to avoid their loss in the "bottomless pit" that was the Turkish customs house. She set up a system for keeping hospital statistics and saw to it that an army medical school was established in Scutari, so that the grim value of these days would not be wasted. And all during the winter of 1855, she was, to all practical purposes, running the hospitals. "Nursing," she wrote to Sidney Herbert, "is the least of the functions into which I have been forced."

Yet the sick men at Scutari would not have agreed with her. They neither knew nor cared what went on behind the closed doors of the northwest tower at night. They did not see their Miss Nightingale as the woman of genius with a will of iron, with a mind—and pen—as sharp as tempered steel. They saw her only as the nurse who somehow managed to be around when they most wanted her there.

"If the soldiers were told that the roof had opened," wrote Richard Monckton Milnes to a friend, "and she had gone up to Heaven, they would not be the least surprised. They quite believe she is in several places at once." It is easy to see why they thought so. Sometimes it seemed the only possible explanation. The power of being in two places at once would have been a most convenient gift, Florence must have thought on many a bitter cold night, as she walked across the long, wind-swept field that separated the General Hospital from the Barrack Hospital.

There was another touch of the superhuman about her. She had an uncanny way of knowing where and when she was most needed. "I believe," wrote a civilian volunteer, Dr. Pincoffs, "that there was never a severe case of any kind that escaped her notice, and sometimes it was wonderful to see her at the bedside of a patient who had been admitted perhaps but an hour before, and of whose arrival one would hardly have supposed it possible she could be already cognisant."

Her effect on the men was enormous. "If the Queen was to die," said one victim of the Alma, "they ought to make *her* Queen, and I think they would." Another man wrote, "She was wonderful at cheering up any one who was a bit low." And, "She was all full of life and fun when she talked to us, especially if a man was a bit down-hearted."

Another soldier records this great tribute, perhaps the greatest of all, considering that she was living in an army barrack. "Before she came, there

was cussing and swearing, but after that it was holy as a church."

She never let a man die alone. If she could not stay with him to the end, she sent Selina. "The more awful . . . any particular case," wrote a chaplain, "especially if it was that of a dying man, the more certainly might her slight form be seen bending over him, administering to his ease by every means in her power, and seldom quitting his side till death released him."

She became the center and the hope of the sick men's lives. Their letters home were filled with her, and through these letters her name became a byword in thousands of English homes. "What a comfort it was to see her pass even," wrote one of her men, in the most famous of all letters about Florence Nightingale. "She would speak to one and nod and smile to as many more; but she could not do it to all, you know. We lay there by hundreds. But we could kiss her shadow as it fell, and lay our heads on the pillow again, content."

This was the passage that inspired the American poet Longfellow to write the poem on which the popular image of Florence Nightingale is based.

> Lo! in that hour of misery
> A lady with a lamp I see
>   Pass through the glimmering gloom,
>   And flit from room to room.
> And slow, as in a dream of bliss,
> This speechless sufferer turns to kiss
>   Her shadow as it falls
>   Upon the darkening walls.

A bleak February passed, but in March two things happened that finally ended the crisis. The first was inevitable. Spring came, and the bitter snows of the Crimea melted away.

The second event was not so simple. It had to be arranged.

A Sanitary Commission of three men was sent from England by the new Prime Minister, Florence's old friend, Lord Palmerston. The three men had orders not only to investigate the abuses in the army but to *do* something about them. The orders under which the Commission sailed had a certain familiar ring. In fact, said the historian of the Crimean War, Mr. Kinglake, "The tone of the instructions is peculiar, and such as to make one believe that they owed much to feminine impulsion. The diction of the orders is such that, in housekeeper's language, it may be said to have 'bustled the servants.' " The orders did indeed have "a feminine impulsion." Florence had all but dictated them from three thousand miles away.

Everything that she had urged and entreated in her reports was now done. Orders began to fly. Someone had finally appeared in Scutari ready to take responsibility for something! The sewer under the hospital was cleaned out; the drains were opened; the floorboards were disinfected; the rats were driven out; the water supply was purified. It had taken six months of misery before these things were done, but the commission, Florence later said, "saved the British army." The effect was felt immediately. The death rate in the hospital quickly dropped from 420 to 22 per thousand.

In May of 1855, Florence decided to go for the first time into the Crimea and inspect the hospitals there. She knew very well that with the coming of spring the fighting before Sebastopol would be renewed. If the hospitals in Balaclava could be put in proper condition, the wounded men could be cared for on the spot and thus escape the awful sea voyage to Scutari.

She was not encouraged by what she had heard of the Crimean hospitals. Nurses from Mary Stanley's party had been installed there by Dr. John Hall, the chief medical officer of the campaign. Since he had been working in the Crimea, Florence had not yet met him, but she had been an extremely painful thorn in his side ever since her arrival in Scutari. The report of the Sanitary Commission had been an added blow to the surly pride of Dr. Hall. Every fault the Commission had found with his hospitals he regarded, quite correctly, as a slap in the face.

Naturally Dr. Hall had taken sides with Mother

Bridgeman and her followers, since by doing so he could cast doubts on the authority of the hated Miss Nightingale. And when he heard that Miss Nightingale was actually invading the Crimea, he produced another weapon against her.

Florence's original orders, issued by Sidney Herbert in October of 1854, appointed her "Superintendent of the Female Nursing Establishment in the English Military General Hospitals in Turkey." *In Turkey.* Aha, said Dr. Hall, triumphantly, the Crimea was not in Turkey but in Russia! Miss Nightingale therefore had no authority in any hospital in the Crimea. Obviously the orders had been worded as they were because in the beginning Herbert had not supposed that any nurses at all would be sent so close to the fighting front. Dr. Hall, ignoring this simple explanation, used the technicality to harass Florence for the next eleven months.

When she landed at Balaclava, Dr. Hall was not among the crowd that hastened to the ship to greet her. But reports of her reception must have infuriated him. The afternoon of her arrival, accompanied, it seemed, by every high officer and every government official in the Crimea, she rode out to visit the encampment before Sebastopol.

She looked like "a genteel Amazone," according to her traveling companion, a famous French chef named Soyer who had come out to cook for the troops. She rode, he wrote, "a very pretty mare which, by its gambols and caracoling, seemed proud to carry its noble charge, and our cavalcade produced an extraordinary effect upon the motley crowd of all nations assembled at Balaclava, who were astonished at seeing a lady so well escorted."

When word spread that the "genteel Amazone" was none other than Miss Nightingale, the men rushed out to greet her. The traditional British cheer, the "three times three," all but rattled the enemy windows in Sebastopol.

As soon as she began her hospital inspection, Florence could feel that she was in enemy territory. The nurses were hostile and in no hurry to follow her directions about the sadly needed improvements in their hospitals. There was no doubt in her mind about who was behind all this. It could only be a matter of time, she realized, before she came to a head-on clash with Dr. John Hall.

But the clash did not come immediately. A few days after her arrival in Balaclava, she suddenly collapsed, after complaining of unusual fatigue. The doctors who rushed to her side found that she was suffering from the severe infection they called simply "Crimean fever."

Terrifying rumors spread from Balaclava to Scutari, and from there to England. In Scutari the men in the hospitals turned their faces to the wall and cried. In London strangers stopped strangers on the street to ask whether they had heard the terrible news that Miss Nightingale was dying.

13

National Heroine

When Florence sailed for Scutari in October of 1854, she was well known only to her own rather select circle of friends. But within six months she had become a national heroine. From the very beginning, her adventures had stirred the imagination of the public. Newspaper writers could not have asked for a more perfect "human interest" item. They ground out pages of appealing, if inaccurate, stories about the brave young lady who had unwillingly left her beloved family, and her life of ease and pleasure, to tend the suffering soldiers.

The Victorian era was a sentimental one. Within a few months of Florence's departure the song writers of London had flooded the market with heart-rending ballads in which melody and lyrics combined to bring tears to the eyes. "Angels with Sweet Approving Smiles," "The Shadow on the Pillow," "The Woman's Smile" were among the favorite songs about Miss Nightingale. But the most popular of all was "The Nightingale in the East." ("So forward my lads, may your hearts never fail. You are cheered by the presence of a sweet Nightingale.")

A lady author rushed into print with a pamphlet claiming to be "The Only and Unabridged Edition of the Life of Miss Nightingale, Detailing her Christian Heroic Deeds in the Land of Tumult and Death, which has made her name most deservedly Immortal, not only in England but in all Civilised Parts of the World, winning the Prayers of the Soldier, the Widow, and the Orphan."

China statuettes and color engravings of a lady wearing a pink dress and a lace cap, labeled "Florence Nightingale," were sold by the thousands. Ships and streets were named after her. In one of the major English horse races of the year, "Miss Nightingale beat a horse named "Barbarity" by a nose. And all over the world baby girls by the hundreds were being named Florence.

"Yes indeed," Parthe wrote her, "the people love you with a sort of passionate tenderness that goes to my heart!"

Everything about Flo's adventures in Turkey went straight to Parthe's heart. Her role as sister of a heroine delighted her, and at last she had something to occupy her time. She was in charge of answering letters from the hundreds of people who wrote the Nightingale family to inquire whether knitted socks or mittens would be more useful in the Crimea. "I am quite *done* with writing," she wrote to her girl friend, "a second blast of linen and knitted socks was nearly the death of me, and 'hints,' my dear—oh, my horror of being asked for hints, such as 'can newspapers be put in the post free' . . . It sounds very ungrateful, I am afraid, but when one's wrist aches over the two hundredth repetition of the matter, I do wish the public would apply to the nearest post-office and use their sense, not their pens." It is a wonder that Parthe survived the Crimean War.

It is easy to see, then, why the news of Florence's illness was such a blow to the people of England. And when further news came that she was out of danger and eager to be back at work, a fresh wave of love and gratitude swept over the country. Some kind of public tribute, her friends decided, was long overdue.

But what should it be? One of Florence's committee ladies suggested a properly inscribed bracelet. Another thought a silver tea service would be more suitable. Liz Herbert shuddered at the thought of what Florence would say to all this. She would never, the Herberts knew better than anyone, accept anything as a personal tribute. The gift would have to be something that could be used to further her work.

After several months of planning, a public meeting was called for November 29, 1855. Never, the *Times* said the next morning, "had a more brilliant, enthusiastic, and unanimous gathering been held in London." At this meeting, Sidney Herbert announced the foundation of the Nightingale Fund to be used for the establishment of a school to train nurses.

"It is very late, my child," Mrs. Nightingale wrote Florence that night, "but I cannot go to bed without telling you that your meeting has been a glorious one. I believe that you will be more indifferent than any of us to your fame, but be glad that we feel this is a proud day for us. For the like has never happened before, but will, I trust, from your example, gladden the hearts of many future mothers."

"If my name and my having done what I could for God and mankind has given you pleasure," Florence replied, "that is real pleasure for to me . . . . Life is sweet after all." There were volumes of unspoken meaning in the last line, but Mrs. Nightingale probably did not notice it.

A letter from Sidney Herbert formally offered Florence the use of the fund for establishing a school of nursing. He asked her how she would like the committee to go about starting the project. If Florence had been the storybook heroine of the Nightingale legend, she might have started to draw up plans for the nursing school. The real Florence wrote a very polite letter of thanks to Sidney Herbert, expressing her appreciation and thanks. Then she added, just a bit impatiently, that she really did have a few other things on her mind at the moment. She would accept the committee's offer only if it was clearly understood that she would get around to thinking about it later. And she had no idea of just when this would be!

While enthusiastic Nightingale Fund meetings

were being held all over England, Florence herself continued to fight her own bleak battle in the Crimea. The hardships of the early days were replaced by the galling annoyance of petty jealousy and intrigue.

Sebastopol had fallen in September of 1855. The end of the war was only a matter of time. Now that the crisis was safely passed, some of the very people who had turned to Florence for help gradually began to feel that she really was not so important after all. "Everything's going to be all right now," they seemed to think; "so we don't need Miss Nightingale. any more. We can go back to running things *our* way."

For six months after her recovery, Florence lived in a state of constant warfare with Dr. Hall. He still argued that she had no authority in any Crimean hospital. "Dr. Hall," she wrote furiously, "does not think it beneath him to broil me slowly upon the fires of my own extra-diet kitchen and to give out that we are private adventurers and are to be treated as such."

Her work in the Crimea was hard enough even without the obstacles put in her way by Dr. Hall. The Crimean hospitals were widely scattered through rugged country. She had to spend hours of every day on horseback, often in rain and snow, in order to visit them all. Yet the work she was trying to do was hindered at every turn by her opponents.

In February of 1856, Lord Panmure, the new Secretary of State for War, finally issued a General Order stating exactly what Florence's position was. "It appears to me," he wrote, "that the Medical Authorities of the Army do not correctly comprehend Miss Nightingale's position. . . . Miss Nightingale is recognised by Her Majesty's Government as the General Superintendent of the Female Nursing Establishment of the military hospitals of the Army. . . . The Principal Medical Officer will communicate with Miss Nightingale upon all subjects connected with the Female Nursing Establishment and will give his directions through that lady."

It was a bitter moment for Dr. Hall. It was a great triumph for Florence. What a lot of trouble she would have been spared if the War Office had not taken quite so long to clear up the point!

Florence had come to Scutari to nurse the sick and wounded. But before she had been there very long she had seen enough of the British soldier's life to realize that he needed help when he was healthy almost as much as he needed it when he was sick. "What the horrors of war are," she wrote to her family, "no one can imagine. They are not wounds, and blood, and fever, and cold, and heat, and famine. They are intoxication, drunken brutality, disorder on the part of the inferior; jealousies, meanness, indifference, selfish brutality on the part of the superior."

The British private soldier, for all his marvelous fighting ability, was considered by his superior officer to be one of the lowest forms of human life. Yet what Florence had learned of the courage and natural goodness of these men did not support this view. The officers assumed, for example, that the soldiers all drank because it was the nature of a soldier to be a drunkard. Florence had realized almost at once that the men in Scutari drank from sheer, desperate boredom. To the mixed horror and amusement of the officers, she set up a fine coffee house, called "The Inkerman Cafe," and opened reading rooms where the men could obtain writing materials and the latest books and magazines from England. She had been solemnly assured that they would steal the writing paper and sell it for drinks, but not one piece was ever lost in this way.

Florence was the first person to solve another

vexing problem for the soldiers. Pay day was the day on which the greatest number of men were carried in half dead from the cheap, nearly poisonous liquor sold in the native grog shops. "Why don't you send your money home to your families before you have a chance to throw it away here?" she had asked the men soon after her arrival. The answer was straightforward. "Because if we gave it to the purveyor to send for us, he'd steal it." Florence was not sure this was true but the men were absolutely convinced of it. So she agreed to act as a private banker. She sent the money home to her Uncle Sam Smith, who then routed it to the soldiers' families.

Eventually the government was stung into action and opened a money-order office in Constantinople to remit the soldiers' money home. "But it will do no good," grumbled Lord Panmure. "The British soldier is *not* a remitting animal!" Within six months, to his Lordship's surprise, over £71,000 ($350,000) had been sent home. The explanation was simple. "I promised *her* I'd send my wife the money," and "I promised *her* I wouldn't spend everything on drink," the men said. And whatever promises they made to *her,* they kept.

When word of the Nightingale Fund reached

the army, the men immediately subscribed over $45,000 to it. Dr. Hall, meanwhile, was pointing out with keen delight that very few of the medical officers had given so much as a penny.

The success of the reading rooms was so great that Florence next tried to start a night school for the men. But this was too much for Lord William Paulet, the Military Commandant. "You are spoiling the brutes!" he snarled at her when she asked permission to open the school. Fortunately a new commandant came to Scutari at the end of 1855 and held a directly opposite view. Two school-

masters and about two thousand school books were sent from England, and there was standing room only at every class held in Scutari.

"She has taught officers and officials to treat the soldiers as Christian men," wrote one observer. Of all that she accomplished in the Crimean War, this was surely the greatest achievement.

The peace treaty with Russia was signed on March 30, 1856. The troops began to be sent home, and soon the last patient had left the hospitals. Toward the end of July, England was buzzing with the news that Miss Nightingale too would soon be returning home. Committees were formed to arrange for her triumphant reception. The bands of the Fusiliers and of the Coldstream and Grenadier Guards planned to meet her at the station in London, day or night, to play her all the way home to Lea Hurst. They begged the Nightingales for information about her expected time of arrival. But no one knew anything about it. Florence had too much sense to let her family in on her travel schedule.

At eight o'clock on the morning of August 7, a heavily veiled lady, traveling under the name of "Miss Smith," was ringing the doorbell at the

Convent of the Sisters of Mercy in Bermondsey. The Sisters had just begun their annual retreat, so the convent was even more quiet than usual on that morning when Florence and her beloved Bermondsey nuns were reunited. Months before she had promised them that if she lived to return to England she would go to them before she saw anyone else. She had not forgotten the promise.

Florence spent most of the day praying with the Sisters. Later that afternoon she left for home. The little station near Lea Hurst was deserted, and no one paid any attention to the lady who got off the afternoon train and walked up to the manor house. The housekeeper, looking curiously out of her window at the visitor strolling up the driveway, suddenly called out, "It's Miss Florence!" and rushed to open the front door.

Florence's homecoming had worked out exactly as she had planned it.

Adviser to Statesmen

In Florence Nightingale's own day, her great fame was based almost entirely on her heroic adventures in the Crimean War. And to a certain extent, so it still is. Yet she herself regarded her war service as the least of all the things she accomplished. It had been a useful starting point for her real work, she believed, but nothing more. It would take a long book indeed to give a detailed account of everything that Florence Nightingale accomplished during the remaining years of her long life.

This work began about a month after Florence's return to England. The weeks immediately following her homecoming had been rather difficult. She had changed so much, and everybody else had changed so little! Well-meant advice about her health poured in from all sides and annoyed her dreadfully. "You have done more than your share!" people told her. "Now you must rest."

Everyone from the Secretary of State to the upstairs maid at Lea Hurst was urging her to rest, to relax, to take the cure, to do nothing, to think about nothing, to forget everything but her health. They were all perfectly right in thinking that she needed a rest, since her health was broken beyond full repair. But how *could* she rest? How could she relax? How could she forget, when she was haunted day and night by her memories of the past two years?

"I stand at the altar of the murdered men," she said. "And while I live, I fight their cause."

The time to begin the fight was *now,* while the conscience of the country was still aroused over the horrors of the war. It would not be aroused very long, she knew. People like to forget such things as quickly as possible. But "these people," she wrote bitterly, ". . . have fed their children on the fat of the land and dressed them in velvet and silk. . . . I have had to see my children dressed in a dirty blanket and an old pair of regimental trousers, and to see them fed on raw salt meat; and nine thousand of my children are

147

lying, from causes which might have been prevented, in their forgotten graves. But I can never
forget!" And she vowed that she would not let
the rest of the country forget. Such a tragedy as
she had seen must never be allowed to happen
again.

She was offered a rare opportunity to launch
her attack. Queen Victoria was summering at Bal-
moral Castle in Scotland. Word came to Lea
Hurst that Her Majesty had a great desire to see
Miss Nightingale personally and to talk with her
about her war experiences. Florence immediately
packed up and left for Scotland, determined to
talk of many other things than her own experiences.

"She laid before us," Prince Albert wrote in his
diary, "all the defects of our present military hospital system and the reforms that are needed."
The Queen herself was awed. *What a head!"* she
exclaimed. "I wish we had her at the War Office!"

What Florence urged on the Queen was the
formation of a Royal Commission to investigate
every detail of the health of the British Army—
the health of the soldier in peace as well as war.
The Queen and her husband were completely won
over both by Florence and by her arguments in

favor of the investigation. But, according to British law, the Queen could not simply order a thing to be done; the monarchy was a limited one. What she *could* do, however, was use her influence on her ministers, as she had recently done in the matter of the sick soldiers' pay.

Only the Secretary of State for War could order the investigating committee into being. The Secretary of State for War was still Lord Panmure, who had once stood up for Florence's rights in his General Orders to the army. This was surely a good sign, but neither Florence nor the Queen was over-confident. Lord Panmure was nicknamed "the bison." He had won the title partly because of his huge head and great mane of hair, but mostly because of his stubborn slowness in acting on any matter that might cause him unpleasantness. But the Queen was sure that if Florence were turned loose on him, the Bison would not be able to resist. She already knew something about him that Florence would soon learn. The Bison was easy to bully.

Florence's first meeting with Lord Panmure was most promising. "You may like to know," wrote a mutual friend gleefully, "that you quite overcame Pan. We found him with his mane absolutely silky, and a loving sadness pervading his whole being." The "Nightingale Power" was still working at full strength.

But it was a slow, weary process to move the Bison to action, even by constant bullying and cajoling. He had to be bullied into forming the Commission in the first place. Next he had to be bullied into agreeing on Florence's choice of the Commissioners. (What good would it do to have men like Dr. Andrew Smith and Dr. John Hall conducting the investigation? They would go right on saying, "Everything is fine as it is. Nothing new is needed.") Next he had to be bullied into setting a date for the hearings to begin. The poor Bison was really in a cruel position. Miss Nightingale was pulling and tugging on one ear, and the old guard at the War Office were pulling and tugging at the other. Whenever the pulling and tugging became too painful, he would simply retire to his estate in Scotland, where it was hard to reach him, and shoot grouse. Or else he would suddenly develop gout in both hands and be unable to answer letters. "His gout," Florence said cynically, "is always very handy!"

Six months passed and still no definite action had been taken. Florence then unleashed her secret weapon. She had been holding it in reserve until the moment it was most needed. "Three months from this day," she wrote, "I publish my experiences of the Crimean Campaign . . . unless there has been a fair and tangible pledge by that time for reform."

This terrible threat went beyond routine bullying. One set of government officials had already been hounded out of office because of a mere newspaper's stories about the Crimean campaign. Lord Panmure groaned at the thought of what might happen if Florence Nightingale, the national heroine, ever released her story to the public. On May 5, the Royal Commission to investigate the health conditions of the army was officially appointed. Its chairman was Sidney Herbert. Its other members had also been hand-picked by Florence.

Now the fighting began in earnest. The amount of work she had done at Scutari was "mere child's play," she said, compared to this. From her stuffy little room in the old Burlington Hotel, she directed every step that was taken by the Commissioners. She knew exactly who the best witnesses would be, and she knew every question that should be asked of each witness. She knew when to be gentle with a witness and when to heckle him. Yet during most of that summer she was lying breathless on her couch, too weak to go out, too sick to eat. Letters and memoranda flew back and forth at a ferocious rate. Sidney Herbert, or some other member of the Commission, was in and out at all hours of the day, asking questions and being coached for the next session. The men called her the "Commander in Chief," and with reason. These were exhausting but exciting days. A great comradeship and loyalty grew up between the members of the "little cabinet," as they called themselves.

Such was the force of custom that Florence, who knew more about the subject than anyone else in the world, did not appear as a witness before the Commission. (Nowadays, of course, she would have been the chairman of it.) Appearing in public before a male audience would be unladylike. She sent her testimony in the form of a written report that bristled with damning facts and figures.

All during these exhausting months, Florence was also writing the book called *Notes on Matters Affecting the Health, Efficiency, and Hospital Administration of the British Army*. It was an incredible feat of strength to turn out those 567 closely printed pages during the same six months that she was running the Royal Commission from her couch. A century later, reading through one of the few remaining copies of the monumental work, one can almost feel the pages sizzling with the white-hot fury in which they were written. The *Notes* were a crushing, unanswerable accusation against the system she had vowed to destroy.

Yet the book was never published. A few copies were privately printed. One of them was sent as a confidential report to Lord Panmure. He put it up on a very high shelf and tried not to think about it.

The core of the book survived in the final report of the Royal Commission, written by Florence and Sidney Herbert in August of 1857. The six-month investigation had produced some terrible statistics. It was not only in wartime that the death rate of the army was high. In the barracks town of St. Pancras, the Commission discovered, the civilian death rate per year was 2.2 per thousand people. But in the barracks themselves the rate was 10.4 per thousand. In another barrack the death rate was 17.5, compared to a civilian rate of 3.3 in the surrounding town.

These figures were eloquent testimony to the conditions of life in the British Army. The civilian population included old people, sick people, and infants, who in those days had a high death rate. But the army, as Florence wrote, "are picked lives. Yet . . . the army dies at twice the mortality rate of the general population. Fifteen hundred good soldiers are certainly killed by these neglects yearly, as if they were drawn up on Salisbury Plain and shot."

Exactly one year to the day after Florence Nightingale's return from the war, Sidney Herbert sent Lord Panmure a confidential report on the findings of the Royal Commission. In his smooth, always courteous way he suggested that the public would not really care for the report. Perhaps the government would like to be ready with *immediate* plans for reform before it was made public? As a matter of fact, he just happened to have on hand a fully-worked-out plan (worked out, of course, by Miss Nightingale) for correcting every single abuse found by the Commission.

Another half a year was wasted before Lord Panmure agreed to the drastic measures called for by the Commission. Another year, filled with discouraging stops and starts, passed. And then something happened that even Florence could not have arranged without the help of Providence and the House of Commons. The House expressed a lack of confidence in the government. In England such a vote in the House of Commons is all it takes to change the government. This meant that the Bison was free at last to shoot grouse in Scotland as long and as peacefully as he wished. The office of Secretary of State for War was now vacant. On June 13, 1859, Sidney Herbert was asked to fill it.

Now at last everything the "little cabinet" had fought for was theirs. Military hospitals were remodeled and barracks were completely rebuilt. They were ventilated and heated and properly lit. These things were all unheard-of luxuries. The terrible army diet was revised; the kitchens were made civilized; the water supply was made drinkable. Even the Purveyor was remembered, and for the first time his duties were set down in black and white. An army medical school was founded to give proper training to the medical officers. The medical department itself was reorganized so that it could care for the health of the soldier *before* he became sick as well as after. The off-duty hours of the soldier were finally brought to the attention of the War Office. All the reforms that Florence had tried on a small scale in Scutari now became part of the regular army.

Florence's health was by now completely shattered. She spent the rest of her life in semi-retirement, lying on her couch and doing the work of ten strong men. For many years she was convinced that she was on the point of death. She drove herself all the harder because there was still so much she wanted to do before she died.

It was not only herself that she drove. She was

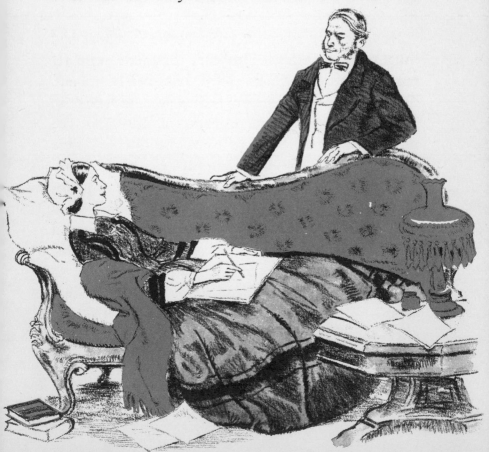

a hard, often cruel, taskmaster to the loyal handful of people who quite literally had handed over their lives to her. Dr. Sutherland had met her in Scutari when he came out as a member of the Sanitary Commission. He became her confidential secretary and was seldom away from her for a whole week in thirty years. Arthur Hugh Clough, the poet, lived and died in her service. He would be good for odd jobs, such as mailing packages and buying railroad tickets, he had told her when they met for the first time. Aunt Mai cut herself off from her family and friends for two years in order to guard the invalid from the outside world. When she finally went home, Florence was furious with her for deserting her post. And Sidney Herbert—

Sidney Herbert knew even when he took the post as Secretary of State for War that he was dying. A lingering, incurable disease made his last years of life a misery. But Florence, whose neurotic illnesses and weaknesses were *not* caused by an actual disease, never really believed that Sidney Herbert was sick. She would not permit him to be sick. Without him the work would fall apart. And surely no sacrifice was too much to ask if it furthered the work!

In 1860 she set out on the most crushing and

heartbreaking task she had yet assigned herself and Herbert. The reforms they had brought about would last as long as Sidney Herbert was in office. But who could be sure that some new Secretary would not simply sweep them aside, if he happened to be an enemy of reform? Only one thing could safeguard the advances they had made: the complete reorganization of the War Office.

Sidney Herbert knew that he was mad even to think of undertaking such a thing. The dust and cobwebs of generations clung to the War Office. He would not be the first minister who went down in defeat before the task of shaking them loose. But who could resist the fierce zeal of Florence Nightingale? Not Sidney Herbert. "One fight more, the best and the last!" she urged, and she really believed that this dying man could carry it off, if only he would *try* a little harder.

It was indeed his last fight. He died in August of 1861. He had already admitted defeat to Florence, and she had treated him in a way that hung over her conscience for the rest of her life. "Poor Florence," he murmured in his last semiconscious moment, "poor Florence! Our joint work . . . unfinished." He had been faithful literally to his last breath.

Founder of
Modern Nursing

Florence's influence at the War Office lasted through several new Secretaries. But her great dream of reforming the Office itself died with Sidney Herbert, whom she mourned for the rest of her life.

There was much to take its place. She had already begun the staggering task of reforming the conditions of army life in India. In those days the whole of India was under British control, and Indian affairs were the greatest problem of the Empire. Florence herself considered her work for India the most important thing she accomplished. This invalid woman, who rarely left her bedroom in London, became known as one of the world's leading authorities on India. For many years it was the unfailing custom for any newly appointed viceroy of India to go and be briefed by Miss Nightingale before leaving England.

In 1859 Florence had published her *Notes on Hospitals.* Her ideas on hospital construction and sanitation were revolutionary. Today we take for granted hundreds of details of hospital life first thought of by Florence Nightingale. Between 1850 and 1900, scarcely a hospital in the world was built without Florence's direct advice and assistance. Her correspondence during these years was a life's work in itself.

Let us now return to this year 1859 and follow the fortunes of still another Nightingale revolution. It is the one that means the most to us a century later.

This was the year in which Florence was working hardest to enforce the report of the Royal Commission. It was also the year in which she published *Notes on Hospitals.* In the midst of all this she somehow found time to write a little book called *Notes on Nursing.* Of all her writings, it is the one that is most read and appreciated today. In its own day it created a sensation. Within a month after publication it had sold 15,000 copies and a new edition had to be rushed into print. A revised paperback edition was brought out called, in the forthright manner of the day, *Notes on Nursing for the Labouring Classes.* For this edition Florence wrote the famous chapter called "Minding Baby." It begins: "And now, girls, I have a word for you. You and I have all had a great deal to do with minding baby, even though 'baby' was not our own baby." This was the first bit of practical advice ever written for the guidance of baby-sitters.

At the time the *Notes* appeared in print, four years had passed since Florence's return from war. Many people during those years had wondered, "Whatever became of Florence Nightingale?" But few people knew the answer. The heroine of the Crimea, it was generally believed, had simply retired to a well-earned rest. What she had really been doing during those years was kept a well-guarded secret. How surprised the people of England would have been if they had known that every piece of army reform achieved since the end of the Crimean War had originated in the Burlington Hotel, and had been forced into existence by Florence Nightingale—the gentle "Lady with a Lamp."

When *Notes on Nursing* appeared, all the tender memories of the lamp-carrying lady were resurrected. Florence Nightingale, the would-be reorganizer of the War Office, was unknown. But Florence Nightingale, the nurse, was still known and loved all over England.

The book is a small masterpiece, as fresh, as biting, as full of wisdom today as it was in 1859. The chapter on what to do and what not to do when visiting the sick should be handed out at the door of every hospital during visiting hours. In its own day the book was unique. It was not only a practical, common-sense handbook on how to take care of the sick, but also a treasury of advice on how to stay healthy. "I am delighted with the *Notes*," wrote a leading doctor of the day. "They will do more to call attention to household hygiene than anything that has ever been written." "Household hygiene" is something we take very much for granted today. A hundred years ago it was a novel idea. Florence herself was delighted with the hundreds of letters she got from readers who just wanted her to know that from then on they planned to open their windows at night.

The huge public response to *Notes on Nursing* once more focused attention on the Nightingale

Fund for establishing a nurses' training school. With contributions of $200,000 to start with, the fund had been well invested at high interest and was growing alarmingly each year.

All during her exhausting years of work for the army, the thought of the Nightingale Fund had been hanging over Florence's head and conscience. She *must* do something soon to start the work that had once been the great ambition of her life. By the end of 1859 she was in such poor health that she fully expected to be dead within a few months. She did not want to die with the matter of the school still unsettled.

Florence could not even consider running the school herself. She could barely leave her couch. Hopefully she wrote to Elizabeth Blackwell, begging her to undertake the post of Superintendent of Nurses. But Elizabeth declined. She was unwilling to give up the practice of medicine for which she had fought so long and hard.

Florence had already decided to make the new school part of an already established hospital. She had been swamped with offers from institutions only too eager to get their share of the rich Nightingale Fund. Her choice was old St. Thomas' Hospital near London Bridge. The medical staff of St. Thomas' was sympathetic to her ideas and offered a wing of the building for use as a nurses' home. But what really decided her in favor of the hospital was its Superintendent of Nurses, a rare treasure of a woman named Mrs. Wardroper.

This Mrs. Wardroper, Florence decided, was exactly what the situation called for. She was part nurse, part gentlewoman, and part dragon. Years after their training was over, old Nightingale nurses still turned pale at the mere mention of Mrs. Wardroper.

Arrangements were basically simple. The hospital would undertake to train the nurses. The Nightingale Fund would pay all the expenses of room and board, laundry, uniforms, and pocket money. In May of 1860 the newspapers carried the first advertisement of the school. Florence and Mrs. Wardroper then began to weed out the most promising applicants. On June 24, 1860, fifteen probationers were admitted to the Nightingale School.

From this small beginning grew the modern art and practice of nursing.

Florence Nightingale did not invent nursing. Women had been caring for the sick since the beginning of human history. Nor was she the first woman to nurse soldiers in a hospital. Catholic Sisters had been doing it for years. She was not even the first person to urge reforms among the hospital nurses of England. But she is unquestionably the founder of modern nursing.

What single characteristic of a Nightingale nurse set her apart from her predecessors? Until very recently people always referred to graduate nurses as "trained nurses." The phrase is still used. It was Florence Nightingale who put in the adjective "trained."

The opening of the Nightingale School was not greeted with loud praise on all sides. In the long history of medicine, not one single step forward has ever been taken without objections from somebody. Who objected most to the idea of trained nurses? Doctors. It would take a long essay on the pure contrariness of human nature to explain why. Of a hundred doctors questioned at the time the school was opened, only four were in favor of it. Why did anyone think that nurses required any special *training?* Training for *what?* And whose outlandish idea was it to have nurses attend lectures on medical subjects? It was an impertinence, as well as a waste of time!

166

"Nurses," explained one anti-Nightingale doctor, "are in much the same position as housemaids and need little teaching beyond poultice-making." Another one said, "A nurse is a confidential servant, but still only a servant. She should be middle-aged when she begins nursing, and if somewhat tamed by marriage and the troubles of a family, so much the better."

An aura still surrounded the name of Florence Nightingale, but it did not help very much. Florence Nightingale doing heroic deeds in a war three thousand miles away was an admirable creature. But Florence Nightingale trying to upset the old, comfortable, civilian ways of doing things at home was simply a nuisance.

Florence was not surprised by this attitude. She had not really expected anything else. The sheer contradiction of it amused her. "An uneducated man who practices medicine," she wrote acidly, "is justly called a quack, perhaps an impostor. Why are not uneducated nurses called quacks and impostors? Simply, I suppose, because there are few who think a man can understand medicine and surgery by instinct. But till the last ten to twenty years, people in England thought that every woman was a nurse by instinct."

The opposition of the medical profession put an extra burden on the brave fifteen who entered St. Thomas' Hospital in June of 1860. They were real pioneers of nursing, just as the nurses who had gone to Scutari in 1854 had been. Since so much depended on them, a great deal was expected of them.

In the early days of the school, the training period was one year. In order to be admitted as a probationer a girl had to come bearing letters of good character from a clergyman, doctor, teacher, or other respectable citizen. Once she was installed in the school, her character became the personal responsibility of the eagle-eyed Superintendent of Nurses. An impressive "Monthly Sheet of Personal Character and Acquirements" was drawn up by Mrs. Wardroper and forwarded to Florence. The girls were marked under nineteen different headings, such as "Neatness," "Quietness," "Trustworthiness," and "Observation of the Sick." Each heading could have as many as twelve subheadings.

Mrs. Wardroper frowned mightily on anything smacking of "Levity of Conduct." And of all the things on which she frowned, she frowned most darkly on flirting with medical students. In fact, the surest way to be expelled from the school was to be caught flirting with a medical student. It was simply not done.

On their afternoon off, the girls were permitted to leave the building only if they went in pairs. "Of course we always parted as soon as we got to the corner," one of the early probationers reminisced in later years.

All of this may sound foolish to us, but we must remember that a hundred years ago girls had far less freedom of action than girls of today. Besides, Florence was trying to win for her nurses a reputation exactly the opposite of the bad reputation of English hospital nurses. With this goal in view, no amount of supervision seemed too great.

The girls' working hours were strenuous. They got up at 6:00 in the morning and were in the wards by 7:00. Beds had to be made in half an hour, at the rate of one bed every two minutes. At 7:30 the patients were washed, and at 8:00 the ward Sister, or supervisor, came on duty. Her first activities would be a bit unusual in a modern hospital, but at that time they were standard procedure. First she read the Collect of the day from the *Book of Common Prayer;* then she poured a

shot of brandy for each patient. Her next chore sounds more familiar: she took everybody's temperature. After this, the probationers dusted the ward and washed the glasses.

At 9:30 the girls went back to their rooms to make their own beds and change their uniforms. They wore plain brown dresses and white caps. They were back in the wards by ten to serve the patients a meal called "lunch." (The eight o'clock brandy seems to have been breakfast.)

Next the house physicians arrived, and the real work of the day began. The girls made the day's rounds with the doctors and helped with the dressings. They stopped for a quick dinner at 12:45 and were back at work by 1:30. At two o'clock the "honorary lecturer" of the day arrived to teach a class and show the girls special cases. One of the probationers was chosen each day to carry a basin of water around so that the great man could wash his hands *after* he had finished examining the patients.

When the lecture was over, the probationers went around with the house surgeons to watch the dressing of surgical wounds. At five o'clock, after a short rest, the girls were revived with tea. Teatime, that great English institution, lasted for an hour, except for one day a week on which choir practice was held at 5:30. From 6:00 to 8:30, the girls fed the patients and got them ready for the night. Then they retired to their own rooms and wrote up their lecture notes for the day. Mrs. Wardroper and Miss Nightingale were extremely fussy about lecture notes.

A rough schedule? Undoubtedly. Even the hard-working nursing student of today might be awed by it. But it served its purpose very well. It was a most effective way of sorting out the serious students. Victorian girls were sentimental. Many of them applied for entrance to the school out of a romantic desire to follow in the footsteps of Florence Nightingale and become a "ministering angel" to the sick. They viewed the new career of nursing as one in which they could spend their days doing lovely or heroic deeds, such as smoothing down pillows and bravely facing contagious diseases.

Florence knew better than anyone how outlandish such a view really was. "A woman who takes a sentimental view of nursing," she wrote, "is, of course, worse than useless. A woman possessed with the idea that she is making a sacrifice will never do; and a woman who thinks that any kind of nursing work is 'beneath a nurse,' will simply be in the way."

Now if ever a system had been invented to knock sentimental notions out of the head forever, it was the average day of a Nightingale probationer. And if ever a person had been born who could keep a girl's feet on the ground, it was Mrs. Wardroper.

It is greatly to the credit of the original class that thirteen out of the fifteen stayed to graduate at the end of the year-long course.

Although Florence could not be present on the actual premises of the school, she was its guiding spirit as long as she lived. She never lost track of a graduate, and in her lonely old age—she lived to be ninety—it was the companionship of her girls that meant the most to her.

Early opposition to trained nursing soon died away. Within a few years the school was besieged with requests for its graduates. There were never enough to go around. Florence took an extremely dim view of private nursing as work for her graduates. She did not want them to waste their training on only one person at a time. They were expected to go into other hospitals, or into workhouses and district nursing, to pass along their knowledge and training. As other hospitals added schools of nursing, graduates of the original Nightingale School were sent in to act as Superintendents. Thus the great work grew and flourished.

Visitors from all over the world came to study the methods of the Nightingale School and to apply them in their own countries. Two Nightingale-trained nurses introduced the methods in the United States. During the Civil War, a committee from Bellevue Hospital in New York went to St. Thomas' to study the school as a model for its own.

Florence had always been lucky in the matter of timing. Trained nursing began to come into its own just at the time that the greatest steps forward were being made in the field of medicine. The twin discoveries of anaesthesia (the control of pain) and asepsis (the control of infection) had created a new kind of surgery. It had been undreamed of just a few years before. Morton and Simpson and Lister, who pioneered these discoveries, were all contemporaries of Florence Nightingale. So were Pasteur and Koch and Roux and Ehrlich and Behring and Parke and the other giants of nineteenth-century medicine. These men brought about a totally new concept of the practice of medicine. And Florence Nightingale pro-

vided them with a new kind of nursing that went hand in hand with their work.

In 1890 the London representative of Thomas Edison called at 32 South Street, where Florence lived for the last fifty years of her life. He asked her a great favor. Would Miss Nightingale just say one or two sentences, and her name, into his machine? By doing so she would put her voice forever onto his tinfoil "phonogram." He told her that he had recently recorded the voice and bugling of Kenneth Landfrey, who had blown the charge for the Light Brigade on that fatal day of battle in the Crimea. Landfrey had sounded the charge for the phonogram on the very same bugle he had blown at Balaclava.

Florence agreed to the engineer's request, and spoke sixteen words into Mr. Edison's marvelous machine. The phonograms were sent to America, but they dropped out of sight and were forgotten. Then one day, nearly half a century later, an Edison secretary found them hidden away in a cupboard. They were worn and scratchy, but they were perfectly clear.

Very recently these phonograms were re-recorded and put on a record called *Voices of the Twentieth Century*. It is a strange and wonderful feeling to turn on a switch and hear the voice of Florence Nightingale speaking to you. It is the voice of a seventy-year-old woman you hear. If you think back over the turbulent, heartbreaking, superhuman labors through which the old woman has lived, you are glad that the voice sounds so mellow and so gentle in its old age.

"God bless my dear old comrades of Balaclava," Miss Nightingale's voice says to us, across the bridge of so many years, "and bring them safe to shore. . . . Florence Nightingale." So at the end we find her once again on the heights of the Crimea, where her life really began.

Author's Note

Florence Nightingale had two life-long habits that have been a great help to her biographers. She liked to write down her ideas, her opinions, her feelings, and even her stray thoughts, in what she called "private notes." And she never threw anything away.

Thus Sir Edward Cook, who wrote her official two-volume biography after her death, found himself faced with a positive mountain of Nightingale papers: official documents, letters, copies of letters that she herself had written, diaries, notebooks, and the sheets and scraps of paper on which she had recorded the thoughts of eight decades.

Florence's mother and other members of her family were also ardent letter-writers and letter-savers. Some of these letters were not shown to earlier writers on Florence Nightingale because too many of the people mentioned in them were still alive. But some years ago Cecil Woodham-Smith was allowed to examine this and other valuable material and to use it in her magnificent biography *Florence Nightingale* and in *The Lonely Crusader,* a version of the book for older girls. Anyone interested in learning more about Florence Nightingale should consult these works. I am most grateful to their publisher, McGraw-Hill Book Company, for permission to use some points of information not available elsewhere.

Here is a partial list of sources consulted during the writing of this book:

Notes on Nursing, What It Is and What It Is Not
by Florence Nightingale

Notes on Matters Affecting the Health, Efficiency and Hospital Administration of the British Army by Florence Nightingale

The Life of Florence Nightingale by Sir Edward Cook

Florence Nightingale, 1820–1856 by I. B. O'Malley

Florence Nightingale by Cecil Woodham-Smith

The British Expedition to the Crimea by W. H. Russell

Eastern Hospitals and English Nurses by a Lady Volunteer

Experiences of a Civilian in Eastern Military Hospitals by Peter Pincoffs, M.D.

Scutari and Its Hospitals by the Rev. Sydney Godolphin Osborne

A Narrative of Personal Experiences and Impressions During Residence on the Bosphorus Throughout the Crimean War by Lady Alicia Blackwood

Reminiscences by Julia Ward Howe

Memoir of Sidney Herbert by Lord Stanmore

Monckton Milnes by James Pope-Hennessy

Pioneer Work in Opening the Medical Profession to Women by Elizabeth Blackwell, M.D.

A History of Nursing by M. Nutting and L. Dock

A General History of Nursing by Lucy Seymer

Index

LANDMARK BOOKS

WORLD LANDMARK BOOKS